THE ESSEX POLICE

THE ESSEX POLICE

by

JOHN WOODGATE

TERENCE DALTON LIMITED
LAVENHAM   .   SUFFOLK
1985

Published by
TERENCE DALTON LIMITED

ISBN 0 86138 034 7

Text Photoset in 10/11 pt. Souvenir

Printed in Great Britain at
The Lavenham Press Limited, Lavenham, Suffolk
© John Woodgate, 1985

Contents

To my wife Joan
for her unceasing support
and to my four children
who have never known anything else
but a policeman for a father

Acknowledgements

IN ACKNOWLEDGING my sources of information I must express my heartfelt gratitude and thanks to the County Archivist, Mr Victor Gray, and the staff of the Essex Record Office, Chelmsford, for without their unfailing courtesy, guidance and efficiency my task would have been impossible.

For an authoritative background and record of Parliamentary legislation going back 150 years I cannot recommend too highly T. A. Critchley's classic *History of the Police in England and Wales.* The painstaking work he undertook has produced what must surely now be regarded as a "bible" for all serious students of police history.

No story of the Essex Police would be complete without a glimpse at the fascinating history of the borough forces which existed from the 1830s. Despite the fact that they are no more, their records are nevertheless still carefully preserved in their respective archives. I am indebted therefore to Mr Malcolm White of Saffron Walden, Mr Len Weaver of Harwich, Mr J. Allen of Colchester, Mr Edward Robinson of Maldon, and the staff of the Southend Record Office, all of whom were unstinting in their help and ever anxious to assist me in compiling as accurate a history as possible.

My thanks are also due to Mr Robert Bunyard, Chief Constable of Essex, for his courtesy and assistance in providing material which is still on file at police headquarters.

CHAPTER ONE

Law and Disorder

IT IS often said that in Britain every citizen is a policeman and every policeman a citizen. There is much truth in this, but at no time more so than the hundred years leading up to the formation of our present police.

Law and order, for the want of a better expression, was maintained by the centuries-old system of parish constables. The office of parish constable goes back to the Middle Ages when villages were close-knit communities, insular, self-sufficient and almost minor principalities in their own right. It was then the compulsory duty of every citizen to act for one year as the constable for his parish.

The office was both unpaid and unpopular. For the constable it was an unnecessary intrusion into his working life. For the public it entailed keeping that constable well within bounds so as not to encroach upon their liberty.

As society became more complex the situation of the parish constable became more and more undesirable. It was by no means uncommon for a parishioner, unwilling to undertake such time-consuming and unpopular duties, to pay another to do it for him. Many constables became semi-professional, holding the office of parish constable for year after year. Most of these "professional" constables were unintelligent, generally inefficient and always the cheapest available. Their powers were extremely limited.

Going back to the twelfth century it had been the voluntary duty of Gentlemen and local squires to assist whenever possible their local constable. It was certainly in their interests to do so, for a law-abiding community was a great asset to a landowner. In the fourteenth century these Gentlemen received statutory recognition as Justices of the Peace, and later as Magistrates. After 1688 they were allowed to implement the law in a manner they thought most fitting, being given enormous powers and becoming not only the local authorities with power to levy rates and allocate public money but virtually the Chief Constables of their day. They not only ordered arrests but were very frequently in charge of operations leading to the arrests of law-breakers. The parish constable in effect became the Magistrate's personal assistant, doing his bidding and executing his warrants.

This system of policing was generally accepted by the population as the best that could be expected under the circumstances, and it operated well in most rural districts. However, country areas were quite different from the fast-growing towns and cities, for events were moving swiftly by the eighteenth century. Drunkenness, vice, corruption, theft, burglaries and highway robberies reached epidemic proportions and the constable found himself hopelessly outclassed by an even more professional criminal and menaced by marauding gangs which infested the streets by day and night. Totally unprotected by legislation, which seemed bent on curbing his

Police constable Thomas Dewberry, of Saffron Walden Borough Police, in the mid-1850s. The crown of his top hat is reinforced to provide additional protection.

1

powers while at the same time affording all the protection of the law to the wrongdoer, the constable saw public morale (and morals) slump.

The government responded with severe penalties for those convicted of all types of crime. The death penalty was extended to cover no fewer than two hundred and twenty-three offences. Such were the standards of detection and public apathy that a criminal considered himself unlucky to be caught, and for the most part carried on his evil trade unmolested. In the end the penalties imposed by the courts became counter-productive, for few people would inform on another, well knowing that the hangman's noose awaited the wrongdoer. Justices themselves actively persuaded aggrieved persons to reduce the value of their stolen goods to below that which was laid down as the minimum required for the death penalty.

The constable's powers were still strictly limited. He was powerless beyond the boundaries of his parish. He had no power to enter or search, and unless he actually witnessed a crime being committed experience taught him not to arrest without a warrant.

Whichever way the constable turned he found himself hemmed in by legal restrictions, designed to ensure the freedom of the individual. Henry Fielding, the true founder of our modern police system, once said, "Officers of Justice have owned to me that they have passed by such criminals, with warrants in their pockets, without daring to apprehend them, and indeed they could not be blamed for not exposing themselves to sure destruction, for it is a melancholy truth that such a rogue no sooner gives the alarm than twenty or thirty armed villains are found ready to come to his assistance".

Quite apart from the forces ranged against the parish constable, there were other defects in the system of parochial policing. Not only were people not getting the police protection to which they were entitled but the system was forcing upon constables a situation where they could not afford to pursue crime. Many constables became very ill-disposed to following up a crime unless they were supplied with, or at least guaranteed, the financial backing with which to do so.

A socially dangerous outcome of this was that a wealthy man could offer his constable financial support for following up his case, while the poor man learned the futility of reporting a crime unless he was pretty certain who was responsible.

Amid all this, though, were men of sound principles and incorruptible morals such as Henry and John Fielding, Thomas de Veil and Saunders Welch, who foresaw chaos and anarchy unless something were done to combat the ever-rising tide of lawlessness. Men like these used their positions as Magistrates to gather around them small bands of totally honest men (and they were few and far between), trained them and sent them out to fight organised crime. Despite a heartbreaking lack of support from the public and to some extent from the Government, they achieved incredible successes.

The official salaries paid to Fielding's men were no more than the pittances laid down by law. The government quickly realised, however, the worth of these few men, often not more than six in number, who took their lives in their hands when they sallied forth, and found ways of paying them "under the counter" by way of the Secret Service List. These few men operated from the house of the Magistrate in Bow Street and were later to become famous as the Bow Street Runners.

SEVEN POUNDS
REWARD.

Associations of gentry and well-to-do farmers were formed in the last quarter of the eighteenth century and later to secure the preservation of property and the prosecution of felons. This notice was issued by an association formed in 1837 and remaining in being until at least 1870. One such association still exists at Colchester, although its only function is to hold an annual "Thieves' Dinner."

Essex Record Office

GREAT BADDOW ASSOCIATION
For the Prevention of Crime and Prosecution of Felons.

WHEREAS some Person or Persons did, on the Night of Wednesday last, the 14th of May instant, BREAK INTO the HEN-HOUSE of Mr. JOHN SMITH, a Member of the above Association, at CANNON BARNS FARM, East Hanningfield, and STEAL THEREFROM

SEVEN HENS

Any Person giving such Information as shall lead to the Conviction of the Offender or Offenders, shall receive the above Reward in the proportions following, viz. :—£5 from Mr. SMITH, and £2 from the said Association, upon application to the Secretary. If more than one informant the Reward to be apportioned.

W. W. DUFFIELD,
Secretary to the said Association.

GREAT BADDOW, 16th May, 1845.

21

MEGGY & CHALK, PRINTERS, CHELMSFORD.

As soon as it became apparent that crime was being driven from the streets and people could walk freely by day, and more unbelievably by night, the Government assumed it had cured the problem and withdrew its financial support for the police. Those few Magistrates who had organised their little bands of thief-takers (as they had become known) were forced by their principles to continue paying them out of their own pockets.

The first two decades of the nineteenth century were noted for their turmoil and industrial unrest; many historians see this period as the closest this country has been to revolution. The stern measures taken during the Napoleonic Wars, such as the suspension, in 1794, of the Habeas Corpus Act (the right of trial soon after arrest), and the passing of the Combination Acts of 1799, making it illegal for workers to form unions for the betterment of their conditions, did nothing to endear the Government to the working population, and unrest grew at an alarming rate.

England was soon to discover, as have other countries through the years, that law enforcement can succeed only with the consent of the population. No army, however great, and no legislation, however oppressive, can endure in the face of determined public opposition.

By 1820 it was becoming obvious that the military could not be relied upon to maintain order, and in that year, indeed, there was a threat of mutiny among the 300 Guards stationed in London. The Duke of Wellington, who was then a member of the Cabinet, wrote to the Prime Minister, Lord Liverpool: "In my opinion the Government ought, without loss of a moment's time, to adopt measures to form either a police in London or military corps, which should be of a different description from the regular military force, or both".

When Robert Peel became Home Secretary in 1820 he set about reforming the criminal law. He was instrumental in removing over a hundred offences from the list carrying the death penalty, and by 1826 was actively engaged in creating a police force for the Metropolis and drawing up plans for similar forces throughout the country. By 1829 he had proposed to Parliament a force of 2,000 men, controlled from a central office in Westminster, with himself at its head.

Thus was born the Metropolitan Police, upon which many county and borough forces were later to be modelled.

In Essex political indecision, failed harvests, a soaring cost of living and agricultural mechanisation all combined to create an atmosphere of unrest in the early years of the nineteenth century. The ending of the Napoleonic Wars was followed by an agricultural depression which was in no way alleviated by the actions of successive governments, and many farmers found themselves facing ruin as the economy plunged.

Farmers not already crippled saw in mechanisation their last hope. Agricultural machinery, and later the steam engine, brought great benefits to the farmer, for one machine could do the work of a dozen men, in a fraction of the time and at much less cost. More and more labourers were thrown out of work, joining the 200,000 men who had been demobilised from the Army and the Navy with the coming of peace.

The workers finally reacted with rioting and widespread acts of incendiarism and machine breaking. It is significant that many instances of public disorder occurred during the winter, when long periods of unemployment resulted in mass hunger and poverty among the labouring community.

The most seriously affected parts of Essex were in the central and northern areas, although the south also had sporadic outbreaks of disorder. A particularly serious riot occurred at Halstead in May, 1816, when a mob tried to rescue four prisoners lodged in Halstead Gaol on charges of machine-breaking at Sible Hedingham.

Next day labourers streamed into the town from the surrounding villages and further window-breaking and damage took place. When the reading of the Riot Act by a local magistrate had no effect the Halstead Yeomanry Cavalry was called in and ordered to disperse the mob, only to be driven back under a hail of stones. The enraged mob barricaded the roads leading into the town in order to prevent reinforcements arriving, but a squadron of Dragoon Guards accompanied by sixty "Constables" from Colchester fought their way into the battered town. The situation was finally brought under control with heavily manned patrols covering all the streets for a week afterwards.

William Pitt declared, after a visit to Halstead, that he had "no conception that any part of England could present a spectacle of such misery."

During the 1820's mobs collected wherever farmers attempted to use their new machinery, particularly the threshing machine. Many farmers capitulated under threats of violence; others who ignored the threats found their machinery sabotaged during the night or their crops and hay-ricks destroyed by fire. Losses from fires were so severe in 1829 that one insurance company suspended all cover on farm buildings and stock, thus unintentionally aiding the rioters, for the farmers then had nothing to fall back on in their resistance to the workers' pressure. The following year the

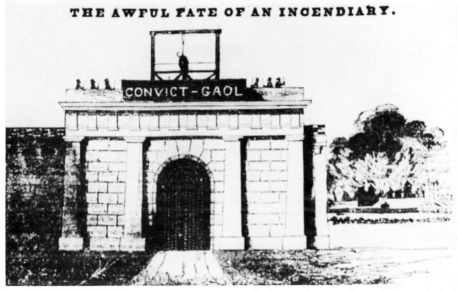

An engraving of the execution of sixteen-year-old James Cook, a cow boy on a farm at Witham, who had been convicted of arson. The farm buildings to which he had set fire are represented on the right.

Essex Record Office

company relaxed its suspension, but only on condition that the farmers ceased using their threshing machines.

Both magistrates and judges reacted with customary severity on those convicted of arson or machine-breaking. In 1829, a sixteen-year-old agricultural apprentice named James Cook was publicly executed at Chelmsford Gaol for setting fire to his employer's farm at Witham. On 24th December, 1830, James Ewen was hanged at Chelmsford for a similar offence. The following year William Jennings was executed, followed by James Pasfield and George Canfield.

At the Essex Assizes of 1830 no fewer than sixteen machine-breakers were sentenced to transportation to Van Diemen's Land (Tasmania). In January, 1831, a further eight were convicted and transported, with forty-three other defendants suffering lesser punishment. Machine-breaking and incendiarism reached a peak in Essex in 1830, and such convictions were still being recorded until 1850.

Columns of unemployed men, most of them hungry, many of them starving, all of them desperate, roamed the countryside pleading for work, begging relief from the parishes or applying for admission to the workhouse. The situation deteriorated at an alarming rate and on 27th November, 1830, the Secretary of State, Lord Melbourne, wrote to the Lord Lieutenant of Essex indicating his awareness of the deteriorating situation in the county. On 8th December, 1830, the Lord Lieutenant and county magistrates met at the Shire Hall in Chelmsford, and there determined to exert pressure to maintain the law and put down the outrages which were disturbing the public peace. Magistrates' clerks were instructed to compile lists of men who

Petty Sessions,
MANNINGTREE,
DECEMBER 7, 1830.

A printed notice issued by the Tendring Hundred Justices in 1830 at a time of widespread unrest.
Essex Record Office

The Magistrates of the **HUNDRED OF TENDRING** having received Information of **ILLEGAL ASSEMBLIES** of the **LABOURERS**, have deemed it expedient to swear in **SPECIAL CONSTABLES** in every **Parish**; and the Magistrates recommend that the Special Constables so sworn, will select one Person in each Parish through whom Orders may be communicated. Should any Outrage occur, information is to be forwarded by a Horseman to the Chief Constable of the Division, and a Notification to be given to a Constable of each Parish through which the Horseman will pass, and such Constable to assemble all those of his Parish.

In the preservation of the public Peace, it is expected many of the Residents in the Hundred will unite, who may not form part of the Constabulary Force; especially to them, the Magistrates earnestly inculcate the necessity of Order and a uniform system of Action in unison with the Chief Constables, to whom the Magistrates' instructions will be regularly communicated.

It is hoped that the Remonstrances of the well-disposed may have had due effect on the misguided Populace, but should any in future assemble and commit Outrage, the Constables will use all possible exertions to procure the aid of contiguous Parishes.

The Mounted Force, of which the Magistrates doubt not a large Body will be formed, will not advance, except in cases of immediate necessity, beyond that on foot, and on coming up to the Multitude they will require them to select three or four Individuals to state their grievances to the Magistrates, and then to disperse; but should they unfortunately refuse to comply, and commit any Acts of Violence, the Ringleaders must be secured, in order that they may be dealt with according to Law.

The Chief Constables will assure the misled People that the Magistrates are always ready to redress every Grievance in their power, and that acts of Outrage and Tumult necessarily tend to augment the Distress of which they complain, and of which all Classes in a greater or less degree now participate.

The Magistrates most earnestly recommend to the whole of the Constabulary Force, the strictest observance of good Order and Sobriety.

27   THOMAS NUNN,   H. R. SOMERS SMITH,
       R. W. COX,   THOMAS NUNN, Jun.

BURKITT, PRINTER, BOOKSELLER, BINDER, & STATIONER, MARKET-PLACE, MANNINGTREE.

6

were willing to assist the authorities as temporary constables in putting down what many considered to be insurrection. Thus was born the Special Constabulary.

On 9th December, 1830, a resolution was passed by the Justices of the Tendring Hundred that "in consequence of the riotous and tumultuous proceedings which have recently taken place, accompanied by the daring acts of incendiary" consideration should be given to raising subscriptions among householders "for the detection and punishment of the authors and perpetrators of these and similar offences."

Both the public and the magistracy were clamouring for a protective force to combat this rising tide of lawlessness, and eyes turned to London where the Metropolitan Police, established the previous year, was beginning to come to grips with the problem. But it was to be some time before anything effective was done.

In May, 1839, a Royal Proclamation empowered magistrates to "take the most prompt and effectual means for putting down and suppressing unlawful meetings." Groups of law-abiding citizens, Special Constables, even Chelsea Pensioners, were armed and the military put on standby for instant removal to any part of the country. Insurrection grew as the summer of 1839 wore on and it became increasingly obvious that the Government was almost powerless to suppress the rising tide of public disorder.

Major-General Sir Charles Napier, commanding the Northern District of England, wrote to the Home Secretary, Lord John Russell, on 20th July, 1839, "My belief is that concessions must be made to the people's feelings, or the establishment of a strong rural Police Force hurried on. I would do both, thinking them absolutely necessary. If the Police Force be not quickly increased we shall require troops from Ireland." The Home Secretary acted swiftly and four days later, on 24th July, 1839, he introduced before Parliament his County Police Bill, proposing that Justices in Quarter Sessions, with the consent of the Home Secretary, should be empowered to establish a police force for the whole or any part of their county, and that the number of constables should not exceed one for every thousand of the population. All appointments into the Constabulary would be in the hands of the Justices but the Home Secretary would retain the power to approve the appointment of Chief Constables. The cost of such policing would fall upon the county concerned.

The Bill was welcomed by the Justices, who had become increasingly concerned that the Government intended imposing upon the country a centrally-directed national police force, thus stripping the magistracy of their centuries-old responsibility for law enforcement in their areas.

Needless to say, the passage of this Bill through Parliament was stormy. A strong body of dissenters, led by Disraeli, attacked it bitterly and accused the Government of sinister motives. The Home Secretary won the day.

Meanwhile, in Essex similar demands were being made for a more efficient system of policing. At the General Quarter Sessions on 15th October, 1839, the inhabitants of Dunmow presented a petition praying for the more efficient policing of that area. The matter was raised again at the Adjourned Quarter Sessions in November of that year.

The Justices at these Quarter Sessions declared "that ordinary officers appointed for preserving the peace within the county were not sufficient for the peace and protection of the inhabitants and for the security of the property within their county" and resolved to take advantage of the new Act by raising 115 constables and superintendents and appointing a Chief Constable for the county at a salary of £400 per annum. Their decision was placed before the Secretary of State, Lord Normanby, for his approval, which was granted by the end of the year.

Essex was one of the first to avail itself of the County Police Act, the effects of which were to be seen throughout the country within two years. During that time twenty-four counties raised their own regular police forces. Of these eight were raised in 1839, twelve in 1840 and four in 1841, the original eight being Durham, Essex, Gloucestershire, Hampshire, Lancashire, Leicestershire, Wiltshire and Worcestershire.

Within a short time it became apparent that this form of regular county-wide policing was proving more costly than anticipated. At this early stage every county was expected to pay for its own police, for Government assistance was not to come until later.

A ludicrous situation developed, with the new county and borough forces operating in what amounted to scattered pockets around the country while large areas of rural England still relied on the old parochial police system of parish constables supported by paid watchmen.

A leader in *The Times* early in 1842 declared with ill-disguised relish, "We perceive with great satisfaction that a strong feeling is gaining ground in different parts of the country, and in most respectable quarters, against the continuance of the rural Police system."

In the face of opposition the Government conceded some ground by introducing the Parish Constables Act of 1842, providing the opportunity for each authority to raise and maintain its police force either under the old parochial constable system or by way of the new county police.

Essex was already operating an efficient and much admired regular police force. At a hearing of a House of Commons Select Committee in 1853 examining the efficiency of the various types of policing, a Mr D. Smith, who had served ten years with the Essex Constabulary before being appointed Superintending Constable of Oxfordshire, was called upon to give evidence. When asked to comment on the calibre of the parish constable he declared that "half a dozen regular Essex policemen would be equal to the seventy parish constables now under me."

CHAPTER TWO

McHardy's Men

A COMMITTEE of county magistrates was appointed in 1840 to elect a Chief Constable for the county. There must have been prolonged discussion beforehand as to the type of man to attract, for the successful applicant would be required to shoulder enormous responsibility.

No fewer than twenty-seven candidates gathered at the Shire Hall in Chelmsford in response to the advertisements placed for this position. Of this number, seventeen carried commissioned rank in the Army or Navy. The interviews lasted all day, the applicants being called before the Justices in the order in which their applications had been received, and at the end of the interviews votes were cast. Those applicants with the fewest votes were immediately informed, the remainder being again put up for ballot and the procedure repeated until there were just two candidates remaining.

It was not until the following day that the Justices were able to announce that the first Chief Constable of Essex was to be a naval captain, John Bunch Bonnemaison McHardy. He had been number twenty-six on the list of twenty-seven candidates. It is interesting to note that this ex-service strain continued in Essex for something like a hundred years, for McHardy (who retired as an admiral*) was succeeded by Major Poyntz of the Royal Marine Light Infantry; he was followed by Captain Showers of the 95th (Derbyshire) Regiment, then came Captain Unett of the East Yorkshire Regiment, who in turn was succeeded by Captain Jonathan Peel of the Royal Field Artillery.

Before his retirement on half pay in 1840 McHardy had had a most distinguished career in the Royal Navy, which he had joined at the age of eleven as a First Class Volunteer. His first ship was the 32-gun sloop H.M.S. *Tartarus* under Captain John Pasco, who took young McHardy with him when he later transferred to the fifth-rate H.M.S. *Rota* which had been captured from the Danes at Copenhagen in 1807.

McHardy showed his determination when H.M.S. *Rota* paid off in 1815. Now aged fourteen, he paid his own passage in an outgoing merchantman to the West Indies, where he applied for service aboard H.M. ships. He served in a succession of vessels before becoming second-in-command of the schooner H.M.S. *Lion* in 1823 with orders to assist in the suppression of piracy in the Caribbean. He was soon in action both in the *Lion* and in other vessels to which he was later appointed, and in 1824 his promotion to lieutenant was confirmed.

*McHardy left the navy as a full captain on half pay, remaining on the active list of officers and thus being eligible for promotion. As the years went by he found himself moving up through the senior ranks, becoming an admiral in 1870.

His capture of the pirate schooner *Diableto* earned McHardy a commendation from the Admiralty, and in 1828 he was given his first command, the schooner H.M.S. *Pickle*, in which he took part in another spirited action, capturing the slaver *Bolodera* in spite of his crew of thirty men and six boys being outnumbered two to one. For this outstanding action he received his second commendation from the Admiralty.

A little more than a year after his action with the *Bolodera* McHardy married Horatia Victoria Aitchison, the daughter of Rear-Admiral Pasco, under whom the young McHardy had served in the *Tartarus* and the *Rota*. H.M.S. *Pickle* had been paid off at Plymouth in October, 1830, two months before the wedding, and when inspected there the standard of discipline and efficiency so impressed the commander-in-chief, Sir Manley Dixon, that he communicated the fact to the Admiralty. On 20th December, 1830, McHardy was promoted commander "for his meritorious services to the Navy."

He spent nine years in the Coastguard service, for six of those years being Inspecting Commander of the Norfolk District, before being promoted captain on 1st January, 1840, and placed on half pay.

Such was the man who was entrusted with the organisation of a police force for Essex.

McHardy found himself in a county in which no fewer than four separate borough police forces were then operating; Saffron Walden, Colchester, Maldon and Harwich had taken advantage of a recent Act empowering them to raise their own police. Dedicated as he was to the principle of a national police force, McHardy must have viewed the prospect of five Chief Constables in one county with some distaste.

Although McHardy was in overall command and responsible for the day-to-day running of the force, it was still the Justices who were responsible to the Government for the efficiency and smooth running of the force. This centuries-old system was to remain for nearly fifty years until it was transferred by the County Councils Act, 1888, to the newly-formed police standing joint committee. Even then, this committee still comprised fifteen magistrates elected at Quarter Sessions and fifteen lay-members elected by the county council, so the magistrates did not entirely relinquish their authority.

McHardy turned out to be a shrewd and perceptive man, disciplined, organised and efficient. He could be both ruthless and generous to those under his command, and his enthusiasm for the task ahead was boundless. It irked him considerably when he saw something less than this great enthusiasm among his superintendents, and he was always reminding them of their responsibilities. He was a man totally dedicated to the formation of an efficient and disciplined police force and part of his success lay in his ability never to be out of touch with those who served under him. The slightest misdemeanour seemed never to escape his notice; neither did those acts which were worthy of praise.

The new Chief Constable's most difficult task involved the selection of his men. He knew that his reputation and all his hopes rested on his ability to choose the right material, both in patrolling officers and those who must supervise them. He aimed his sights high and gambled on a policy of having fewer numbers at the outset, but of a higher calibre, rather than a full complement of mediocrity. This policy manifested

Admiral J. B. B. McHardy, a portrait dated 1877 when the first Chief Constable was seventy-six.

itself later in high wastage, but thus did he lay the foundations upon which the force grew to become the envy of so many.

An applicant for the post of constable was first interviewed by the Chief Constable. If that went well he was handed a form on which his previous employers had to certify how long they had employed him, that he was "sober, honest and of Good Temper, that his Connexions and Associates were respectable." They had also to certify that he could read and write.

On completion of this the candidate took the form to a Justice of the Peace who certified that the employers named thereon "were worthy of confidence." The aspiring constable was then subjected to a medical examination, the surgeon completing his part of the form by certifying the applicant's age, height, physical description and the fact that "he is fit for police duties."

11

The recruit then attended the Shire Hall, Chelmsford, where he was sworn in before the magistrates. Only then did he report to headquarters at Springfield.

At this point the cautious Chief Constable had to be sure in his own mind that the newly-fledged constable was fit and properly instructed before letting him out on the streets. Before any uniform was issued the constable was subjected to a fifty-six-day probation period.

Along with his uniform the constable was issued with a pair of handcuffs, a truncheon decorated with the arms of the county, a wooden rattle (later replaced by the whistle) and a book entitled "Orders and Instructions for the Government of the Essex Constabulary." He had been required to study this in great detail during his period of training, for it laid down in explicit terms how he was expected to conduct himself both on and off duty, how to patrol his guard* (beat), his powers of arrest, how to serve summonses and execute warrants, how to give evidence in a court, and many other items. Not least was the stern warning that any neglect or violation of his duty would incur a fine of up to £10 or imprisonment for one month with hard labour.

He learned that "Constables are always to take the outside of the footpath, and when walking along the streets should not shoulder past respectable people but give way in a mild manner, for the more respectful and civil the Constabulary are, the more they will be supported and respected by the public."

He was advised also to familiarise himself with the various lock-ups situated in his division, for these were still the only means of confining prisoners until they were dealt with by summons or brought before a court. Later, as properly constructed cells were built into all the new police stations, the lock-ups gradually fell into disuse. Whenever a prisoner was brought to a police station the arresting officer had to ensure, if possible, that the complainant accompanied him in order to substantiate the charge. These instructions, and many more, had to be thoroughly digested before any constable was allowed to take his place on the streets of his division.

Thus did McHardy form and train his tiny force. In the meantime the parochial constables remained, for there could be no sudden transition from one to the other. There were simply not enough county constables to take the place of their parochial colleagues. Indeed, the transfer of responsibility was to take more than thirteen years to complete.

McHardy, always a believer in a national police force, introduced a uniform very similar to that being worn by the Metropolitan Police, a royal blue tailcoat, dark blue trousers and a black stove-pipe hat reinforced with a thick layer of leather around the crown. The coat collar was of stiff, upright design, buttoned to the neck and bearing on each side of the throat a crown and the number of the constable.

In June, 1840, McHardy instructed that each member of the Constabulary "provides himself with two pairs of white drill trousers and that they do appear in them whenever the Superintendent may direct, between 1 May and 1 October." The constable, even at this very early stage, possessed what amounted to a summer and a winter uniform. Each constable was made aware that if he resigned or was dismissed

---

*A term which McHardy brought with him from the coastguard service.

the sum of five shillings would be deducted from his wages for the purpose of altering his uniform for use by his successor.

In February, 1840, the County Justices had agreed to the employment of a hundred constables at twenty shillings a week and fifteen superintendents at £80 a year. By October of that year McHardy realised the need for an intermediate rank and introduced the rank of inspector. It was agreed that the numbers of constables be increased in order to select from them twenty suitable candidates to be made inspectors. Their salaries were agreed at twenty-five shillings a week.

The recruitment figures for that year clearly show that March and April produced the bulk of the intake, indicating that advertising had taken place earlier, the applicants being put on "standby" until sufficient numbers were available to launch the new force.

Month	Constables	Inspectors	Supts.
February			3
March	45	4*	6
April	43	5*	5
May	15	5*	4
June	8		1
July	8		
August	5	1*	
September	6	1*	
October	7	1	
November	9	5	2
December	6	2	1
Total:	152	24	23

*Joined as constables in the month shown and made up to inspectors in October, 1840

The totals of each rank, exceeding as they do the authorised figures, indicate that McHardy was catering for wastage. As it turned out he under-estimated the problem, for of those constables actually appointed twenty-five had left by the end of their first month and a further sixty had resigned or been dismissed by the end of their first year. He seems to have had a more delicate finger on the pulse so far as the inspectors and superintendents were concerned, for of the twenty-four inspectors appointed only six left during their first year, six of the twenty-three superintendents leaving during the same period.

The total strength of the Constabulary by December, 1840, was seventeen superintendents, eighteen inspectors and sixty-seven constables—administratively a little top-heavy. The rank of sergeant was not introduced into the county until 1855.

From the outset McHardy demonstrated in practical terms his concern for the welfare of his men by introducing a superannuation scheme. Realising how much finance such a fund would require and how little his officers could contribute, he obtained permission from the Justices to finance it as follows:- (1) direct contributions from the members by way of stoppages from pay amounting to 6d a week from superintendents, 5d a week from inspectors and 4d a week from constables; (2) all stoppages of pay brought about by sickness; (3) all disciplinary fines imposed by him on his officers; (4) a proportion of all fines imposed by the magistrates on persons brought before them by the constables; and (5) all proceeds from the sale of cast-off or worn-out uniforms.

However, even this worthwhile contribution to welfare had its sting in the tail, for the pension was dependent on a man's good behaviour. Some twenty years later we find instances of constables having their pensions reduced by as much as a half as a direct result of having been disciplined for one or more offences during their years of service.

In October, 1840, McHardy devised a grading system for constables. They joined as 2nd Class and were later promoted to 1st Class on merit, drawing pay of nineteen shillings and twenty-one shillings a week respectively. By April, 1842, he had added a 3rd Class at seventeen shillings a week. He also divided the superintendents into similar grades at £100, £90 and £80 a year respectively.

A constable on joining would automatically be classified as Constable 3rd Class, and after six months could apply for upgrading to 2nd Class. After eighteen months in that grade he could then apply for 1st Class status. It took an average of two years to advance from 3rd to 1st Class—a period of time identical to today's probationary period. Advancement was by no means assured or automatic, for it depended entirely on whether the man's superintendent considered him worthy of being so raised.

The system of duties and the responsibilities of the constables were then very much as they are at present. They were paraded for duty, inspected, had their beats allocated by the inspector (later the sergeant) and items of interest pointed out for attention during the patrol. In many areas of Essex, particularly during the early days when numbers available were limited, it was common for the inspector or superintendent to convey a number of constables in the County Cart, dropping them off at various locations where it was thought their presence would be most needed. Even so, every officer was required to make a number of conference points during his patrol. At a prearranged time and location he was expected to present himself and remain there for thirty minutes to be visited by another patrolling officer or any of his senior officers. To neglect to attend such a point was considered a grave disciplinary offence punishable by a fine or dismissal. There are many such instances in Essex Police records.

The county constable worked long and hard. His duties were, of course, dictated by the environment in which he found himself but generally he worked a split shift incorporating three or four hours during the day followed by a longer period at night—always between 10p.m. and dawn. The average working day was ten to twelve hours duty seven days a week. A weekly rest day was not to be granted until the turn of the twentieth century. There were no refreshment breaks during these periods of duty and it was generally left to the expertise of the constable to fend for himself without getting caught. He was granted one week's holiday a year—unpaid, of course.

Attendance at Divine Worship was not simply encouraged but, in many forces, made compulsory. So far as Essex was concerned the Chief Constable directed only that "duties would be so arranged as to allow the attendance of the Constabulary at

Divine Service, and Constables are expected to show an example of due respect for the observance of the sabbath day, and strict attendance to their religious duties."

A constable living in a Station House was not allowed to leave that building even when off duty without the express permission of the superintendent or senior officer. Similarly, constables in rural areas required permission before they could leave their beats.

All patrols were on foot, and it was not uncommon for constables, particularly on rural beats, to walk over twenty miles a day.

It was at weekends, when the public houses discharged their oft-drunken customers, that the constable found himself with more than he could handle. Drinking was by no means confined to the general public and there was no doubt that the constables also enjoyed the odd tipple.

McHardy, the stern, religious Victorian, dealt ruthlessly with any constables guilty of bringing the force into disrepute. Police dismissals for offences involving alcohol reached a peak during the 1840's and early 1850's, falling off during the 1860's; by the 1870's it became extremely rare to find such a case.

Constables of the new county force quickly discovered that they had room to move and could pursue the wrongdoer over many parishes while still retaining their authority. This one factor alone must have resulted in many successful arrests.

Another interesting part of the constable's duty was connected with that great product of the Industrial Revolution, the railways. The criminal classes quickly realised the rich pickings to be had by this new mode of fast travel; they could board a train in London, be in the Home Counties within the hour, burgle a few houses and

The opening of Grays railway station in 1855 showing two policemen on the platform. This early photograph has obviously been retouched somewhat crudely.   *Thurrock Central Library*

be back in the Metropolis again before the hue and cry could be raised. Knowing this full well, the Chief Constable directed that every constable who had a railway station on his beat should meet as many trains as possible to survey the emerging passengers for any sign of known criminals or suspicious persons. These visits he had to record in his daily journal.

Night duty presented its own problems, for there was little or no street lighting and in rural areas the moon provided the only source of illumination. Constables were issued with brass oil-lamps with a bulls-eye lens complete with a foldaway

handgrip and spring-clip on the back, thus enabling the lamp to be carried by hand or secured to the constable's belt. To avoid the inconvenience of having to light the wick every time the lamp was needed an ingenious sliding shutter mechanism opened or closed the lens at will, allowing the lamp to burn continuously. The constable was responsible for the care and maintenance of his lamp and for the purchase of oil and wick. For this he was paid an extra one shilling a month.

If the inspectors provided direct supervision of constables, this did not mean that the superintendents were allowed to become desk-bound. They received instructions from McHardy to visit their constables at irregular hours—and particularly at night.

16

McHardy was constantly "grieved to observe that some superintendents entirely neglect to visit the patrols between midnight and daylight" and directed that all visits made should be recorded in the superintendent's journal in red ink.

The worthy superintendents, despite being granted a handsome forage allowance of two shillings a day for their personal steed, were still not averse to travelling in the comparative comfort of the County Cart when visiting their men. This little practice did not escape the eagle eye of McHardy, who observed "that County Carts are being unnecessarily used by superintendents when visiting night

Opposite: A police oil lamp of 1840 with the back open to show the oil reservoir.

Right: The same oil lamp, "The Crescent Lamp" made by Dolan and Company, of London, seen from the front.

patrols, instead of on horseback. I direct that such carts should never be used, day or night, and that in addition horses should not be driven at more than six miles an hour."

It was essential for McHardy to stamp his will and authority on this new body of men. Being a naval captain, he was used to instilling discipline. One cannot help but smile at some of the little escapades which failed to escape his notice. For example, he learned "accidentally", he says, that three constables of the Dunmow Division, having performed duty at a fair at Thaxted, were on their way back to Dunmow when they chanced upon a public house. It was July (1840) and the weather warm. Throats were dry and the beer-house beckoned. These three constables were seen to be actually dancing in the place! The Chief Constable, ever mindful "of the general good conduct of the force and the high compliments recently paid by the Justices", was not amused. He rapped the superintendent, who was miles away at the time, and posted the happy constables to other divisions!

It was the Chief Constable's dictum that if you kept a man busy you improved his efficiency. With this in mind he persuaded the authorities to permit various officers of the force to become Inspectors of Weights and Measures, Inspectors of Nuisances, Inspectors of Common Lodging Houses and Assistants to H.M. Revenue Officers.

The shrewd Chief Constable knew full well that these offices were held and administered by local authority officials. He argued that not only would it improve the efficiency of his men to give them such jobs, bringing them into greater contact with the public, but if the county was paying these officials then the sums saved could be offset against the cost of the police.

Yet another task undertaken by McHardy's men came in October, 1840, when the Boards of Guardians of the Poor Law Unions appointed members of the Constabulary as Relieving Officers for Casuals in an effort to stem the ever-growing flood of vagrants pouring into the county and wandering from parish to parish begging relief. The duty of these Police/Relieving Officers was to persuade as many vagrants as possible to return whence they had come. The officers were empowered to search any such person claiming relief and either grant that relief or turn him back. Any money or other property found on such a person who had been granted relief was handed over to the Poor Law Guardians to offset that relief.

So effective was this work of the police that applications to the Chelmsford Union alone dropped by a staggering five thousand. McHardy later stated that one thousand vagrants had been taken before the courts in a three-year period and quoted figures showing that in one half-year (1849) seventy-nine persons were granted relief against two thousand six hundred and five relieved in the previous half-year.

Another duty thrust upon the constable involved the repatriation of paupers as far afield as Scotland, Ireland, the Isle of Man and the Scilly Isles.

As the first year wore on it became obvious to McHardy that the initial figure of something over a hundred constables was going to be nowhere near enough if he was to police the entire county efficiently.

Under constant pressure to keep costs to a minimum, McHardy had to allow the parochial constables to remain in those areas not yet policed by the county force. In addition, he required some form of temporary constable until such time as he could build up a regular force. In October, 1840, he wrote to all divisional superintendents instructing them to submit lists of those areas which had been covered under the parochial system and were now without cover of any description and to forward details of any person who was both qualified and willing to act as local constable. The object, said McHardy, was "to provide at least one efficient Peace Officer in every hamlet and village in the county, who by cordial co-operation with the county police, may render it truly efficient without incurring the necessity of increasing the county police." A table of fees and allowances was worked out so that these volunteers would not be out of pocket, and an approach made to the Secretary of State for approval of this stop-gap measure.

By the second week in December a reply was received from the Home Office approving the employment of such persons and setting out regulations concerning these candidates. This measure, if successful, would give McHardy the breathing space to consolidate his force and the opportunity to apply for a further increase in manpower. He knew though that such an increase must depend on proof of efficiency. Both his ability and the calibre of the constables already pounding the beat was under scrutiny, not only from County Justices and the people of Essex, but from those other counties who had not yet decided on the style their own forces would take.

It must have given McHardy some pleasure to present to the Justices at Quarter Sessions the first overall crime return compiled by the Essex Constabulary. It covered the period 7th April to 30th June, 1840, and showed how his men were coming to grips with their problems.

Persons apprehended or summoned:	males	142
	females	16
	total:	158
Committed for trial:	felony	19
	assault	7
Dealt with at Magistrates' Courts:	vagrancy	26
	trespass	3
	assaults	10
	disorderly conduct	6
	simple drunk	5
	drunk & disorderly	17
	drunken assault	6
	wilful damage	5
	suspicious characters	2
	furious driving	1
	deserting family	1

Few people could doubt, as this historic first year drew to its close, that McHardy was the right man for the job and that this brave experiment was really beginning to work.

During the early months of 1840 discussions took place between the County Justices and the new Chief Constable to find suitable accommodation for a police headquarters. Various sites were discussed before agreement was reached on Old Court, the disused depot of the West Essex Militia in Arbour Lane, off Springfield Road, Chelmsford. It comprised "an Armoury, four Lodges or Dwelling Houses, two Magazines, a Guardroom, two Prisons, a Forge, Workshops, Sheds and Garden." The four lodges were, in fact, two pairs of buildings facing each other across the barrack square. The "prisons" were, of course, military cells.

The county had purchased the entire site and buildings from the Crown for £3,000 in 1819, plans being prepared for the conversion of these buildings into a lunatic asylum for some 350 patients, but the cost proved prohibitive and the site stood idle.

It was agreed that tenders should be invited to build a house for the Chief Constable and to convert the four existing buildings into a police headquarters complete with cells, sleeping accommodation and superintendent's quarters. While this work was put in hand Captain McHardy was found temporary offices at the recently built Springfield Gaol, just across the road. He and his secretary, Mr Walter Burke (another retired naval officer who had been granted the post at a salary of £100 a year) moved into the gaol, only to find the offices not furnished. The

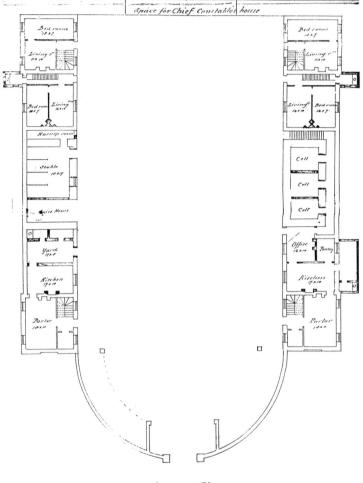

The ground floor plan of the original Essex Police headquarters at Springfield Court, Chelmsford.

Ground Plan

magistrates hastily ordered desks, cupboards and other office furniture to be transferred from the barracks. Unfortunately, the Colonel of the Militia got to hear about this and protested that while the county might have purchased the buildings, the transaction did not include the furnishings!

By March, 1840, a tender had been accepted from a builder named Thomas Moss "from the hamlet of Moulsham" to convert the depot and build the Chief Constable's house for a total cost of £3,260. The plans show a large three-sided complex of buildings, the north and south wings being of two storeys and containing a number of large bedrooms, living rooms, kitchens, parlours, three cells,

An early police rattle, the predecessor of the whistle.

guardroom, stables, harness-room, cart-shed and offices. A very fine three-storey house for the Chief Constable completed the third side of the square. These buildings, which were to remain the headquarters of the Essex Constabulary for the next sixty years, incorporated the divisional headquarters of the Chelmsford division. They stand to this day, used by various departments of Essex County Council.

Lengthy discussions took place on the subject of where constables in other parts of the county should be housed. Some Justices on the Police Committee considered that every constable should operate from his own lodgings or house and be paid a suitable allowance.

McHardy disagreed, for he had visions of greater things and could foresee the extent of Constabulary growth in years to come. He appreciated also the absolute necessity of being able to post men from one part of the county to another and realised only too well the difficulties involved if every man were living in his own lodgings. In June,1841, he submitted a carefully prepared report to the committee advocating a mobile workforce and the advisability of building police stations with accommodation for officers at carefully selected places throughout the county.

He argued that the efficiency of the force depended on the men being housed in public buildings and not in private lodgings, and pointed out that the only real question was whether so important an advantage could be obtained without a disproportionate expense. "I believe it is not practicable to efficiently carry out the Act with the whole force in private lodgings," he stated unequivocally.

McHardy's ability to change official thinking and to imbue even those magistrates who had had no idea that a police force could be anything but static and unchanging with just a little of his own vision and enthusiasm was a mark of his genius.

To reinforce his argument McHardy produced a breakdown of the cost for providing police stations and station houses. He also suggested how the county could recoup its expenditure. This is how he went about it:–

	£
Purchase of land	50
Two Strong Rooms (cells)	100
One Guard Room 15ft × 15ft	100
One Stable 13ft × 12ft and Cart Shed 13ft × 8ft	130
Total	380

The interest on this sum, at 4%, is £15.4s.0d. The £3 now allowed for stabling being saved would subject the county to the annual expense of £12.4s.0d.

Accommodation required:-
For Superintendent:-
    One living room 15ft × 10ft
    One kitchen 12ft × 10ft
    One bedroom 12ft × 10ft
    2nd bedroom 12ft × 9ft 3in
    One office 16ft × 8ft 300

For Two Constables:-
    Two living Rooms 13ft × 10ft
    Two bedrooms 9ft × 8ft 6in
    2nd bedrooms 9ft × 6ft 220

A well, pump, boundary wall, yard-gates, drains, cesspool and incidentals 180

Total 700

Four per cent on this sum would amount to £28, which by the superintendent paying £15 per annum, and the constables £5 each, with the saving of the £3 now allowed for an officer, would amount to £28—which is the interest on the capital invested.

I propose also, with reference to the County Constabulary Station now being erected at Springfield, the following scheme of rent be adopted:-

Chief Constable	£50 pa
Secretary	£15 pa
Superintendent	£15 pa

16 rooms for accommodation of Inspectors & Constables at 1s.0d a week for each room

Another of McHardy's initial tasks was to divide the county into manageable area. His first consideration was to place his constables in those areas where they were most needed, the quieter areas having to wait until he could increase his establishment to provide the county-wide cover he so wanted.

There was already in existence a system of division which had been operating quite efficiently since Saxon times, the hundreds and parishes. A glance at a "Hundreds Map" of Essex gives a very clear picture of how, through the ages, the county was for civil administrative purposes divided first into hundreds and then sub-divided into parishes. Since time immemorial each parish had had its constable and each hundred its High Constable. Here then was the solution to McHardy's problem, a ready-made, widely-known and recognised system of boundaries. It was quite obvious to McHardy that he could not use each of the hundreds as a separate division, so he amalgamated the smaller hundreds and formed the fifteen divisions as follows:–

Division	Div. HQ	Superintendent
Brentwood	Brentwood	A. Martingale
Chelmsford	Springfield*	T. Coulson
Colchester	Colchester	R. Johnston
Dengie	Latchingdon	J. Hawkins
Dunmow	Dunmow	M. Deacon
Epping	Epping	T. Godwin
Freshwell	Gt Bardfield	J. Anderson
North Hinckford	Sible Hedingham	T. Redin
South Hinckford	Braintree	S. Malings
Ongar	Ongar	J. McInnes
Rochford	Rayleigh	A. Low
Tendring	Thorpe	E. Evans
Walden	Newport	J. Clarke
Witham	Witham	C. Cooke

With the scant forces available McHardy could do no more than place a token presence in each of his divisions.

Within each of these divisions a site had to be found to establish a divisional headquarters. Logically, the largest town would have been the natural choice, but such a choice was impossible where a borough force was already operating there. Such was the case in the Walden Division which entirely surrounded the largest town, Saffron Walden. This town maintained its own borough force, so the divisional headquarters was sited a few miles away at Newport. In the Dengie Division the obvious choice would have been Maldon, but this too had its own borough force, so McHardy placed his divisional headquarters at Latchingdon. Harwich was no great

*It quickly became apparent that the headquarters buildings at Old Court, being half a mile from Chelmsford town centre, were too far away for the town to be efficiently administered by its constables, particularly as regards the walking of a recalcitrant prisoner from the High Street to the cells in Arbour Lane. Within a short while Chelmsford Division was transferred to the Shire Hall, in which there were already a number of cells; it continued to operate from there until a police station was built in 1903 in New Street.

problem, situated as it was on the coast in the extreme east of the county, and a more natural choice for the headquarters of the Tendring division was Thorpe-le-Soken.

McHardy had no need to concern himself with the west Essex parishes of Barking, Chingford, Chigwell, Dagenham, East Ham, Little Ilford, Loughton, Low Leyton, Waltham Holy Cross, West Ham, Walthamstow, Woodford and Wanstead. These had been transferred in 1834 to Metropolitan London and were already being administered by the Metropolitan Police.

Not only was it necessary to man these divisions but plans had to be made for suitable premises to house the superintendent and officers who were to operate those areas. McHardy approached the Justices for permission to take over any county-owned property which could be easily converted to police use. Where this was not practicable alternative accommodation was to be rented on a temporary basis until permanent premises could be found.

The first conversions of county property involved Newport and Halstead gaols, and part of the County Gaol at Colchester. The first two had been declared surplus to requirements following the building of the new Springfield Gaol at Chelmsford.

Instructions were given to the keepers of Newport and Halstead gaols that all their prisoners were to be transferred to Chelmsford, the women going to the old

Newport Gaol, near Saffron Walden, which was the headquarters of the Walden Division for forty-four years from 1840.

gaol and the men to the Springfield Gaol. The keepers were also informed that they would have to clear their gaols of all prisoners by 31st August, 1841, so that the police could take over on 1st September.

There is nothing on record to show the response of George Wright, the keeper of Halstead, but reaction was forthcoming from John Mead, keeper of Newport, in the form of beautifully written letters (whether written by a clerk or by himself is not known) begging to be allowed to stay on a short while longer. Such a letter, dated 20th July, 1841, is reproduced here:

"I must humbly beg pardon for the liberty I have taken in presuming to address you, but having received a letter from Mr Parker stating that my services would not be required after the 31st of next month, and inferring from this that I should be compelled to quit the House of Correction at that time, I would humbly beg leave to say that I have been using my best endeavours to procure a dwelling, but after all my exertions have been unable to do so, as none will become vacant until Michaelmas*, at which time I have engaged one. I beg to say that it is by the advice of the Visiting Magistrates of this Gaol, who are well acquainted with the difficulties of my case, I have presumed to address Your Worships. I would beg to state also that, in addition to my being rendered houseless by so short a notice, there are a quantity of potatoes and other vegetables in the garden which I had hoped to have laid by for the winter, but which would be spoiled were they removed so early in the month of August.

Trusting that I have always endeavoured, to the utmost of my powers, to discharge the duties of my Office to the satisfaction of the Magistrates, I would humbly beg Your Worships to take my case into your most serious consideration and that you will be pleased to allow me to remain at the House of Correction, as at present, until Old Michaelmas, at which time I can procure a dwelling.

I beg to be allowed to remain, Gentlemen,
Your most obedient, humble servant,
John Mead

The magistrates replied that as Superintendent John Clarke was living close by in rented accommodation it might benefit Mead to approach the owner of that property and apply to take over Clarke's rooms. To this Mead replied on 16th August, 1841, that he had approached the owner but "he told me positively that he could not allow me to go into it, it already being let to another person, so that Sir, I am still without the prospect of a house until Michaelmas. I shall be entirely destitute of a dwelling." There is nothing to show whether the Justices gave way on this or not, save that by November of that year Superintendent Clarke was certainly in residence at Newport Gaol and paying £11.14s.0d rent per annum for that accommodation.

In the meantime, Mead had been granted £31.6s.8d which represented two-thirds of his annual salary. No mention was made of his potatoes and other vegetables. George Wright at Halstead was granted his full salary until Michaelmas of that year, then an annuity of £20 a year for life and "allowed to keep the apples now growing at Halstead."

In March, 1841, a building known as Market House in Billericay was offered to the county as suitable for use as a stationhouse and lock-up. The owner agreed to accept a rent of £8 a year for the use of his house until more suitable premises could be found.

*29th September

Dunmow police station, built in 1842 and still in use more than 140 years later. *David L. Lipson*

The first land to be acquired for the building of a divisional headquarters was at Latchingdon in the Dengie Division. Within a short time inquiries were being made with landowners at Rochford and Dunmow. Although negotiations took place in November, 1840, it was to be a full year before contracts were prepared and work commenced on the first purpose-built police station in the county at Dunmow in June, 1842; within a year a police station, cells and stables had been completed at a cost of £1,100. The builder was a Henry Hammond Hayward, who was to go on to build a number of police stations throughout the county. The negotiations in respect of Latchingdon were more protracted than those at Dunmow, for it was not until 1846 that a suitable site was purchased and a police station built by the same Henry Hayward for the same cost as at Dunmow. Dunmow station remains fully operational to this day and ranks as the oldest in the county.

In June, 1842, three plots of land were offered at Braintree and Bocking, in the Halstead Division. The Justices decided to hold their next meeting at the White Hart Inn, Bocking, in order to view this land and decide on its suitability. Accordingly, on 8th June, after a doubtless convivial meeting, they agreed to purchase a plot owned by a Mr Laver, who happened also to be a builder and was granted the contract to build Braintree police station for the sum of £1,060. This building stood for many years in Rayne Road, next to St Michael's Hospital, before being demolished when the present police station was built in Fairfield Road at the turn of the century.

Finance was proving something of a problem, for in addition to purchasing land it was costing in the region of £1,000–£1,300 to erect the police stations. The Chief Constable had fourteen divisions and this represented enormous outlay. The county therefore sought financial backing from various businesses and finance companies at four per cent interest. Advertisements were placed in 1840 for the sum of £5,000, in January, 1844, for £2,000, in July, 1844, for £3,000 and in October of the same year for a further £3,000.

26

By April, 1843, the Chief Constable and Justices had decided that Castle Hedingham should be next on the list for a stationhouse. A very handsome police station and magistrates' court were operational by October, 1844. This building still stands.

Other Justices throughout the county were soon applying to be considered for police stations in their areas. More important than the actual buildings was the prospect of a regular, permanently based police presence, for there were still far too few constables to go round. In May,1843, Epping applied for such consideration and this was quickly followed by a similar request from Ongar. The approach of Ongar was accompanied by a letter from no less a person than the Under Secretary of State who declared that a lock-up should be built at Ongar with a superintending constable in charge. This weighty argument failed to move the County Justices, who decided that priority should go to Epping.

However, Ongar did not have very long to wait, for by 1855 a fine police station and magistrates' court costing £1,500 had been built on land purchased for £205. This police station and court were in constant use until 1962 when the court was transferred to Epping. The police station remained in operation until 1964 when it was demolished and a new one costing £30,000 built on its site.

By February, 1844, plans were approved for a station house and lock-up at Orsett and consent given for the purchase of land at Brentwood. By May of that year Orsett police station was rising under the hands of builder Thomas Hill, who had contracted to complete the building for £716.2s.5d. This building stood in Rowley Road, Orsett, and was operational for very many years before being demolished in 1976. The police station at Brentwood stood in what is now called Library Road and was the divisional headquarters for the Brentwood Division until 1937, when the present police station was built on the main London Road. The original building has been converted into a library.

Despite being one of the first sites to be considered in 1840, Rochford saw no positive steps to build a police station until 1846. In August of that year a plot of land was purchased for £219, the contract being awarded to William Carter, whose final figure for the building amounted to £805.13s.0d. On its completion towards the end of 1847 Inspector Henry Flood was moved in and Rochford thus became a sub-divisional station under Rayleigh, which was then operating from temporary premises in that town under Superintendent Algernon Low.

In August, 1850, Superintendent Low resigned. One of the original superintendents, he had joined the Constabulary in June, 1840, and had spent the whole of his ten years' service at Rayleigh. It is just possible that his decision had something to do with the new police station at Rochford, for within four months the divisional headquarters moved from Rayleigh to Rochford, this move having undoubtedly been in McHardy's mind when he had built the new station.

Inspector Flood was promoted superintendent and remained where he was at Rochford. Flood, then aged thirty-one, had joined the force in December, 1842, and went on to complete nearly forty years' service before retiring on pension in 1882.

Rochford police station in North Street remained operational until 1914 when the present, and much grander, police station was built in South Street. The original building is now the town's Post Office.

Some parishes, not altogether happy with the number of constables allocated to them, applied to McHardy for an increase in their establishment. They were told that if they wanted more constables they would have to pay for them, providing their salaries, uniforms, equipment, accommodation and allowances. Undeterred by this, Braintree "bought" two extra constables, Halstead one additional constable, Great & Little Coggeshall one additional constable, and Brentwood two constables to patrol the parishes of South Weald, Brook Street, Gildables and Great & Little Warley.

By 1849 Manningtree and Witham had received approval for their police stations, and the usual advertisements were placed for financial backing. The Essex Provident Society provided the £1,500 required for Witham, and by August, 1849, the building of that station commenced. The building in Guithavon Street took only seven or eight months to complete. This particular building still stands, although no longer a police station.

Despite the fact that the Constabulary had been operating for some ten years there were still powerful forces who made clear their views that the new police were an expensive luxury which should be speedily abolished. In July, 1850, the Billericay Guardians of the Poor petitioned the County Justices "that the County Constabulary have superintendance over so large an extent of the County as makes it quite impossible for them efficiently to protect the property situated in it, that for this inefficient Force the ratepayers are very heavily burthened, the outlay which is required for its support now amounting to sixteen thousand pounds a year. That it is impossible, without a ruinous expense to the County, to increase the Force so as to render it efficient. That for these reasons it is highly desirable that the said Force be forthwith abolished."

Looking at the situation from the ratepayers' point of view, it cannot be denied that this new constabulary force was proving very costly indeed. During the years 1840–1845 the county had borrowed no less than £14,000 at four per cent interest to build police stations costing an average of £1,200 each. Considering the cost of furnishing and maintaining each of these stations, the purchasing of horses, carts, uniforms and equipment, a wages bill of around £800 a month and Divisional Contingency Accounts averaging £80 a month, it is easy to see how the sum of £16,000 was spent.

But what was the ratepayer getting for this outlay? One hundred-and-sixty-three constables spread very thinly indeed throughout the county, with most of the fourteen divisions still boasting no more than a dozen men. With a population then of 396,298, this represented a ratio of one constable to 2,265 people. Despite continued efforts on his part to keep costs to a minimum McHardy was under pressure to justify the expense of this style of policing.

The County Justices voiced their support for McHardy by declaring that "the Essex County Constabulary is a highly valuable force, and is essentially necessary for the protection of property and the proper administration of Public Justice."

The building programme continued. The existing police stations at Dunmow and Latchingdon were extended to include magistrates' courts costing just under £200 each, and Halstead gaol was sold for £750 and the proceeds used for the building of Halstead police station. Early in 1851, the Justices of the Hinckford Hundred petitioned for the building of a courthouse attached to the new Halstead

Above: Halstead Gaol, which was divisional headquarters of the North Hinckford Division from 1840 until the building of Halstead police station in 1851. The photograph was taken in 1970 when the building was in use as a mill; it has since been demolished. *Mr Osborne, Halstead Historical Society*

Below: Ongar police station, built in 1855 and demolished in 1964–65 to make way for a new police station. The last court sitting there was held in March, 1962. *West Essex Gazette*

police station. Since £200 was paid for the courts at Dunmow and Latchingdon, it was considered that the same amount would suffice for the building of a courthouse at Halstead. Not a single reply was received to advertisements.

The Constabulary Committee was obliged to approach the County Justices with a suggestion that a further £200 be made available. That did the trick. The building went ahead and was finished by August, 1852. It remains to this day, still an operational police station, with the court still sitting twice weekly.

Not very far from Halstead, at Castle Hedingham, the local Justices made a similar application in respect of the police station built there in 1844. A plot of land

Old Harlow police station, built in 1852.

adjoining the police station was purchased for the princely sum of £25 and a courthouse added to the existing building. Again, both are operational today.

By October, 1852, approval was given for the erection of similar police stations and courts at Thorpe-le-Soken and Manningtree. The County Justices wisely decided to use the same sets of plans and to budget for the same sum as for the building of Halstead. The cost of these two buildings was estimated at £2,500–and the county simply did not have that amount available. Once again it was resolved to advertise for the money at the usual rate of four per cent interest.

What followed must have given McHardy the greatest possible pleasure. He offered the full £2,500 from the Constabulary Superannuation Fund. Taken aback the Justices certainly were, but they nevertheless accepted the offer gratefully. These stations thus share the distinction of being the first to be financed from the pockets of constables throughout the county. The contract for these two buildings was awarded to Mr Henry Hayward, who had built Dunmow and Latchingdon police stations. This same builder was also responsible for Ongar police station, built in 1854, and other police stations in the county.

By 1850, as the force stabilised and the building programme progressed, McHardy was able to satisfy the Justices that a substantial increase in manpower was justified. The token presence in each of his divisions was now swelled by a further sixty-three constables.

30

CHAPTER THREE

Death at Hutton

AS THE first streaks of dawn filtered through the trees of Norsey Wood, Billericay, the peace of that Thursday morning, 21st November, 1850, was shattered by the sound of men crashing through the undergrowth and the snarling of a fierce dog. William Waylett and George Amos, gamekeepers for Lord Petre, had tracked down and caught red-handed a well-known poacher from Ramsden Heath, twenty-year-old William Wood.

Well knowing the fate which awaited him if taken, the young poacher was determined to make a fight of it, first threatening the keepers with his shotgun and then drawing a vicious-looking knife. At this Waylett released his bloodhound. No match for the two men and their dog, Wood was quickly overpowered, bound and delivered to the police at Billericay along with two freshly killed pheasants found in his possession.

Later that morning the prisoner was taken before the magistrates, Captains Spitty and Ede. With scant ceremony he was sentenced to three months' imprisonment.

In those days at Billericay any person sentenced to a term in gaol had first to be conveyed to Brentwood and from there taken by County Cart or train to Chelmsford Prison. Inspector John Rough gave the task of escorting William Wood on the seven-mile walk to Brentwood to forty-three-year-old Pc Robert Bamborough, an officer of seven years' service. Now, it must certainly have occurred to Bamborough, if not to the inspector, that a prisoner of Wood's reputation merited an escort of two constables. Be that as it may, the officer had been ordered to take the man, and take him he must.

The manacles used on the prisoner comprised a length of stout chain with a handcuff at one end and a handgrip at the other. Bamborough locked the handcuff around Wood's right wrist and, taking the chain, led him out into the High Street. Turning left, they made their way up to the *Rising Sun* public house and then downhill out of town on what is now Rayleigh Road.

With little to occupy their minds but the surrounding countryside, prisoner and escort trudged along the quiet road as it twisted and turned on its way to the village of Hutton. After two miles the junction of Church Lane came into view on their left, and opposite stood the large, red-brick residence called Hutton House. Near the Church Lane junction was a small stagnant pond, shallow and unpleasant, with oozing black mud around its edges. A short distance further on stood the maltings (now demolished) owned by Mr Offing, inside which the labourers were preparing to break off for their midday meal.

Inside Hutton House, eleven-year-old Sarah Ann Hatch stood at a window overlooking the road. Her curiosity aroused, she craned forward to watch the two men pass by. Suddenly, to her horror, she saw the prisoner push the officer violently to the left.

Tripping over the grass verge, the constable fell on his back into the pond, still managing to retain his grip on the manacle chain. Wood was pulled into the water with him but regained his balance quickly and leapt on to the officer's chest, demanding that he release his grip on the chain.

Pc Bamborough's only reply was to tighten his grip as he struggled to extricate himself. At that Wood trampled the officer into the muddy water, forcing his head below the surface. Then, holding his victim's head and nose with one hand, he thrust

Hutton House, from a window of which Sarah Ann Hatch watched the events of 21st November, 1850.

black mud into the constable's gaping mouth. Within seconds Bamborough had lost consciousness.

Leaving him in the water, Wood leaped from the pond and took to his heels. Within yards, though, he stopped, returned to the pond and hauled the officer's head and shoulders clear of the water. He turned again and fled down Church Lane towards All Saints' Church, Hutton.

By that time the girl's screams had alerted the workmen in the maltings some thirty yards away. Swiftly they hauled the policeman from the pond. Pc Bamborough was placed in a cart and driven the three-quarters of a mile to the *Chequers* public house in Hutton, while another worker sped to Billericay to summon the police and a doctor.

Within a short time surgeon Mr W. Carter and Inspector Rough were at the *Chequers*. At first believing him to be dead, the surgeon was surprised to see the constable begin to vomit. His surprise turned to consternation, though, when he saw that Bamborough was bringing up nothing but black mud. He told the inspector that his lungs were obviously congested with this filthy substance and that he could not have long to live. Hearing this, the inspector returned to Billericay and summoned the magistrates who had only that morning dealt with the case.

Arriving at the public house, Captain Spitty and Captain Ede questioned the unfortunate constable as best they could, taking his account down as a form of Dying Declaration.

The police quickly discovered that the escaped prisoner had made his way to Brentwood and then on to Tilbury. From there his trail was followed across the river to Gravesend and Chatham. On their arrival at Chatham the officers found their quarry already under lock and key, for Wood had been recognised from the description published in that morning's newspaper. Within twenty-four hours of his escape he was back in Billericay.

It was then common practice for the accused to be confronted by his victim, both for identification purposes and to hear for himself what his accuser had to say. Accordingly, in company with magistrates and Superintendent Coulson from Brentwood, the prisoner was taken to Pc Bamborough's bedside, where he heard the officer relate what had happened. Wood had no questions to ask, as he was entitled to do, and said only that he had no intention of killing the constable. He was taken away and charged with attempted murder. Pc Bamborough died the following day.

A little over a week later at an inquest held at the *Three Horseshoes*, Billericay, during which Inspector Rough came in for some very uncomfortable questioning, the jury returned a verdict of wilful murder against William Wood.

During the second week of March, 1851, the accused stood before Mr Baron Parke in the Nisi Prius court* of the Lent Assizes, Chelmsford. Represented by a Mr Hawkins, he heard the damning Dying Declaration of Pc Bamborough read to the jury. His entire defence revolved around the subject of intent, for had he intended the death of the officer, he said, he would never have returned to pull him from the water. How could the jury accept this without corroboration? Paradoxically, it was the evidence given by the chief prosecution witness, Sarah Ann Hatch, that was to save him from the gallows, for she told the truth.

At the end of the day the jury returned a verdict of manslaughter. The Judge remarked to the prisoner, "The jury has taken a very merciful view of your case, and with that I cannot find fault". He sentenced Wood to transportation for life.

John Rough, called to give evidence, did so as ex-Inspector Rough, his resignation immediately after the death of his constable having been accepted. One of the original inspectors appointed in 1841, his police career had lasted just nine years.

Thus did the constabulary, just ten years old and 138 strong, suffer its first loss of life.

The *Chequers* public house still stands as it did in 1850, as does Hutton House and the old police station. Rayleigh Road is much wider now and carries considerably more traffic than it did then. Church Lane remains, and apart from its tarmac surface looks the same today as it did 130 years ago. The *Three Horseshoes* public house has long since disappeared but the pond itself, the scene of this murderous attack, remains to this day and forms part of the garden of a nearby house.

---

*Nisi Prius: a special court convened to try cases which, for whatever reason, could not be dealt with by the Assize. In this particular case William Wood was the last on the Assize list, and when it became apparent that time would run out before his case came before the Assize (thereby enabling him under a medieval Act to ask for trial at Westminster) a Nisi Prius court had to be convened to try this one case.

CHAPTER FOUR

Expansion

WITH THE Government paying around £9,000 a year to maintain 127 Revenue Officers in Essex, McHardy, a former Coastguard and anti-smuggling officer himself, recommended that the 200 police officers in the county could make a valuable contribution to this service. On 31st December, 1850, he wrote to the Justices "with a view to the more effectual protection of the Revenue I suggest that officers of the Essex Constabulary should be empowered to make seizure of any contraband goods which they may discover while in the execution of their normal duties." This recommendation was agreed by the Justices and forwarded to the Home Office for sanction by the Revenue services.

During April, 1851, a certain Inspector Daunt (later to become superintendent) in company with Pc Samuel Duce arrested three smugglers and seized a cart laden with contraband tobacco. Both smugglers and goods were handed over to the Excise authorities and in due course the diligence of the police officers was recognised by a reward of £31.0s.4d. which went to county funds. Doubtless Daunt and Duce received two or three guineas each as reward for their diligence.

McHardy now faced a dilemma, for his proposals of December, 1850, had not yet been approved. Inspector Daunt and the constable had technically exceeded their authority. Nevertheless, £31.0s.4d represented about thirty weeks wages for a county constable then and McHardy was loathe to lose such a sum.

He wrote to the Justices explaining the situation and quoting the rules and regulations governing the Essex Constabulary, namely that "all Chief and other Constables appointed under the Act shall be restrained from employing themselves in any office or employment for hire or gain other than in the execution of their duty." Without a doubt these officers had "gained" from an act which was not within the execution of their duty. The Chief Constable went on to suggest that the issue could be resolved by a simple amendment to the rules and regulations in that the words "except with the sanction of the Secretary of State, the Court of Quarter Sessions (ie Justices) or the Chief Constable" be added to that sentence.

He was doubtless pleased to hear that the Justices concurred with his solution, but probably not quite so pleased to learn that they had deleted the words "Chief Constable". All future rewards would therefore require to be sanctioned by the Justices!

An interesting situation existed in the Blackwater and Crouch estuaries concerning the protection of the renowned oyster beds of that region. As far back as Roman times this area of tidal estuaries had been famed for its oysters and shellfish, and by the turn of the nineteenth century it was providing a valuable contribution to the wealth of the county.

So valuable were these beds that watchmen were employed to guard against poachers, and in 1842 the Burnham Oyster Company approached the Chief Constable with a suggestion that the police should take over, or at least assist with these duties. McHardy agreed on condition that the company contributed towards the cost of maintaining these officers. He subsequently transferred to Burnham an inspector and four constables for this duty. The inspector was Andrew Rome, who had joined the constabulary at the outset. He was to remain at Burnham until he retired at the age of seventy-nine, still an inspector, in 1897. This incredible span of fifty-seven years continuous police service constitutes a record never since equalled.

The deterrent effect of uniformed police officers patrolling these creeks and marshes was such that within a few years other oyster companies were investing in the "hire" of policemen. The Tollesbury & Mersea Oyster Company maintained four constables, and the Paglesham Oyster Company paid for a sergeant and two constables.

Always looking for ways of improving the service given by his police force, McHardy proposed to the County Justices in July, 1851, that yet another duty could well be performed by his men. The toll-gates around Chelmsford (no fewer than twenty-three in number) could be manned and operated by his constables, a task which would "increase their efficiency" and give them an opportunity of learning who was out and about on the county roads. The tolls collected could be used to finance an increase in manpower for the Constabulary.

He did not go into details as to how he could immediately replace twenty-three officers (an omission totally out of character with his normally meticulous mind), but the question did not arise, for the Justices dismissed the idea out of hand.

During the summer of 1852, McHardy was approached by the County Justices and military authorities for assistance in their attempts to increase the strength of the Essex Militia. He conferred with the Colonel of the Regiment and agreement was reached that the Constabulary would be paid five shillings for every eligible volunteer obtained by its members. McHardy wrote to all his divisional superintendents instructing them to use their best endeavours, through their constables, to persuade as many as possible to volunteer for the Militia. "It is my intention," he wrote, "to devote this procuring money towards the foundation of divisional libraries for the general benefit of the Constabulary—more particularly for the subordinates who, I regret to say, are very deficient in general knowledge and evince little desire to acquire it..." He followed this rather sad observation with a declaration that the libraries would be established only if the members desired it, a county-wide referendum being proposed to ascertain the views of the Constabulary.

In December the following year he wrote that his "efforts to furnish the Constabulary with this aid and stimulant to mental improvement had been frustrated by the unqualified negative return by the Epping Division and Ongar Detachment," and under the circumstances he felt "reluctantly compelled to abandon the scheme and to refrain from any further interference with the Militia procuring money."

He could never be accused of not having the welfare of his men at heart. It is rather surprising that in an authoritarian age he allowed this setback to occur as a result of putting the matter to a democratic vote; this sense of fair play was a hall-mark of his character.

McHardy was often to express his annoyance at what he called "lack of knowledge." Indeed, it was not uncommon for him to adopt measures reminiscent of a schoolmaster. On one occasion he urged his superintendents to use every means in their power "to instruct those under your orders to increase their mental qualifications, and to improve their handwriting, for I regret to notice that I have frequently been much disappointed... You will cause every member of the Constabulary to copy out this memorandum and transmit them to me by the end of this month."

It was not only the problems of limited education that worried the Chief Constable, who seized any opportunity that presented itself to improve the efficiency of his force. When he heard in January, 1854, that the County Gaol at Colchester was to be demolished to make way for a new barracks for the East Essex Militia McHardy immediately wrote to the Justices suggesting a new police station should be built on an area of land not earmarked by the military authorities.

The County Gaol had been the home of the Colchester Division since the formation of the Essex Constabulary, the basing of the county police in the building being possible because it was on the Ipswich road about a mile east of the town centre and was both owned and maintained by the county. The Colchester Borough Police operated from rooms in the basement of Colchester Town Hall, which also housed the borough gaol.

The Chief Constable's proposal was approved and plans prepared for a new police station, the builder Henry Hayward being given the contract to build both the barracks and the police station in April, 1854. He was instructed to use the old bricks and other material salvaged from the gaol, this helping to keep the cost of the station house and lock-up down to £1,533.

During October Hayward reported finding the level of water in the gaol well unusually low, and it was discovered that construction of a nearby railway cutting, owned by the Eastern Counties Railway Company, had drained away the water. A deeper bore would have to be sunk and a new pump fitted at a total cost of £58.10s.0d. Hayward was told to go ahead and the Justices resolved to send the bill to the railway company.

The police station was completed in early 1855 and remained the divisional headquarters of the Colchester Division until 1946, when the borough police amalgamated with the county. The merged forces then operated from the police station in Queen Street which had been used by the borough force since 1940.

Later in 1854 a long and wide-ranging report heralding a number of changes, one of them being the introduction of the rank of sergeant, was submitted to the Justices by McHardy. The cost of policing the county was clearly a major preoccupation, McHardy complaining that the growth of the county constabulary was being retarded by a lack of finance and going on to say that he trusted "that the Government and Legislature will yet recognise the justice and expediency of aiding Local Police Rates by an annual grant from the National Funds." Two years later, with the passing of the County and Borough Police Act, such Exchequer grants were introduced.

The difficulty of "procuring and retaining men of honour and ability" as divisional superintendents had impaired the general efficiency of the force, McHardy said, proposing the reduction of the fourteen divisions to ten and the raising of the superintendents' salaries in relation to their grades. He proposed three First Class Superintendents at £85 a year, three Second Class at £75 and four Third Class at £65, and went on to recommend the establishment of an intermediate grade of sergeant at twenty-three shillings a week, just two shillings more than the wage of a First Class Constable. Ten First Class Constables should, he said, be promoted to sergeant and the authorised strength of the force be increased by that number.

Since his proposals would effectively wipe out any financial gains brought about by the reduction in the number of superintendents he suggested making good the loss by increasing rents paid by members of the force.

The scheme for local constables introduced at the end of 1840 in an effort to bolster the thinly spread police presence had not been a success as the numbers of volunteers coming forward had been nowhere near as high as McHardy had hoped.

The original police station at Thorpe-le-Soken, built in 1853 as the headquarters of the Tendring Division. It is still in use today.

At the time of his report there were fifty-four regular First Class Constables, fifty-eight Second Class and fifty-six Third Class operating in Essex.

Changes in uniform were also recommended in his report, his suggestion being that consideration should be given to a new style of uniform being introduced into the Metropolitan Police at the time. He suggested the following styles for each rank:

Constable: A coat of blue cloth, single-breasted with eight buttons down the front and a further two buttons on the hips, all buttons bearing the county arms; an embroidered collar bearing a crown and the number of the constable.
Sergeant: The same uniform as the constable but with only a crown on the collar.
Inspector: The same as the sergeant except that the coat was double-breasted, with eight buttons in each row; there should be black braid, half an inch wide, around the collar.
Superintendent: The same as the inspector but with silver braid, half an inch wide, around the cuffs.

After being considered at great length by the Justices, McHardy's report was agreed in principle and despatched to London for approval by the Secretary of State. By April, 1855, Lord Palmerston had replied that he had examined the issues raised and offered no objection to their implementation.

The way was clear for McHardy to put his plans into effect. Freshwell, Ongar and Tendring divisions were amalgamated with neighbouring divisions and North and South Hinckford were merged to form a new Hinckford Division.

The Essex Constabulary now comprised the following divisions:

Division	Location	Sub-Division	Superintendent
Brentwood	Brentwood	Billericay Orsett Romford	William Bridges
Chelmsford	Springfield	Nil	Joseph Rhymer
Colchester	Colchester	Thorpe Manningtree Copford	Thomas Daunt
Dengie	Latchingdon	Burnham	Inspector J. Bauser
Epping	Epping	Ongar Harlow	William Pattisson
Hinckford	Halstead	Braintree Castle Hedingham	Jeremiah Raison
Rochford	Rochford	Rayleigh	Inspector H. Ackers
Walden	Newport	Saffron Walden Stansted Chesterford	Henry Flood
Witham	Witham	Coggeshall	Joseph Catchpole

Of the sixteen sub-divisions those at Billericay, Romford, Copford, Burnham, Harlow, Rayleigh, Stansted, Chesterford and Coggeshall were still operating from rented accommodation.

Mention of Romford raises an interesting and somewhat puzzling question: why was it not chosen as a divisional headquarters back in 1840? In 1841 the population of Brentwood was just 2,362, whereas Romford boasted 5,317. The latter was a thriving town with much of its industry catering for the Metropolis. Famed for its leather-working, its large brewery and its busy cattle market, to say nothing of a workhouse built to accommodate 500 (a sure indication of the size and importance of a community), Romford was decidedly worthy of consideration.

It is probable that the town was considered to be situated too close to the Metropolitan Police area to render it effective as a divisional headquarters, although this fact did not prevent Romford Division being formed in later years. Its importance was acknowledged from the outset with the stationing of an inspector in the town during the 1840s, and through the years the police strength grew steadily until in 1900 Romford became a division in its own right.

Meanwhile, the County Justices were rearranging the police districts within the county. These had been created earlier for administrative purposes and are not to be confused with police divisions. The districts formed were seven in number and are set out here only to show the strength and distribution of the force and the population and acreage of the various parishes:-

District	Parishes	Acres	Population	Constables
1.	Braintree	2,500	4,340	1
	Bocking	3,800	3,846	4
2.	Halstead	6,230	6,982	3
3.	Gt. & Lt. Coggeshall	830	430	2
4.	South Weald	5,200	1,383	
	Brentwood	730	2,205	
	Great Warley	1,990	952	
	Little Warley	2,140	344	5
	Shenfield	1,430	938	
	Ingrave	1,220	521	
	Childerditch	900	209	
5.	Chelmsford	1,750	7,796	6
6.	Havering	4,290	423	
	Hornchurch	4,920	2,378	
	Romford	3,340	5,868	8
7.	All other Parishes within the county	840,640	235,712	140
	Totals:	881,910	274,327	169

These figures for population do not, of course, include the boroughs of Saffron Walden, Colchester, Harwich and Maldon.

With the ratio of constables to population now one to 1,623, the Justices approved an increase in the force of a further thirty-two constables. District 1 was to receive two constables, District 2 would receive two constables, Districts 3 and 4 would be sent one constable each and District 7 a total of twenty-six constables. They also approved the increase in rents and the creation of the new rank of sergeant; he was to pay the same rent as a married constable, two shillings a week.

The total strength of the force, in 1855, was therefore:-

Chief Constable	1	
Superintendents First Class	3	
Superintendents Second Class	3	
Superintendents Third Class	4	10
Inspectors First Class	3	
Inspectors Second Class	3	
Inspectors Third Class	4	10
Sergeants	10	10
Constables First Class	54	
Constables Second Class	58	
Constables Third Class	56	
Constables newly authorised	32	200

Although McHardy had succeeded in doubling the strength of his force in fourteen years, the strength of his divisions still averaged only one superintendent, one inspector, one sergeant and ten constables. It is interesting to reflect that McHardy's total number of constables was less than the present-day Chelmsford Division alone.

In less than fifteen years McHardy had succeeded in providing no fewer than thirteen custom-built police stations for his original fourteen divisions. Only Walden remained without new premises; its officers were comfortably housed in the sturdy Newport Gaol and adequately equipped with offices, sleeping accommodation and cells.

Of the original divisions, only Freshwell remained unprovided for, the superintendent working from rented accommodation at Great Bardfield. The need

The village lock-up, known as the Cage, at Great Bardfield. This was unusual in having two cells, one of them for females.

for new premises disappeared in 1855 when Freshwell was amalgamated with the Dunmow and Hinckford Divisions, yet two years later approval was granted at the request of local magistrates for the building of a court, cells and accommodation for one constable at a cost of £850.

This achievement signalled the end of the initial building programme in the county. Police stations were henceforth to be built only when the surrounding population grew to such proportions that the existing police cover was deemed inadequate. Saffron Walden was given its own police station in 1884 when it was considered necessary to move the divisional headquarters from the village of Newport to a more sensible location in the much larger town. Maldon, too, saw its own police station built soon after the amalgamation of the borough and county forces in 1888.

When one considers the enormous extent of police building over the length and breadth of the county today, it is somewhat amusing to reflect that McHardy was instructed back in 1840 that his police stations should be so designed as to render them easily convertible to private dwellings should the new system of policing fail.

The year 1866 began with McHardy complaining to the Justices that recruitment was being seriously affected by the low rates of pay. Since 1840 there had been only

40

one review, in 1855. He proposed substantial increases, particularly for the supervising ranks, and the abolition of the Third Class grade in all ranks except that of constable.

By April the following increases were approved:-

	Old	New
Chief Constable	£450	£500
4 Superintendents 1st Class	£130	£150
6 Superintendents 2nd Class	£115	£125
4 Inspectors 1st Class	£ 65	£ 90
6 Inspectors 2nd Class	£ —	£ 80
4 Sergeants 1st Class	23s. pw	28s. pw
10 Sergeants 2nd Class	—	25s. pw
50 Constables 1st Class	21s. pw	23s. pw
100 Constables 2nd Class	19s. pw	21s. pw
56 Constables 3rd Class	17s. pw	19s. pw

The same year also brought about a considerable improvement in the comfort of the constabulary with the installation of gas lighting in the police stations at Chelmsford, Brentwood, Castle Hedingham, Dunmow, Halstead, Rochford, Witham, Epping and Ongar.

It was to be expected, perhaps, that local Justices should see no reason why the public rates should be burdened with this additional expense. Some, including those at Epping and Ongar, proposed that deductions should be made from the policemen's pay to help pay for this new form of lighting.

That year of 1866 brought to public notice the price that policemen were called upon to pay in the course of maintaining law and order. Such a price was paid by Pc Edward St Clair, stationed at Saffron Walden.

Dawn was breaking on a fine April morning when the peace was shattered for Pc St Clair as he patrolled his lonely beat near Wimbish. Screams and the crashing of furniture from a nearby house brought the officer running to the scene. On entering the house he found a stranger savagely attacking a man and wife who had been aroused from their beds by the sound of the stranger entering the house. It later transpired that the assailant, who had walked in his bare feet all the way from Saffron Walden, was an escaped lunatic.

St Clair tackled the man and managed after a fierce struggle to get him downstairs, but in the struggle the officer was bitten on his right thumb with such ferocity that the flesh was opened to the bone. Later that morning the local magistrates ordered the man to be removed to an asylum and Pc St Clair was instructed to carry this out. Only after he had handed over the patient could Pc St Clair obtain treatment for the injury to his thumb, by the simple expedient of having hot water run over the wound. Unfortunately the hand became badly infected, and doctors diagnosed gangrene. Without hesitation the unfortunate constable was conveyed to the operating theatre, where the lower half of his right arm was amputated.

These sad facts were communicated to the Chief Constable, who subsequently recommended to the Justices that Pc St Clair, although an officer of only six years' service, should be awarded the highest pension possible. This was unhesitatingly approved and a pension of 1s.6d a day, roughly half-pay, was awarded. Edward St Clair was then just thirty-two.

While the injuries to this constable were quite exceptional, the subject of violent physical attack on police officers was not. McHardy was informed of every instance in which his men were subjected to serious assault, and ideas were beginning to form in his mind on the subject of recognising bravery in the course of duty.

Until 1871 the only reward normally granted for exceptional conduct was a monetary grant of two or three guineas made by the magistrates as a mark of their appreciation. However, McHardy felt that something of a more tangible nature was required, something which would identify an officer who had shown particular courage. After considerable thought he approached the Justices and put to them his idea for a Merit Class officer.

He proposed an emblem in the shape of a star, embroidered in silver thread, and to be worn on each side of the officer's collar alongside his number. He suggested limiting the award to a handful of men who had shown "highly distinguished conduct in the discharge of duty, particularly when accompanied by a risk to life, personal courage and coolness, aided by marked intelligence." Only ten sergeants and twenty constables could bear this distinction at any one time, the constables receiving an extra shilling a week and the sergeants an extra two shillings a week; both badge and extra pay were subject to forfeiture for misconduct.

The magistrates were delighted with the proposal and instructed McHardy to implement the scheme, but so discerning was the Chief Constable that over six months were to go by before he made his first award. The recipient was Pc John Street, stationed at Foxearth in the Hinckford Division. Pc Street was patrolling his beat at Pentlow, an isolated spot near the Suffolk border, at about two o'clock in the morning of 7th January, 1872, when he was suddenly confronted by three men who had just broken into a chicken-house and stolen no fewer than seventeen fowls which were contained in a large sack carried by one of the men. The officer challenged them and demanded to know what was in the sack. Without warning all three men attacked him. Fortunately, in addition to his truncheon the constable was carrying a stout stick (by no means uncommon in those days for officers on night duty) and set about the three men with such vigour that they eventually turned and fled.

He set off in pursuit and caught up with them, whereupon they again turned on him. A rather one-sided battle took place on that deserted road before the three again took to their heels and fled. This time, although injured, Pc Street retained a tight hold on one of the men and the sack containing the chickens. Within a short space of time he had this man under lock and key, and one of the others whom the officer had recognised quickly joined his companion. The third man was never traced.

McHardy decided that here was just the situation he had in mind. He wrote to Pc Street's superintendent informing him of this, and then personally ordered a tunic to be prepared by the tailors displaying the Star of Merit. He ensured that the tunic was

Members of the Rochford Division in 1873. The men are wearing the frock coat which replaced the original tail coat from 1855.

delivered to Pc Street on the very day that he appeared at Castle Hedingham Court, where the two thieves were appearing on remand. McHardy was fully aware of the publicity that such action generated and of the boost it gave to police morale.

Pc Street was entitled to describe himself as "Constable Merit Class," for this was now a grade in its own right irrespective of whether the officer was first, second or third class at the time. Its infrequent use by McHardy ensured that it remained an exceptional and highly prized award. It continued to be awarded until well into the present century, the star being later transferred from the collar to the lower half of the right sleeve.

The growth of the Essex Constabulary by no means kept pace with the growth of population in the county during the nineteenth century. In 1840 an inspector and two constables was considered sufficient for the growing seaside resort of Southend, which in that year had a population of 5,279 if one includes Leigh-on-Sea and the other five parishes which eventually made up the borough of Southend-on-Sea. At the 1871 Census the population of that same area had risen to 9,747, but the strength of the police had not increased in proportion.

In April, 1873, the ratepayers and inhabitants of Southend petitioned the County Justices not only for an increase in the number of policemen but also for the building of a permanent police station and magistrates' court. Every summer Southend saw its population swollen by an influx of holidaymakers brought by steamer and by train from London, and it cannot be wondered at that the inhabitants pressed for a substantial increase in police cover.

The Justices fully supported the application and by October land in what is now Alexandra Street had been purchased for £450 and a contract for a station house incorporating four cells, a magistrates' court and accommodation for a superintendent and four married constables had been put out to tender. The contract was awarded to a Maldon builder named Saunders who undertook "to complete the work within ten months from 3rd September, 1873," but it is obvious that difficulties were encountered and the building was not completed until the end of 1875. No less than £4,500 of the £4,568.18s.4d the building cost was borrowed from the Police Pension Fund at the usual four per cent interest.

Realising the potential of this thriving community McHardy was already making plans to transfer the divisional headquarters from Rochford to Southend. From the moment of transfer the police presence in Southend grew apace, with sub-stations being established at Shoeburyness, Westcliff, Hockley and Great Wakering.

New pay scales came into force at the beginning of 1874. They were:-

		Old £	New £
Superintendent	Class 1	150	170
	Class 2	125	140
Inspector	Class 1	90	110
	Class 2	80	90
Sergeant	Merit Class	—	33s. pw
	Class 1	28s. pw	31s. pw
	Class 2	25s. pw	29s. pw
Constable	Merit Class	—	28s. pw
	Class 1	23s. pw	27s. pw
	Class 2	21s. pw	24s. pw
	Class 3	19s. pw	21s. pw

That same year of 1874 saw the introduction of new headgear which has since come to be regarded as the distinctive mark of the policeman. In October McHardy wrote to the Justices saying that as other forces had discarded their hats in favour of helmets he recommended that officers in Essex should be issued with similar headgear, at the same time pointing out that the Metropolitan Police had issued new-style uniforms to their superintendents and inspectors and suggesting the issue of similar uniforms to senior members of the Essex force.

His proposals were accepted, and thus the dress coat which reached almost to the officer's knees and the bowler-type hat he had worn since 1855 disappeared, replaced by a shorter tunic and a helmet whose design has remained virtually unchanged since that time. Superintendents and inspectors found the fronts of their uniform jackets adorned with black frogging which was to remain an essential part of their uniform until well into the present century.

The Chief Constable's thoughts were not so taken up with matters of uniform that he ignored matters of hygiene. He was well aware of the danger of underground sources of water being contaminated by the cesspools and soakaways which were common features.

As far back as the 1840s McHardy was complaining of an open sewer which ran from the police headquarters buildings at Springfield down to the River Chelmer, his protests resulting in the laying of a proper drain at a cost of £90, and in 1849 he commented on the "offensive odour" which prevailed at Dunmow police station, ensuring that a water closet was built at a cost of £5.8s.

This lack of hygiene had not greatly improved more than twenty years later, for in April, 1872, he wrote that, having suspected for a long time that the water drawn from the well at headquarters was impure, he had taken it upon himself to send away a sample for analysis and was not surprised when the analyst reported that the water "was heavily polluted with the products of nearby drains and cesspools." He went on to declare that he had no alternative but to draw the pure water which was then

The original police station at Latchingdon which served as headquarters of the Dengie Division until 1902.

enjoyed by the prisoners at nearby Springfield Gaol, and to cease using the headquarters well until modifications could be made.

More serious than this was a report he submitted in October, 1877, informing the Justices that typhoid fever, also known as drain or cesspool fever, had broken out at Latchingdon police station (one of the first to be built). He had immediately called in the County Medical Officer of Health and instructed him to forward his report to the Justices for necessary action to be taken on "this sanitary evil." McHardy took the opportunity in the same report to inform the Justices that smallpox had struck down the inspector and constables at Orsett police station as a result of an infected prisoner being lodged in one of the cells. He had closed down the station and declared that it would remain thus until thoroughly disinfected and passed by the Medical Officer.

That there had been no permanent improvement for the officers stationed at Orsett became obvious when the County Justices received a report dated 15th August, 1884, from the Chief Constable (then Major Poyntz) in which he angrily reported that smallpox had once again broken out at Orsett. Not only was Sergeant Gifford seriously ill and "lying in a very precarious state" but his wife had also contracted the disease. Because Mr and Mrs Gifford were too ill to look after their five young children the Chief Constable had employed a nurse to care for the family; the Giffords' doctor would not countenance the removal of the parents to the Infectious

Admiral McHardy with members of his force at Old Court, Chelmsford. The photograph was taken between 1875, when superintendents and inspectors were first issued with caps instead of helmets, and 1881, the year of McHardy's retirement. The men fourth from left and second from right in the front row are wearing the Star of Merit introduced in 1871.   *Stan Jarvis*

Ward of the Orsett Union House on the grounds that it was the cause of the outbreak in the first place.

The Orsett police station was until 1878 one of only two custom-built police stations in the whole of the enormous Brentwood Division, covering all of south-west Essex, the other being at Brentwood itself; both had been built in 1844. Even Tilbury with its bustling docks did not boast its own permanent police quarters but was administered from Orsett by way of "detached" constables operating from rented accommodation, as indeed were Grays, Ockendon and Aveley.

Agreement was reached in January, 1878, that Grays should be provided with its own permanent police station, a site being purchased for £387 and plans prepared for a new station house and lock-up. Surprisingly, no provision was made in the plans for a magistrates' court, the local Justices at that time still sitting in rented rooms at the ill-famed Orsett Union House.

By a curious coincidence in April, 1878, the Guardians of the Poor required the Justices to quit their accommodation in the Union House by September of that year as the rooms were said to be required for other purposes, and the plans for Grays police station were hastily amended to incorporate a courtroom. Only £1,450 was allocated for the building, but the lowest of the nine tenders received in October amounted to £1,663. So pressing was the need by then for accommodation that the County Justices had to authorise the increase.

Within eighteen months the new police station, the last to be built during McHardy's long and industrious period of office, was ready for occupation by an inspector and three constables, and the magistrates. The magistrates still sit in the courtroom but the police have moved to a new and very much larger police station built during the late 1970s immediately behind the old building; the old police offices are now occupied by the Probation Service.

Tilbury had to wait another twenty-seven years before being granted its own permanent police quarters.

For forty years McHardy had controlled the Essex Constabulary, building up the infant force and parrying the thrusts of those who sought its early demise. By 1880 he was beginning to accept that the time was fast approaching when he would have to hand over the reins to a younger man.

He had to prepare for retirement. In a letter dated 19th October, 1880, he pointed out to the Justices that his salary of £520 was made up of £400 basic salary plus £100 allowances and £20 paid by the boroughs of Saffron Walden and Harwich. His pension would be calculated only on his basic salary, and he felt justified in asking for a pay rise of, say, £100 a year to offset the allowances and so to increase his pension when he retired. Bearing in mind that his salary had increased by only £100 over the forty years he had served in Essex, the Justices felt this was not asking too much; the Secretary of State also gave his approval on 29th April, 1881.

The superintendents of the Essex Constabulary say farewell to the Deputy Chief Constable, Wallace McHardy, before his departure in 1875 to become Chief Constable of Lanarkshire. The helmets and uniform jackets adorned with black frogging for inspectors and superintendents had been introduced the previous year.

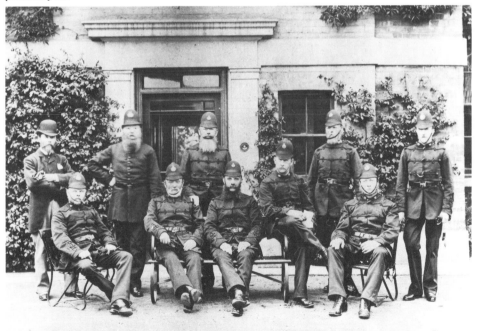

Two months later McHardy sent in his letter of resignation, to take effect on 18th October, 1881. And on the day that he retired he wrote his final letter to the Justices containing not only his farewell but also his last review of the force.

"When first established, the police were viewed with some distrust and disfavour as being an unnecessary expense, but the keen discernment of the British public soon led them to recognise in the policeman a friend to quietude and order, and thus distrust gradually gave way to confidence as was manifested by the applications received from various villages and parishes for a constable to be stationed therein," he wrote. "This confidence has been more than maintained..."

Admiral McHardy was not to enjoy a long retirement. He died at the home of his son-in-law and daughter at Bath on 19th December, 1882, his body being brought back to his beloved Essex for burial in the family grave at Holy Trinity Church, Springfield. When his wife Horatia died the following year her body, too, was brought back to Essex and laid to rest at Springfield.

An Essex policeman of the nineteenth century, Pc James Ballard of Shoeburyness. Taken in the 1870s, this photograph shows him wearing the bowler-style headgear which was replaced in 1874 by the now-familiar helmet.

CHAPTER FIVE

A new Chief Constable

T HE ELECTION of McHardy's successor took place on 21st October, 1881, when ninety-four Justices gathered at the Shire Hall, Chelmsford, to pick one man from the four short-listed from the original 122 applicants. Their choice fell on Major William Henry Poyntz, Chief Constable of the Borough of Nottingham.

With seventeen years experience as an officer in the Royal Marines Light Infantry followed by eight years as chief constable of the fourth largest borough force in the country (in terms of area), Major Poyntz came to Essex with his own ideas on how a police force should be run, and they did not entirely coincide with the views of his predecessor, with whom he had many discussions before McHardy's departure.

Born in Dublin in 1838 of well-to-do Anglo-Irish parents, William spent much of his early life at boarding school, first in Dublin and then in England, completing his education with a year at Trinity College, Dublin. The immediate family numbered among its members an admiral, a naval captain and a colonel, and there seemed to be no question that the sons of the family should follow a naval or military career. William, unable to make up his mind whether to choose the navy or army, opted for the middle road and was commissioned in the Royal Marines Light Infantry, with whom he took part in the capture of Canton in 1857 and the storming of the Taku forts two years later. His service in China was followed by further service in the Far East, in Japan, before his return to England.

His marriage in 1870 was followed two years later by a decision to resign his commission as he felt that the prolonged absences which were so much a part of service life were no recipe for a happy marriage. Seeing an advertisement for the post of Chief Constable of Nottingham, he wrote to the retiring chief constable, who happened to be an old friend and brother officer, and the result was his appointment as chief constable at the age of thirty-four. He held the post for nine years until he became Chief Constable of Essex.

In setting out to review his new command Major Poyntz bore in mind the discussions he had had with McHardy. One of his first tasks was to compile a list of officers now well advanced in years, with a view to their retirement. Many of these men had joined the Constabulary in its early days, had worked with McHardy in establishing the force and had seen it grow to maturity. In such esteem did McHardy hold these men that, aware though he was of their age, he simply did not have the heart to order their retirement, preferring to excuse himself by saying that he was awaiting the result of Parliamentary legislation on police pensions.

While dismissals from the force were the responsibility of the Chief Constable, retirements had to be referred to the Police Committee of Justices (which met quarterly) for them to approve the pension of each officer. In January, 1882, just three months after taking office, Major Poyntz placed before the Justices the names of Superintendent May, who had been with the Constabulary since 1842, Sergeant Stewart (1848) and eight constables. In April the list comprised Superintendent Flood (1842), Superintendent Bridges (1843), Inspector Fox (1844), Inspector Guy (1845) and thirty-two sergeants and constables. July brought similar retirements for Inspector Hicks, Sergeant Moffatt and fourteen constables, bringing the total in six

Major W. H. Poyntz, Chief Constable from 1881 to 1888.

months to sixty-two officers and men. The Chief Constable eventually increased this total to over seventy.

Not all were retiring on full completion of service. Many were found to be incapable of continuing due to illness, infirmity or disabilities brought about by injury on duty. These latter were invalided out on gratuity payments.

For many years Superintendent Bridges had been Deputy Chief Constable under McHardy, and with his enormous experience he had provided Poyntz with support and advice during his first few important months. Now, with Bridges gone, Poyntz wrote to his old force in Nottingham inviting an old friend, Superintendent Raglan Somerset, to join him in Essex. Somerset, who had served in that borough force since 1878, accepted the challenge and joined the Essex Constabulary on 1st April, 1882. By July of the following year Poyntz had made him Deputy Chief Constable, in which position he remained for no less than thirty-three years.

It was only to be expected that Major Poyntz would have different ideas from those of his predecessor. McHardy, for example, having carefully selected each of his superintendents, left them to run their divisions with the minimum of interference, regarding them as natural extensions of his own authority. Poyntz, on the other hand, preferred to get out and about to see for himself what was going on.

He became well known for his habit of walking unannounced into any Magistrates' Court in the county, sitting quietly at the back, observing and listening intently to the evidence being given by the constable. Woe betide any officer who did not conduct himself properly in the witness box or who failed to give his evidence in a factual and impartial manner.

To the annoyance of the superintendents (for the sins of their men reflected on their ability to supervise) and the discomfort of those named, Poyntz developed a system of publicising by way of Force Orders, which every officer was obliged to read, the full details of any disciplinary offence, the name, rank and station of the officer concerned, the punishment awarded and very often his own acid comments.

Poyntz's anger manifested itself after one of his unannounced court visits when it was announced on Force Orders that "at Witham Magistrates' Court he listened with very much dissatisfaction and regret to the highly unsatisfactory and prevaricating manner in which Pc Nottage gave evidence against a man summoned for drunkenness and threatening him. The Magistrates dismissed the case. On cross-examination it certainly appeared that Pc Nottage was animated by a personal grudge against the defendant on account of a previous difficulty with him. The Chief Constable does not consider this officer, either in health, energy or temper, likely to make an efficient constable and has ordered him to resign forthwith."

There were other instances of a somewhat lighter nature in which one's mind conjures up all sorts of pictures. One constable, a Pc Drew, found himself the butt of county humour when it was declared that "this officer's uniform greatcoat, belt and gloves, which he had been wearing on night duty on the 1st instant, having been found in a field at Upminster on the following morning at 7.30, and he being unable to satisfactorily account for this, he has been ordered to resign forthwith."

Even holders of rank, such as the inspectors, could not avoid such publicity when they erred. An example of rather slipshod standards brought not only embarrassment but financial loss to one such officer and his constable when it was declared that

"due to a considerable want of sharpness and intelligence shown by an inspector and constable at Ongar resulting in the escape of a horse-stealer, the Chief Constable publishes the facts as a warning to members of the force to be more careful under similar circumstances. On the night of 30th September, at a quarter to eleven, a man rode into Ongar on a horse with only a common halter and without saddle and bridle. He was stopped by the inspector and challenged as to where he had got the animal and where he was going. His answers being satisfactory the inspector allowed him to pass. He was then met by the constable who, in a similar manner, stopped, questioned and permitted him to go on his way. Next morning it was reported that the horse, of considerable value, had been stolen. This was entirely an error of judgment on the part of both officers considering, (1) the time of night, (2) that horse-stealing is prevalent around Ongar, (3) there was only a common halter on the horse and it was being ridden, (4) that the place the thief stated he had bought the horse was only a short distance from Ongar, and (5) that the county cart and horse were available at the station and could at once have been used to ascertain whether the man's statement was true or otherwise.

"The Chief Constable is of the opinion that both officers acted very unwisely by their mistaken confidence, and as the expense to the county in endeavouring unsuccessfully to trace the thief amounts to £1.17s.9d he directs that the inspector pays two-thirds of this sum and the constable one-third of this sum."

This "error of judgment" cost each officer a week's pay!

The first thing that Captain Showers did when he succeeded Major Poyntz as Chief Constable in 1888 was to abolish this system of identification of offenders, restricting his Force Orders to an outline of the offence, the punishment awarded and the words "a constable was today fined..." Nowadays, dismissals or requirements to resign are confined simply to the officer's name. Minor infringements of the disciplinary code are no longer made the subject of Force Orders but are recorded on the officer's personal record kept at headquarters.

From 1st October, 1884, new rates of pay were approved, based both on length of service and class status. They are therefore rather more difficult to compare with the old scales.

		£	Old
Superintendent:	on appointment	120	
	after five years	135	
	after ten years	150	
	first class	200	170
	second class	175	140
	third class	150	
Inspectors:	on appointment	95	90
	after five years	102	
	after ten years	110	
Sergeants:	on appointment	29s.2d	29s.
	after two years	30s.4d	
	after five years	31s.6d	
	after eight years	32s.8d	
Constables:	on appointment	22s.2d	21s.
	second class	23s.4d	
	first class	24s.6d	
	after two years	25s.8d	
	after five years	26s.10d	
	after eight years	28s.	

CHAPTER SIX

Brutal Murder

IN THE 1870s concern grew in Essex over the number of criminals moving out from London to commit crime in the county. The two areas particularly affected were around Romford, Grays and Tilbury, where poaching and burglaries were reaching serious proportions, and in the Epping and Ongar districts, where horse-stealing was prevalent. The Epping area was particularly favoured by the thieves for the virtually unbroken cover afforded by the forest nearly all the way to London. To make matters worse the criminal was by 1880 resorting to the carrying of firearms, and more and more reports were coming in of their indiscriminate use against both public and police. Indeed, the situation had become so grave in London that Metropolitan Police officers in the East End had themselves been issued with firearms .

It could only be a matter of time before an unarmed Essex policeman faced an armed criminal. And that situation arose on a Tuesday afternoon in 1885 as Inspector Thomas Simmons was driving the police trap through Hornchurch, accompanied by Pc Alfred Marden. As they neared Rainham railway station they were approached by Pc Wilderspoon, of the Metropolitan Police, who told them that he had just seen three men, one of whom he recognised as David Dredge, a well-known criminal, getting off the train from London.

The two Essex policemen eventually caught sight of Dredge and his companions near Blewitts Farm, Inspector Simmons instructing his constable to follow them on foot while he drove off to Rainham to fetch reinforcements. Marden followed the men as far as Ford Lane before losing sight of them, then waited in the Hornchurch road for Inspector Simmons, who when he arrived with another constable set out with Marden to search for the men.

A short while later they saw Dredge and his companions about a hundred yards ahead of them in the Romford road. Hearing the sound of the police horse and seeing the policemen, Dredge dived through a hedge into a field, pursued by Marden. Within moments the constable had caught the man.

In reply to a question as to what he was doing in the area Dredge pulled a revolver from his pocket, pointed it at the constable's head and threatened to blow his brains out.

At that moment there was the sound of a shot. Turning round, Marden saw the taller of the other two men, who had by then been stopped by the inspector, standing with a smoking revolver in his hand. The gun was still pointed at Inspector Simmons, who was staggering back holding his stomach. Without a thought to his own safety Pc Marden ran towards the men, who took to their heels and ran off down the road. The constable found the inspector still standing but obviously in great pain. With Simmons assuring Marden that he could be safely left, the constable set off in pursuit of the men, who were by then running across a nearby field.

As he gave chase Marden saw the taller of the two men, the one who had fired the shot, shake off his overcoat and throw it down; it was obviously impeding his flight. The officer grabbed it on the run and went quickly through the pockets.

Both men eventually disappeared behind a haystack. Within moments they reappeared on the other side both holding revolvers and facing the oncoming constable. Without a word they raised their guns and fired at the officer, who felt one of the bullets fly past his face. Spinning round, he tripped and fell to the ground.

The two men continued their dash, still pursued by the gallant officer, towards a river which ran through the field. On the bank both men again turned and threatened the constable with their revolvers, without actually firing them. With that they leapt

The grave of Inspector Simmons in Oldchurch Cemetery, Romford.

into the river and made their way to the other side. In the gathering darkness the constable lost sight of them.

As Marden turned to make his way back he was astonished to see Inspector Simmons coming towards him. Pc Marden assisted the inspector back to the roadway, for by that time Simmons was totally exhausted and in great pain. Helping him into the police vehicle, Marden then drove to the nearest police station, at Dagenham.

On their arrival the officers gave a description of the three men before the inspector was transferred to a more comfortable vehicle and driven to his home in South Street, Romford. There he lingered for four days before dying on Saturday, 24th January. A subsequent post-mortem revealed that the bullet had penetrated the inspector's abdomen, travelled across the body and lodged in the base of his spine.

An intensive manhunt was now on for the wanted men, with Superintendent Dobson of Brentwood in charge. The discarded overcoat was found and a search of its pockets revealed seven ball cartridges, one cartridge case, large and small skeleton keys and a spectacles case. It was later confirmed that these cartridges were identical to the bullet extracted from Simmons' body.

The public outcry was immediate and widespread, with every newspaper carrying accounts of this atrocity. Meanwhile, the hunt had spread from Romford to the teeming, squalid streets of London's East End. Every policeman was on the lookout for David Dredge, for he, of course, had been positively identified.

The funeral of Inspector Simmons took place on Tuesday, 27th January, watched by an enormous crowd which lined the streets from the centre of Romford to the cemetery in Oldchurch Road. No fewer than 160 mourners representing the Liberty of Havering preceded the cortege, which was followed by the officer's family, Major Poyntz and the Assistant Chief Constable, Raglan Somerset, every county divisional superintendent, and 140 inspectors, sergeants and constables, their silver helmet badges draped in black crepe, followed by a contingent of a hundred officers of the Metropolitan Police.

Shortly after 9 a.m. on 3rd February, Detective Sergeant Rolf of H Division, Metropolitan Police, was in Burdett Road, Stepney, when he saw and recognised David Dredge. The wanted man surrendered quietly and was taken to the local police station, where a telegram was despatched to Superintendent Dobson informing him of the arrest. Sergeant Rolf was ordered to convey his prisoner by train to Romford. Their arrival was obviously anticipated, for an excited crowd followed the group from the railway station to the police station, which in those days incorporated the Magistrates' Court.

Dredge was charged at that stage with threatening to shoot Pc Marden and was remanded in custody to Chelmsford Prison. He appeared again before the same court on 19th February, where he was also charged with the wilful murder of Inspector Simmons. Dredge's assertion that he was nowhere near the inspector when he was shot brought from the prosecution the argument that where two or more persons are engaged in a common enterprise to commit an unlawful act, and one or more of them is armed with the intention of resisting arrest or if they agree to offer violence to any person who attempts to impede them, then it matters not who actually pulls the trigger. Dredge pleaded not guilty, and applications were made on his behalf for the trial to be transferred from Essex to another Assize on the grounds that public feeling was running so high that a fair trial would be impossible. Much to the annoyance of the Essex people, and particularly the county newspapers, the prisoner was ordered to stand trial at Hertford Assizes.

Meanwhile, the hunt continued unabated for the other two men. On 10th March an alert pawnbroker in Euston Square, London, managed to send a message by one of his staff to the local police station to the effect that a man answering the description of one of the wanted men was in his shop offering for sale a revolver. Within minutes two constables entered the shop and there encountered James Lee, alias Menson. Immediately he saw the constables Lee attempted to escape and a furious struggle took place, the police officers being assisted by members of the public. Lee was eventually overpowered and taken to Platt Street police station. Because of the struggle no attempt had been made to search the prisoner, who was placed under guard in the interview room. As he sat there Lee surreptitiously withdrew from his pocket a handful of cartridges, which he threw on to the open fire. As the cartridges exploded he made another attempt to escape in the confusion, but was again overpowered.

Protesting his innocence, James Lee was taken to Romford and there charged with wilful murder. He pleaded not guilty, declaring that he had been nowhere near the town on the day in question and that his identification was false. During the committal proceedings Pc Wilderspoon positively identified Lee as one of Dredge's companions.

As with Dredge, applications were made for Lee to be tried outside Essex. This was eventually agreed and he was committed, somewhat surprisingly, to the Old Bailey. Efforts had to be made for both men to be tried together, and eventually both Lee and Dredge were ordered to stand trial at the Central Criminal Court.

On Monday, 27th April, 1885, Lee and Dredge stood together in the dock at the Old Bailey before Mr Justice Hawkins. Among the witnesses called on the first day of the trial was a Charles Henry Woodcraft, who testified that he had seen Lee wearing the overcoat in question on previous occasions. Another witness, a Mrs Salmon, told the court that she identified the spectacle case found in the overcoat pocket, she being the wife of the optician who had actually sold the article to Lee, whom she identified in court. Other witnesses, such as David Kemp and Joseph Hawkins, both labourers, testified that they had witnessed the shooting.

The second day was taken up with the defence, with Dredge basing his argument on the fact that he did not fire the fatal shot, was speaking to a police officer some distance away from the shooting and had no idea that his companion intended shooting his way out of trouble. Lee, for his part, steadfastly denied being at the scene, protesting that he had been falsely identified.

At the end of the day the jury acquitted Dredge but unhesitatingly found Lee guilty as charged. In passing sentence of death the Judge ended with the usual intonation, "and may God have mercy on your soul," to which Lee retorted, "I have had none from the Judge, nor justice either." On his leaving court Dredge was immediately re-arrested and conveyed back to Romford to face the charge of threatening to shoot Pc Marden.

At 8 a.m. on 18th May, 1885, James Lee suffered the ultimate penalty at Chelmsford Prison, becoming only the fourth person to be hanged within the privacy of the gaol since the Capital Punishment Act of 1868 had prohibited the public execution of felons.

At the Essex Summer Assize in Chelmsford on 28th July, 1885, Dredge again pleaded not guilty and alleged that Pc Marden "being in a state of excitement at the time had made a mistake in believing him to be armed." At no time, declared the prisoner, did he have in his possession a revolver, least of all did he point it at the officer.

Nevertheless, the evidence against him was too strong and the jury found him guilty. The Judge, Mr. Justice Huddleston, commented that he had been properly acquitted of murder "but the evidence now was perfectly convincing." The court heard of Dredge's previous convictions, which included assault on the police, and was told that he had been sentenced to seven years penal servitude in 1878 for horse-stealing. This sentence had just expired at the time Inspector Simmons was shot. For threatening to shoot Pc Marden Dredge was sentenced to twelve months hard labour.

But what of the third man? To identify him we must return to the criminal career of Irishman James Lee, who had been born James Menson. His life of crime started at an early age and he served three prison sentences before quitting the Emerald Isle. Settling in Somers Town, London, he lost no time in joining a gang of thieves and burglars, a prominent member of which was a man named Jack Martin. The two men quickly established a reputation for daring burglaries and were known to carry firearms wherever they went.

Shortly after arriving in London, Menson read a newspaper account of a man named Lee who had been convicted of murdering his mistress in Babbacombe, Devon, and sentenced to death. With the convicted man standing on the scaffold, the executioner pulled the lever but the mechanism failed to operate. Instead of plummetting to his doom, Lee remained standing on the immovable trapdoor while the executioner tried and tried again to activate the mechanism. Finally, the prisoner was returned to his cell and was afterwards reprieved by the Home Secretary. Menson, on reading this, promptly changed his name to Lee, declaring "they couldn't hang him, no more can they hang me" (this confidence was shattered, if only for a few dreadful moments, when his turn came to stand in the same place).

With Dredge and Lee accounted for, few police officers harboured any doubts that the third member of this murderous trio was other than Lee's bosom pal Jack Martin, their suspicions being reinforced by his sudden disappearance from all his usual haunts.

Once again it was Detective Sergeant Rolf, now totally dedicated to bringing these murderers to justice, who came nearest to taking the suspect. One day in August of that same year Rolf was walking down Commercial Road, Stepney, when he suddenly found himself face to face with Martin. "I want you, Martin," said the officer. "My name's not Martin, Rolf," replied Jack. The sergeant told him that he recognised him and that he was being arrested on suspicion of murder.

At this, Martin slid his hand into his jacket pocket and warned the officer to remain where he was. Knowing his man as he did, Rolf was sure that he was facing an armed man. After a few moments, faced with no alternative but to back off, the officer could do no more than grit his teeth as he watched his quarry disappear into the maze of back streets.

The hunt for Martin was intensified, but it was to be two months before police inquiries switched dramatically to the north of England. On 28th October a burglary occurred at Netherby in Cumberland, a large quantity of jewellery being stolen. The police set up road blocks in their search for four men seen nearby at the time of the burglary.

Within a short while four men walked straight into a road block manned by Sergeant Roche and Constables Johnstone and Fortune. One of the four men, none other than Jack Martin, pulled a revolver from his pocket and unhesitatingly shot Sergeant Roche, wounding him in the arm. Another of the gang, Anthony Rudge, shot Pc Johnstone in the chest. A short distance down the road they encountered Pc Fortune, who within moments was left for dead with serious face and head injuries.

Another of the four, James Smith, known as "One Armed Jimmy," decided to separate from his companions and try to make his own way back to London. He set off south. Martin, Rudge and the fourth member of the gang, James Baker, decided to make for Carlisle, about eight miles distant.

They were spotted by a stationmaster near Penrith and the village constable, Pc Byrnes, was summoned. This constable bravely tackled the three men and was promptly shot through the head, his body being flung into a nearby dyke. He was still alive when found about half an hour later but subsequently died.

The three men made their way to Tebay railway sidings where their luck ran out. They were spotted trying to conceal themselves under a tarpaulin on a goods train and a number of railway employees hauled the trio out by their legs, a furious fight taking place before Martin and Rudge were secured. Baker managed to escape by leaping on to a moving goods train as it left the station, but his liberty was short-lived, for the police were waiting for the train when it made its first stop at Lancaster.

With the three now safely under lock and key at Carlisle Gaol Detective Sergeant Rolf travelled north to interview them—particularly Jack Martin. Despite all his efforts, Rolf was unable to extract a confession from Martin regarding his involvement in the Simmons murder. Rolf returned to London disappointed but nevertheless totally convinced that Martin was the man who had pulled the trigger on Inspector Simmons.

After a long trial all three men were convicted and executed on 8th February, 1886. "One Armed Jimmy" disappeared and was never heard of again. Thus died, in all probability, the third man in the murder of the Essex inspector.

For his outstanding bravery and devotion to duty Pc Marden was awarded the Star of Merit. A public collection for Inspector Simmons' widow realised the enormous sum for those days of £1,100.

For those who believe in coincidences it is interesting to note how fateful was the day Tuesday in this story. The inspector was shot on Tuesday, 20th January; he was buried on Tuesday, 27th January; Dredge was arrested on Tuesday, 3rd February; Lee was arrested on Tuesday, 10th March, and convicted on Tuesday, 28th April; and Dredge was convicted on Tuesday, 28th July.

The arrest of Dredge and Lee brought to a head the whole question of arming the police. Poyntz knew that the Metropolitan Police were, in certain areas, armed. The last thing he wanted to see was county officers with holsters on their belts, but he reminded himself that one of his primary duties as a chief constable was to the safety of his men while at the same time maintaining the image of the police as an integral part of the community.

With the growing use of firearms and the cold-blooded murder of Inspector Simmons he felt justified in approaching the Justices and suggesting a compromise whereby officers stationed in areas particularly plagued by London villains should be allowed the right to decide whether they wished to carry arms.

He incorporated these ideas in a report dated 27th February 1885, in which he wrote,

> "I have to bring to your notice a question that demands very careful consideration, the untimely death of Inspector Simmons bringing it prominently forward at the present time. It seems to me that the period has now arrived when some armed protection should be afforded to certain members of the Essex Constabulary doing duty on the borders of the Metropolis, and patrolling in isolated positions, to and from which burglars and bad characters from the East End of London have quick and easy access. It now appears the usual custom for such characters to carry revolvers and use them on the slightest attempt

at interference on the part of the police. I fear that unless some steps are taken to counteract this system, the police on the one hand may to some extent become intimidated, whilst burglars gain confidence in the fact that by shooting a policeman they may increase their chance of getting clear away. The knowledge that officers may be in possession of firearms might have a deterrent effect. I am entirely against the arming of the police generally and I feel such a step would present itself most unfavourably to the public at large. I would confine the issue to the superintendents and inspectors of the Brentwood and Epping Divisions in the following proportion:- Brentwood 3, Romford 3, Grays 2, Epping 3, Harlow 2, Ongar 2, to be kept at each station in their individual charge and issued when deemed necessary, or applied for in accordance with the regulations laid down (hereto attached). In addition, I consider 2 revolvers should be supplied to the Sergeants at Abridge and Matching and one each to the Constables at Nazeing, Rainham and Havering."

Major Poyntz proposed adopting the rules under which revolvers were issued to policemen in outlying Metropolitan areas, the first of which was that revolvers were only to be issued to men "who desire to have them when employed on night duty." The revolvers were to be kept in the police stations and only issued when the constables paraded for duty, the weapons being loaded by the officer in charge. The revolvers were to be unloaded immediately a constable went off duty and were to be handed over to the superintendent or inspector in charge as early as possible the following morning.

"The revolver is to be carried in the holster on the belt on the right side and is not to be taken out of the holster for any purpose whatsoever, except for self-defence," stated the regulations. An officer on going off duty had to report "every instance when he has had occasion to remove it from his holster during his tour of duty," and these reports were to be passed at once to the Chief Constable.

Other regulations dealt with the issue of firearms to men at out-stations, where a locked box was provided for the safe-keeping of revolver and ammunition. Superintendents and inspectors were instructed to examine the box and its contents whenever they visited their men's residences.

The Justices accepted these proposals in their entirety and forwarded the report to the Secretary of State for his approval. The newspapers of the day, while treating the murder of Inspector Simmons with great sympathy, lost no time in highlighting what they considered to be the growing lawlessness of the western areas of the county and strongly advocated a substantial increase in police powers. When they heard of Major Poyntz's recommendations they voiced their total support. The Secretary of State approved the measures in June, 1885, and an immediate order was placed with Webley & Sons for the purchase of twenty-two revolvers costing £1.17s.6d each. These were allocated in accordance with the Chief Constable's instructions, and for the first time in history Essex constables were to be seen at night patrolling their beats with holsters on their belts.

The effect was immediate. The armed criminal knew that he was likely to be shot if he pulled a gun on a police officer. It was to be another forty years before the next Essex policeman was shot and killed on duty, once again at the hands of London criminals.

Following the creation of the constabularies, the Government appointed a number of high-ranking officers whose responsibility it was to visit each police force within his area and report to the Home Secretary his findings as to their state of efficiency. These officers, known as Her Majesty's Inspectors of Constabulary, made annual visits to each of these forces and could spend anything up to a week inspecting buildings, equipment and men before sending off their report to the Government.

It could be said that Saffron Walden owes its fine police station to such a visit by the HMI. In October, 1882, Colonel Cobbe was carrying out his usual inspection of

The police station at Saffron Walden, built in 1884 to replace Newport Gaol. It is still in use in 1985.

the force, which included a visit to Newport police station. This building, once the old gaol, had been taken over by the police in 1840 when Saffron Walden was still a borough force. Colonel Cobbe reported that he had found Newport police station in a very dilapidated state and recommended urgent action on the part of the county.

Agreement was eventually reached that the building should be sold and a new police station built in Saffron Walden itself. Work commenced in 1884 and was completed within a year at a cost of £3,460.7s.11d. The old gaol at Newport was sold in October, 1886, for just £450.

Major Poyntz, having established himself as a man of stern discipline, nevertheless displayed genuine regard for the wellbeing of his men. He was instrumental in bringing about an important change of uniform when, seeing the obvious discomfort of the constables as they perspired through the height of summer in the same heavy serge uniforms that had kept them warm during winter, he introduced a lightweight worsted uniform for use from 1st June to 30th September.

With 1886 came the first signs of the Chief Constable's deteriorating health. Although robust in the physical sense, he suffered from a condition which affected his nervous system. By the end of that year his physician told him that his health was such that only complete rest for two or three months would benefit him. On 4th January, 1887, Poyntz wrote to the Justices, enclosing the doctor's certificate and begging leave of absence until April. The request was granted and Mr Raglan Somerset was instructed to take over his duties.

No great improvement had occurred by April and a further three months leave was granted, but by July the Chief Constable was back with the force invigorated and apparently in good health. Unfortunately, this improvement was to be short-lived.

On 19th September, Colonel Cobbe arrived at Chelmsford to begin his annual inspection of the force. He was met at the railway station by Major Poyntz, who was driving himself in a two-wheeled trap drawn by a horse he had only recently purchased. The two men set off down Duke Street towards the High Street, intending to turn into Springfield Road and thence to headquarters, where the Constabulary was already lined up for inspection*. On reaching Tindal Square the horse suddenly took fright, broke into a gallop and bolted across the High Street towards the coaching entrance of the Saracen's Head Hotel.

With Poyntz struggling to regain control they careered into the hotel yard, where Colonel Cobbe was flung from the vehicle and knocked unconscious. A few yards further on an elderly lady, a Mrs Garmeson, accompanied by her young relative, a Miss Remnant, was walking through the yard towards the High Street. The horse and trap struck the two ladies, Mrs Garmeson being flung violently to the ground, sustaining severe head injuries, while Miss Remnant was dragged along the yard, receiving injuries to her legs. The horse continued its dash down the yard, coming to a stop only when it crashed into another vehicle parked there.

Major Poyntz, thoroughly shaken, ran back and assisted passers-by in getting the three injured persons into the hotel. A doctor was summoned but despite his efforts Mrs Garmeson died an hour later. Colonel Cobbe and Miss Remnant were to remain at the Saracen's Head for another week before they were fit enough to travel.

At the subsequent inquest Major Poyntz, still shattered by this disaster, was closely questioned as to the nature of his horse. In reply to the Coroner, Mr C.C. Lewis, he said that he had bought the horse some four to six weeks before the accident and went on, "I bought it of a most respectable man, a farmer who gave it

---

*Those readers who know Chelmsford may wonder why Poyntz took the High Street route from the railway station, instead of turning left down Victoria Road. The answer is simply that the section of Victoria Road between the station and New Street did not exist in 1888. The only possible way to Springfield was via the High Street and Springfield Road. Victoria Road then commenced where Chelmsford's new police station now stands, ran for two or three hundred yards towards the river and then petered out in the meadows. Only a footpath continued from that point to where the *Three Cups* public house stands in Springfield Road.

The Saracen's Head, Chelmsford.   *Stan Jarvis*

the highest character. When I tell you I bought it for my wife and children you may know I used some precaution."

A verdict of accidental death was recorded, and in reply to the sympathetic remarks of the Coroner Major Poyntz said, "It has been a very grievous thing to me, and I can only say that I have felt it more than I show and shall probably do so for some time."

Within a few weeks the effects of this tragedy had taken its toll on his health, destroying all the good work that six months' leave had achieved. By early 1888, with his condition rapidly deteriorating, Poyntz was forced to accept that he could no longer continue as Chief Constable. The Justices received his letter of resignation on 2nd March, 1888.

Three months were to elapse before the Justices were in a position to interview and select a successor. Major Poyntz's resignation became effective on 2nd July, 1888, and he retired with his wife to Eastbourne. He was later to remark with some bitterness that neither the eight years he had spent as Chief Constable of Nottingham Borough nor the seven years that he was Chief Constable of Essex were sufficient to entitle him to a pension. He died on 21st October, 1892, at Windsor, Berkshire, in a house he had named "Springfield."

CHAPTER SEVEN

Further Growth

FOLLOWING the enforced retirement of Major Poyntz the post of Chief Constable of Essex was advertised, and no fewer than 135 applications were received. The salary offered was £500 a year, plus £100 allowances.

The new Chief Constable, chosen by the Justices on 5th June, 1888, was Captain E.M. Showers, who had for two years been Chief Constable of Exeter Borough, a force with a strength at that time of only fifty-nine men. Impressed by his military background and tradition—his father was an officer in the Madras Artillery, his grandfather was General Edward Melion Gulliver Showers, and he himself had been for seven years an officer in the 95th Derbyshire Regiment—as well as by his assiduous studies and ambition, the Justices confessed themselves equally taken by "his pleasing and gentlemanly manners."

Captain Showers' military career had come to an end when in 1872 he resigned his commission and settled in the West Country to study law and police duties, his eyes firmly fixed on a police career. In 1884 he successfully passed his law examinations and was immediately appointed a superintendent in the Devon County Constabulary.

Some men might have been daunted by the prospect of taking charge of a force more than five times larger than the one he had controlled for two years, but not Captain Showers. He looked on his appointment rather as the natural fulfillment of all his years of study and of the four years already spent in the practical application of those studies.

On taking over his new responsibilities Captain Showers found the strength of his force as follows:-

Division	Supts	Insps	Sgts	Cons
Brentwood	1	2	5	48
Chelmsford & HQ	2	2	6	29
Colchester	1	2	5	40
Dengie	1	2	3	11
Dunmow	1		4	11
Epping	1	4	3	26
Hinckford	1	1	2	33
Rochford	1		1	22
Walden	1	1	1	18
Witham	1		1	17
Total	11	14	31	255

Headquarters staff (under Chelmsford above) comprised one Chief Constable, one Assistant Chief Constable, one superintendent , three sergeants and six constables.

The Constabulary was now, after fifty years, firmly established and growing in proportion to the demands being made upon it.

Maldon Borough Police had fallen victim to the Local Government Act, 1888, which had abolished so many small forces. The Dengie Division, then comprising a superintendent, an inspector, one sergeant and eleven constables (not counting Inspector Rome at Burnham's Oyster Company), still operating from Latchingdon, found itself with a sudden increase of over 5,000 inhabitants. The Chief Constable laid plans before the Justices for the divisional headquarters to be moved to Maldon or Southminster.

The Justices, members now of the newly-formed Police Standing Joint Committee, met at Latchingdon on 25th October, 1889, to look into the situation. Although agreeing that the police station was in a very poor state of repair they nevertheless resolved that with a moderate outlay Latchingdon police station might be rendered sufficient and suitable for the wants of the Dengie Division. They also decided that the business of the Petty Sessions, which averaged not more than four cases a fortnight, was too small to justify the separation, that the purchase of a site at Southminster and the building of a new police station would entail serious expense, and that "the present police station at Latchingdon is centrally placed and adequate."

That the police had to accept this decision was obvious, but if the Justices thought the people of Maldon and Southminster would do likewise they were mistaken, for within a few months a petition was presented by the inhabitants of those towns demanding an increase in police strength and the building of two police stations. The Justices replied "that such buildings would incur an expense of £6,000 to £7,000, that Latchingdon is having over £200 spent on alterations, and that the small number of Petty Sessional cases at Southminster and Maldon does not warrant such expenditure." This reply did little to placate the petitioners, who continued to exert pressure until they finally had their way.

Undaunted by this setback, the Chief Constable applied for approval to build police stations at Clacton-on-Sea and Romford. The former was by 1890 a thriving seaside resort second only to Southend, and the latter arguably the busiest town in Essex. Despite its growing popularity, Clacton's permanent population had grown only minimally over fifty years from 1,296 in 1841 to 1,891 in 1891. Only two constables were stationed in the town, although during the summer months reinforcements were always available from Walton (two constables), St Osyth and Weeley (one each).

As far as Romford was concerned, it was quite obvious that alternative accommodation was needed, for its inspector, sergeant, and eleven constables were still operating from the same rooms in Liberty Hall, Market Place, from where the old parochial constables had sallied forth a hundred years before.

While the committee deliberated over these proposals they found themselves coming under pressure from yet another quarter, this time the Justices and inhabitants of Braintree. In December, 1888, it had been decided that £450 should be spent on additional cells and other improvements to the old police station in Rayne Road. On hearing this the town's magistrates wrote expressing their hope that as the police station was situated half a mile from the centre of town, and on an unlit road, the county would consider putting that money to better use by moving the police station to a central location.

The decision to improve the police station was postponed and a sub-committee formed to report on the situation at Braintree. By January, 1890, this committee reported that the structural defects in the police station were so extensive that only a considerable sum of money would restore its usefulness, that due to the complete

Captain E. M. Showers, Chief Constable from 1888 to 1915.

absence of drainage a number of officers were falling sick, that the water in the station well had been analysed and found to be polluted (an immediate prohibition had been ordered on its use for drinking and cooking and a temporary supply of pure water organised), and that the location of the police station was causing serious problems due to the fact that the courthouse was at Bocking on the opposite side of the town. The station's cell book revealed that no fewer than sixty-one prisoners had been lodged at the station during the year January, 1889, to January, 1890, all of whom had to be marched through the town to court. The committee recommended that the only solution to these problems would be the building of a new police station and courthouse combined, or the siting of the police station close to the existing

Above: Braintree police station, which was completed in 1892.

Right: Romford police station, also built in 1892 and demolished in 1965, soon after the Metropolitan Police had taken over the division.

Below: Clacton police station, built to serve the expanding seaside resort at a time when the town was part of the Tendring Division administered from Thorpe-le-Soken.

court. These recommendations were accepted and advertisements soon appeared in the local newspapers for a suitable site to be offered.

While awaiting the results of this the committee returned to the question of Romford and Clacton. Inspector Willsmer, in charge of the Romford Sub-Division, was called to Chelmsford and questioned as to what would be required. He informed the members that Liberty Hall contained four cells, which were so dilapidated that only two of them could be used. A new police station should contain accommodation for an inspector, a sergeant and at least four constables in addition to four good cells, he said. He went on to suggest that, as the Justices sat in a very old courthouse at Liberty Hall, arrangements should also be made to incorporate a court with the police station. The County Surveyor reported that such a building would cost something in the region of £4,000.

By January, 1891, it had been agreed that Romford and Clacton could have their new stations and courthouses. Romford police station was completed on time in 1892 but without the proposed courthouse. Instead, the Justices moved to premises a little further down South Street in what is now the County Court. The Magistrates' Court was not built on to the rear of the police station until the 1930s and was demolished along with the main building soon after the Metropolitan Police took it over in April, 1965.

The site for Clacton police station had been purchased with sufficient land for the building of a courthouse but the two could not be built together for the simple reason that no Petty Sessional business was then being conducted in the town, all the cases being heard at Thorpe-le-Soken. Delays were experienced because official approval had to be obtained from various authorities, not least of them being the Thorpe Justices themselves, for Clacton to try its own cases. This was not forthcoming until 1898 when a courthouse, costing £960, was built beside the new police station. Ten years later another larger court was built at a cost of £1,893. Both Romford and Clacton police stations were equipped with speaking tubes running from the Charge Room to the sergeant's quarters (a telephone line connecting the Justices' Office at the Shire Hall with Police Headquarters at Springfield had existed since the middle 1880s). Other police stations throughout the country had to rely on the telegraph system.

Clacton was completed in the same year as Romford's building and immediately a sergeant and two constables were posted there to supplement the two constables already positioned in the town. Within five years an inspector was posted to Clacton to supervise the new sub-division and take charge of the court work. By 1898, with 300,000 trippers visiting the town each summer, the police strength had been increased by a further two constables.

The Police Committee were still involved in the completion of Braintree's new police station. In August, 1891, the Justices had purchased the Railway Hotel and two adjoining houses in Fairfield Road for £3,700. Work on the conversion of these properties was put out to tender and twelve replies received ranging from £3,975 to £4,500. The lowest had been submitted by Mr Alfred Brown, the same man who had just finished building Romford police station. He was granted the contract on condition that all building had to be completed within six months of the order to commence. The police station and court were finished by April, 1892, and the

67

superintendent, sergeant and ten constables moved in. Both buildings remain operational to the present day.

Some six miles west of Braintree lies the quiet village of Stebbing, close enough to the town of Dunmow to avoid isolation and yet far enough away to ensure that its centuries-old way of life remained undisturbed. Predominantly farming folk, the villagers suffered with the rest of the country during the terrible depression of the 1820's and 1830's and had been firmly behind the inhabitants of Dunmow when they petitioned for a regular constabulary force. In 1850 the village had turned out to welcome its first full-time constable, smartly uniformed in blue tailcoat and shiny top hat, as he took up residence among them. His hours of duty were certainly long and the area he covered on foot was huge, but apart from that he did not seem to have a lot to do.

So what, these good people asked, had they done in this year of Grace 1888, to deserve a constable like Enoch Raison? Not many knew that he had already served more than his full twenty-five years. Joining the police on 13th October, 1851, he had seen service in various parts of the county until his retirement in June, 1880, brought a pension of two shillings a day. He found it impossible to settle down, and within two years was asking to be allowed to serve a little longer. His request being granted, he was posted to Stebbing.

The villagers found him morose, officious, sharp-tongued and offhand, showing no signs of wanting to settle down, as others had before him, to become an accepted part of village life. As time went by dislike of the man grew to open hatred, and before long a state of undeclared war existed between the village and its constable. Matters came to a head in October, 1888, when the superintendent at Dunmow received the alarming news from his inspector that if he did not make arrangements for the immediate removal of Pc Raison the villagers would likely do it for him! Without delay he consulted the Chief Constable, who ordered that the constable must be removed as soon as possible, preferably at night. Sufficient constables were to be drafted into the village to ensure that his removal was achieved as peacefully as possible.

The superintendent's worst fears were realised when, with the sudden arrival of this nocturnal escort, the word spread like wildfire that Enoch Raison was leaving. Within minutes those carefully laid, but foolhardy, plans were in tatters and the unfortunate constable's departure was achieved only in the face of a fusilade of missiles and hoots of derision from those gathered to witness the spectacle.

Some days later, on 5th November, the local boys carried their own Guy Fawkes to the village bonfire, not this time the infamous perpetrator of "gunpowder treason and plot" but a remarkably life-like effigy of their erstwhile village constable.

Enoch's ill-fated return to the force was doomed. On 23rd November, 1888, Pc Raison was at last persuaded to accept his pension and retire as gracefully as his shattered pride would allow.

In 1891 the Chief Constable set about reducing the two largest divisions in the county, Colchester, which encompassed the whole of north-east Essex, and Brentwood, which covered the entire south-west.

A new Thorpe Division was formed comprising the beats/parishes of Thorpe-le-Soken, Frinton, Kirby, Great Clacton, Little Clacton, Great Bentley, Great Oakley, St

An effigy of Pc Enoch Raison is carried by masked villagers of Stebbing to the bonfire in 1888.

Stan Jarvis

Osyth, Tendring, Weeley and Walton-on-Naze. Thorpe, once the headquarters of the old Tendring Division before being relegated to a sub-division in 1855, became again a divisional headquarters.

If Colchester was to lose eleven of its parishes, Brentwood was to fare even worse, for in April, 1891, the beats of Aveley, Chadwell St Mary, Little Thurrock, West Thurrock, Purfleet, Tilbury, Stifford and Rainham were incorporated into a new Orsett Division, inaptly named, as it turned out, for its headquarters was at Grays while Orsett itself remained in the Brentwood Division. The situation was rectified nine months later when Fobbing, Horndon, Orsett, South Ockendon, and Stanford-le-Hope were added, making thirteen beats altogether, and the enlarged division was re-named the Grays Division.

Brentwood suffered still further reduction when, just nine years later in 1900, Romford became a division in its own right and took the beats of Romford town, Collier Row, Hare Street, Havering, Hornchurch, Harold Wood and Upminster.

CHAPTER EIGHT

The Murder of Sergeant Eves

SOON AFTER nine o'clock on the evening of Saturday, 15th April, 1893, Adam John Eves rose from his supper at his cottage in Purleigh, near Maldon, and donned his uniform jacket and helmet. Telling his wife that he had various calls to make that night, he said she was not to expect him home until about eleven-thirty.

A popular and respected officer, he had joined the Essex Constabulary at the age of twenty in 1877. He was commended for bravery in July, 1891, when he arrested a violent poacher who was later sentenced to two months' hard labour for assaulting him, and again in September of that year when he arrested a gang of corn thieves. He was promoted in February, 1893, and posted to Purleigh.

Most of what Eves did that night will never be known. It is certain he called at the *Royal Oak* public house where he delivered a reward poster to the landlord, leaving there a few minutes after ten o'clock. Meanwhile, his wife had cleared away the supper things and retired to bed. She rose at her usual time the next morning and busied herself preparing his breakfast. As mid-morning approached with still no news she threw the meal away. At noon she went to her front door and gazed along the road. The local carpenter, Herbert Patten, happened to pass by and she asked him whether he had heard of any fires during the night, for this was all she could imagine would have kept her husband away for so long. Patten replied that he had heard nothing. He assured her, though, that he would let her know the moment he heard anything. That promise he was to remember for the rest of his life.

About three o'clock that afternoon, this same man was taking a Sunday afternoon stroll across the fields at Hazeleigh Hall Farm, about a mile from Purleigh. Crossing Pound Field, he reached a spot known as Bell Rope Gate and there saw an area of disturbed ground.

His heart began to pound as he realised that the ground upon which he was standing was saturated with blood. Walking slowly to the nearby ditch, he leaned over and found himself gazing with mounting horror on the dead and mutilated body of Sergeant Eves.

Patten knew it was no use returning to Purleigh, for the nearest policeman lived at Stowe Maries, about two and a half miles away. Running practically all the way, he found Pc Chaplin at Stow Maries and blurted out his discovery. Both men hurried back to Hazeleigh where, as it happened, Inspector Pryke was at that very moment making inquiries at the farm into the theft the previous night of a quantity of corn from one of the barns. He too was hurriedly summoned to the scene.

The injuries to the police sergeant were appalling. He had been savagely battered about the head, face and body, and his throat had been slashed in three places. The inspector and Pc Chaplin noticed that the dead officer's truncheon was still in its pocket and that the shutter on his oil-lamp was in the "off" position. Clearly, whoever had murdered him had either done so swiftly and by surprise, or the sergeant had been confident enough in taking on his man without resorting to the use of his truncheon. Lying beneath the body were three stout sticks, or cudgels, one of them broken into three pieces. These were all bloodstained, as was a spade found lying nearby.

A close examination of the vicinity revealed a set of wheel marks leading across the field directly to the house of a well-known petty criminal named John Davis. By now though the news had spread like wildfire and villagers were gathered around the spot talking in hushed whispers as the body of Sergeant Eves was taken away. Pc Chaplin was later to say that he noticed one man, whom he instantly recognised as Richard, the brother of John Davis, standing alone and silent in that crowd.

The following morning, Monday, 17th April, the police searched the home of John Davis, and shortly afterwards the home of his brother. Both men were arrested. Shortly after that the homes of Charles Sales and John Bateman were also searched and these men taken into custody. When the clothing of all four was examined bloodstains were found on a waistcoat belonging to Charles Sales and on a coat owned by John Davis. More blood was found on a jacket and pair of shoes owned by Richard Davis. Bateman's clothing was also found to be stained, but whether the bloodstains were of human origin was impossible to establish. A further search of

Sergeant Eves' house at Purleigh as it is today.

The *Queen's Head* at Purleigh which served as headquarters of the investigation into the murder of Sergeant Eves. Behind it stood the cottages of John and Richard Davis.

Richard Davis's home revealed three sacks of corn in the bottom of a pond in his garden.

All four men appeared before the magistrates at the Moot Hall, Maldon, and were remanded in custody to Chelmsford Gaol.

The following Wednesday a villager named Thomas Choat went to the police and volunteered a statement concerning a certain James Ramsey, who was the foreman in charge of the threshing machine at Hazeleigh Hall Farm. Three men worked this machine; Ramsey operated it, Choat fed it and Richard Davis sacked the corn. Thomas Choat told the police he had heard a number of threats made by Ramsey against the police sergeant, and went on to say that Ramsey had appeared for work on the Monday morning wearing new clothes and a new hat. This, said Choat, was most unusual, for there had been nothing wrong with Ramsey's working clothes when he had seen him on Saturday. Following this the police discovered that false entries had been made in the farm books with respect to the threshing of corn, it being quickly established that a greater quantity of corn had been deposited in the store barn than was actually shown on the records. The farmer, Edward Fitch, reported that something like thirteen bushels had disappeared from the storage bins.

A quantity of corn found scattered about the scene of the murder was compared with that stored in the barn and found to be identical. Similarly, the corn found in Richard Davis's pond was found to correspond in every respect. The task of the police appeared not too difficult, for whoever had falsified the tally sheets must have been an employee, and whoever had stolen the corn had also murdered the officer.

James Ramsey and his fifteen-year-old son, also named James, were arrested and their home was searched. A pair of blood-stained trousers belonging to Ramsey senior and fitting the description given by Choat as having been worn by Ramsey on the day of the murder was found, and so was a knife which showed signs of having recently been cleaned and sharpened. Concealed under Ramsey's mattress were a number of sacks identical to those found in the pond at Davis's home.

No firm evidence could be found against John Bateman and young Ramsey, both of whom were released. Charles Sales, James Ramsey and the Davis brothers were ordered to stand their trial at Essex Assizes. Their counsel immediately made application for the trial to be moved well away from Chelmsford, part of their grounds for complaint being the inflammatory articles which had appeared in the press, but the application was refused.

From the tiny, intimate courtroom at Maldon's Moot Hall the four accused found themselves on Thursday, 27th July, 1893, standing in the dock of the majestic Shire Hall at Chelmsford before Mr Justice Mathew. To the charge of wilful murder they all pleaded not guilty.

As the first day wore on it became increasingly obvious that the prosecution could offer little evidence against Charles Sales. Mr F.O. Crump, Q.C., who led for the Crown, rose to say that he would not under the circumstances press the charge against Sales. The jury formally returned a verdict of not guilty.

Ramsey and the Davis brothers continued to maintain their innocence, claiming that they had all been at home and sound asleep on the night of the murder. Ramsey's defence was ingenious, for he declared that he had known nothing of the murder until the following day, Sunday, when he had been approached by John Davis who asked him to supply an alibi in the event of the police arresting him. Ramsey replied that he would not contemplate doing so unless Davis told him what it was he had done. To this, Davis replied that he and two others, Richard Davis and Charles Sales, had committed the theft and then murdered the police officer. Ramsey went on to say that Davis had told him that he was bound to be taken and, if he was, would Ramsey speak up for him? Ramsey agreed to do so. It followed, therefore, that any knowledge Ramsey was found to possess came not from his presence at the scene but from what Davis had told him. The fact that not one of the defendants produced a single member of their considerable families to substantiate their stories was not lost on the jury.

In the face of these denials, what could the prosecution offer? The evidence of the cart tracks was introduced. Their existence and the ownership of the cart was never denied by Richard Davis, who went on to explain that he had used the cart only a short time before the murder to pick up stones from that very field. The spade found by the body and identified as belonging to him was produced, and a Home Office pathologist who had carried out the post-mortem on the body of the policeman agreed that a number of injuries found on the officer could have been caused by that spade. What would the defence make of that?

Pure supposition, they said. The opinion of the pathologist was nothing more than that and could in no way be construed as proof that it was so used.

Mr Crump then held aloft the jacket belonging to John Davis. Opening it, he pointed to a home-made loop sewn into the lining. Demanding to know its meaning, he extracted from Davis the admission that it was for securing a concealed cudgel. Again, the fact that Davis was in the habit of carrying such a weapon was not proof of murder, but it succeeded in forming a picture in the minds of the jury of Davis as a desperate and dangerous ruffian.

In their addresses to the jury the defence pointed out that the evidence submitted by the prosecution was purely circumstantial, much of it opinion and inuendo designed to instill in their minds a picture of the defendants as merciless thugs. But where, they asked, was the proof?

It was Mr. Justice Mathew, in his carefully worded and accurate summing-up, who really laid before the jury the issues to be considered. There was, he said, clear evidence that no one had ever called into question that whoever had stolen the corn had also murdered the officer. No reasonable man could ever doubt, he went on, that Sergeant Eves met his death in his efforts to arrest the thieves. The cardinal question must therefore be, "Who were those thieves"?

That the theft was carefully planned there could be no doubt. False entries had been made in the farm tally sheets to show less corn in the barn than had actually been placed there. Who had made out those tally sheets? Richard Davis. Who was the farm foreman responsible to his employer for the accuracy of those records? James Ramsey. That the records were falsified was incontrovertible, for after the murder the grain in the barn was carefully measured and found to agree with the tally sheet–and yet thirteen bushels had been taken away. The defence had attempted to show that this was simply a mistake on the part of the accused, or at worst a fraud perpetrated by Richard Davis of which Ramsey had no knowledge. The Judge commented on this, "You will judge for yourselves whether it is possible that James Ramsey, who was responsible as the foreman to his employer, could have permitted such a fraud to take place without his knowing it."

And what of the prisoner, John Davis? The Judge continued, "How many men were engaged in this? It is said by the prosecution that you should come to the conclusion that there were three persons. There were three weapons and therefore you ought to infer that there were three persons. The one man above all others who was likely to be confided in by Richard Davis and James Ramsey was John Davis."

Another question the jury had to consider was the finding of the bloodstained spade and the marks it was alleged to have made on the body of Sergeant Eves. There was no dispute that it belonged to Richard Davis, but what the jury had to ponder was not only how it came to be there but, just as important, why that particular implement? It was a perfectly common spade, not an agricultural shovel and therefore quite unsuitable for scooping up large quantities of loose corn. The Judge commented, "It does not appear to me that it would occur to anybody to use such an instrument for such a purpose, and it is not likely that it was done. You must judge whether it is likely that they did take it."

The jury retired for just ninety minutes before bringing in verdicts of guilty against the Davis brothers and of not guilty against Ramsey. The judge solemnly intoned the death sentence on the brothers, who were then led away. Ramsey was discharged, only to be immediately re-arrested for the theft of corn.

After all this, there still remained a gnawing question in the minds of those who had so avidly followed the fortunes of the accused. Which of those three men was the murderer? Was it John Davis, Richard Davis or, even though acquitted, could it have been Ramsey? Were all three equally responsible? The public had not long to wait before another dramatic development seemed to provide the answer.

Within days of his conviction Richard Davis lodged an appeal. His brother John, apparently resigned to his fate, sacrificed whatever hopes he had of avoiding the hangman's noose by openly confessing to the murder. Yes, he said, the three of them had gone to Hazeleigh Hall Farm to steal the corn. Filling their sacks, they had made their way back across the field, Richard some distance in front, followed by John, with Ramsey coming up behind. Suddenly in the darkness John was confronted by the figure of Sergeant Eves, who had evidently not seen Richard and was unaware of the approach of Ramsey.

"Hallo there, Jack," said Eves, "it looks as though I am going to find you a bed for the night." With that John dropped his sack and turned to flee, but was quickly grabbed by the officer. The sergeant was a tall, powerfully built man and more than capable of tackling Davis without needing to draw his truncheon. Neither was there any need for his light, for he had instantly recognised his man. Within moments the two men were struggling fiercely, Davis trying desperately to escape but tiring fast under the weight of his opponent.

Suddenly Ramsey appeared out of the darkness and dealt the officer a crushing blow to the head with his cudgel. Eves went down. Ramsey continued to rain blows on the unfortunate policeman while Davis extricated himself. Once clear of Eves' grasp Davis threw himself on the officer and pinned him down while Ramsey drew his knife and hacked at his throat. It was all over.

As they lay there gasping for breath the realisation of what they had done slowly dawned on them. Footsteps were heard approaching and they looked up to see Richard Davis hurrying up. A brief discussion took place as to what to do with the body. One of them suggested putting it on the local railway line, another that it should be buried. Finally, it was decided to dump the body in the nearby ditch. That, at any rate, was John Davis's version of what happened.

Richard Davis's appeal, no doubt strengthened by his brother's confession, succeeded only in that the death sentence was commuted to life imprisonment, for even allowing that John Davis's confession bore any semblance of truth it had undoubtedly shown Richard as an accessory after the fact. The ultimate penalty was suffered by John when he was hanged at Chelmsford Prison on 16th August.

Ramsey was now faced with a formidable task. Davis's confession had not only identified him as a participant in the theft of corn, but had named him as the actual murderer. To make matters worse, he learned that Richard Davis was being brought from prison to testify against him at his forthcoming trial, as was John Davis's widow Selina.

On 10th November of that year, Ramsey stood his trial at Essex Assizes before Lord Chief Justice Coleridge. Mr. F.O. Crump again led for the Crown. That this trial, for the fairly basic offence of theft, would involve a re-examination of the Eves murder became obvious from the very outset. Mr Crump rose for his opening address and declared that everyone in court was no doubt familiar with the defendant's involvement in the murder trial, and went on, "I think, when you have heard the evidence today, you will find that the most guilty of those men engaged in the murder has unfortunately escaped the supreme penalty of the law which, I venture to say, would have been a just penalty for him." He continued by outlining in considerable detail not only the theft but the murder also. He declared his intention of calling Richard Davis as a prosecution witness and went on to state that he "would lend no ear to any suggestion that Richard Davis's testimony should be regarded as tainted, for he was now reconciled to his fate and will now tell the story as it actually happened."

Selina Davis was called into court and there swore on oath that on the evening of the murder she had been at home preparing to go to bed about nine o'clock.

Superintendent C. Halsey, who investigated the murder of the Purleigh police sergeant.

There was a knock at the door and Ramsey entered, carrying a bundle of sacks. He had a conversation with John Davis, only a part of which Selina heard. Ramsey had said to John, "I have the bags." Mrs Davis then retired to bed leaving her husband and Ramsey downstairs. Some time later, she judged it to be about ten o'clock, she heard the voices of three men as they left the house. That third man was Richard Davis.

Cross-examined by Ramsey, she stuck rigidly to her story despite his accusations that she was bearing false witness against him. This, of course, was the first time she had given this evidence for, at the trial of her husband and the other two accused, she had been protected by law from testifying against her husband.

Richard Davis was undoubtedly the most telling prosecution witness of them all, for he confirmed in every detail his brother's confession. Like Selina, he too had gone to bed about nine o'clock. At about ten o'clock he was aroused by the sound of his brother rapping on his ground-floor bedroom window. After a short conversation he followed John to his house where he found Ramsey waiting with a number of sacks. Both Ramsey and John, he said, were armed with sticks.

He went on to describe the theft and then the murder. At the point where he had returned to the scene and found Ramsey and John standing beside the dead body of the officer he was asked by Mr Crump, "What did John Davis say to you?" to which he replied, "He told me he had knocked the sergeant down and that James Ramsey had cut his throat." It was Ramsey, too, he alleged, who had suggested putting the body on the railway line, but John had said, "Let's put it in the ditch and go home."

Ramsey, as was to be expected, reacted furiously to these allegations and a heated exchange took place between the witness and the defendant, with each accusing the other of lying. Richard remained unmoved and insisted, under the most intense cross-examination, that his was the true account of what had happened.

At this, Ramsey rounded on Davis and shouted, "That man was not killed in a minute. You and your brother knocked him about and left him for dead. I never touched him. You went home and got a spade to bury him. When you returned he was still alive. You knocked him about until his poor head was in pieces." This information, Ramsey was quick to explain, was not his eye-witness account of what happened but was what John Davis had told him on the day following the murder.

The jury had to ask themselves, was John Davis telling a pack of lies in his confession? Would a man, knowing he was about to be hanged, deliberately incriminate a friend whom he knew to be innocent? What could he possibly gain by so doing? One would have thought that if Richard's life had meant so much to John then he would have correctly identified the third man, unless of course that man was Charles Sales, a member now of the Davis family. Why indeed should Richard Davis accuse an innocent man? And Selina Davis too? Either Ramsey was the victim of a fiendish and deadly conspiracy on the part of the Davis family (and the only real reason for this could have been to save Charles Sales) or he was indeed that mysterious third man.

The jury had no doubt whatsoever, for without leaving their seats they found the prisoner guilty as charged. The judge, addressing Ramsey, said, "You stand guilty of the crime on the very clearest possible evidence because much of it is your own confession. I should ill-discharge my duty if I shortened by one single hour the sentence which may be passed upon you." He thereupon sentenced the prisoner to fourteen years' penal servitude.

Were those who had followed these trials any wiser as to the truth of the matter?

The mystery of how Richard Davis's spade came to be found at the scene is quite tantalising. John Davis spoke only of a cudgel and a knife as the murder weapons. If the pathologist was correct we must accept that the spade was almost certainly used to strike the officer. Why, then, did John Davis make no mention of it? If it had been Ramsey who had beaten the officer with his cudgel and then gone on to cut his throat, as Davis had declared, why go to the trouble of attacking him with the spade?

These points lead us directly to what the spade was doing at the scene in the first place. Both James Ramsey and Richard Davis worked at Hazeleigh Hall Farm and must have been familiar both with its layout and the whereabouts of the various items of equipment. Assuming that such implements were kept there and were used by the three men, what possible reason could there be for Richard's spade being brought to the scene?

Ramsey had given a perfectly logical and simple explanation. Richard had gone home to get it for burying the body. Yet the body was never buried but simply dumped in the ditch. Had they intended burying it in the first instance then the question of what to use must have been discussed. There was no point in going back to the barn, breaking in again and then using a blunt corn shovel to dig a hole big enough to bury a large policeman when Richard could, just as easily, run home and get a proper spade.

Another point of some importance concerns the three heavy sticks found under the policeman's body. In those days it was perfectly common for a police officer to carry a heavy stick when going out at night. Contrary to police regulations it may have been, but many a policeman had learned to his painful cost the inadequacy of his truncheon when confronted by a ruffian armed with a stout cudgel. We must therefore ask whether the sergeant was carrying such a stick. If he was, then could it have been one of the three found at the scene? We know for a fact that John Davis was in the habit of carrying such a weapon; indeed Richard Davis described seeing his brother and Ramsey carrying sticks on the night of the murder. He made no mention of carrying one himself.

In studying John Davis's confession we find that Sergeant Eves went in to tackle John, apparently unaware of Richard's departure and Ramsey's imminent arrival. Is it likely that the sergeant saw all three men together and bravely tackled them? That is a possibility, for his bravery had already earned him two commendations. He must have known, though, that in so doing there was no chance of his summoning assistance at that time of night in the middle of a field. Is it not far more likely that in the darkness he saw only one figure and confidently went for it? We shall never know.

The funeral of Sergeant Eves took place just a week after his murder. Newspaper accounts of the day declared that every village for miles around Purleigh was deserted as all the inhabitants packed the route to the little church on top of the hill, commanding such a majestic view over the Blackwater estuary, to pay their last respects to a brave and much-admired officer. The cortege was led by the Chief Constable, followed by every divisional superintendent in the county and over 150 sergeants and constables (half the force).

A short while later every policeman in the force contributed his share towards a handsome headstone which once stood proudly over the grave, but now lies flat and neglected.

Mrs Eves was eventually awarded the highest pension permitted at the time, £15 a year, whereupon a public subscription was organised which raised £400, echoing, it was said, the disgust of the people at the miserly provision made for such tragic incidents.

CHAPTER NINE

New Headquarters

WITH THE strength of the force growing year by year the requirements of its administrative staff grew in proportion. Springfield Court, which in 1840 had been sufficient for the needs of the Constabulary, was by the turn of the century becoming decidedly cramped. Increased accommodation for the recruits, who lived in during their basic training, along with similar accommodation for their instructors, was essential and additional offices had to be found for the staff and stores.

In reporting these facts to the Standing Joint Committee Captain Showers also pointed out the state of disrepair into which the Chief Constable's house was falling. Not least of his problems was the drainage system, the odour from which had pervaded the buildings for a long time.

The Justices instructed the County Architect to examine the whole structure from top to bottom and forward them his report. Members of the Police Sub-Committee also visited Springfield Court to view the premises for themselves.

At a special meeting of the Standing Joint Committee on 29th March, 1899, the Police Committee reported that the headquarters buildings had become totally inadequate for the accommodation of staff, that the County Surveyor had estimated that £9,000 would be required to rectify the structural defects and that the entire ground floors would have to be taken up to trace the source of the offensive smell. The sub-committee was convinced that an entirely new site should be considered for the County Headquarters and to this end they had received an offer of a three-and-a-half-acre site in Gaol Lane (now Sandford Road) which could be purchased for £1,500.

Three months later, however this committee reported that negotiations had broken down, but in September Mr G.J. Bolingbroke, who also owned land near Gaol Lane, offered a three-acre site for £1,250.

The chairman of the Standing Joint Committee declared himself not at all satisfied that the expense to which the county would be put for the building of a new headquarters was justified and put down the motion "that as plans have been prepared by the County Surveyor which appear to meet all reasonable requirements of the Chief Constable, at a cost not exceeding £7,500, the Standing Joint Committee is not justified in involving the county in the very heavy expense of the purchase of a new site or of erecting new buildings for the headquarters of the County Constabulary." Fortunately the chairman was defeated and the committee ordered the Police Sub-Committee to proceed with all haste.

On 6th December, 1899, a letter was received from Captain Showers informing the Justices that his wife was very ill. Her doctors attributed her illness to the insanitary conditions then prevailing at Springfield Court. Obviously fearing an outbreak of typhoid, the Justices immediately ordered Captain Showers, his family and staff out of the building.

The County Surveyor moved in and took up all the floors throughout the ground floor of the main building. Underneath he found a number of old disused wells, cesspools, drains and tree roots, all of which had combined to rot the foundations and floor-joists, thereby bringing about the offensive smell. He recommended as a matter of urgency that all the flooring and joists be renewed, the drains and wells filled in with concrete and the entire foundations dried out. Work on this was immediately commenced.

Meanwhile, a competition had been organised carrying a first prize of £100 for plans for a new headquarters. The winner was a Chelmsford man, Mr George E. Clare.

By September, 1902, a most handsome complex of buildings stood ready for occupation. The new headquarters comprised a lodge, the Chief Constable's house and stables, a main block, a recruits' block and further stables. The gardens were laid out that month at an additional cost of £80, bringing the total cost of this undertaking to £19,384. The new headquarters were known as Springfield Court, while the old Springfield Court was renamed Old Court.

During the year that the new headquarters opened at Springfield the strength of the County Constabulary was as follows:-

Division	Supt	Insp	Sgt	Pc
Brentwood	1		4	19
*Chelmsford & HQ	2	1	7	40
Colchester	1	2	4	36
Dengie	1	1	2	14
Dunmow	1	1	1	16
Epping	1	1	4	31
Grays	1	1	6	31
Hinckford	1	2	5	30
Rochford	1	2	8	43
Romford	1		4	23
Thorpe	1	1	3	18
Walden	1		2	20
Witham	1	1	3	14
Additional (Oyster Companies)				4
Total	14	13	53	339

The persistence of the inhabitants of Maldon and Southminster, who had unsuccessfully petitioned for police stations to be built in their areas in 1890, was rewarded when in January, 1899, a deputation of Justices from the Dengie Hundred met the Standing Joint Committee at Chelmsford. They requested that the court at Latchingdon be moved to the Moot Hall at Maldon and that a police station and

*Headquarters staff then stood at 1 Chief Constable, 1 Assistant Chief Constable, 1 superintendent, 2 sergeants and 6 constables.

court be built at Southminster. These Justices obviously put forward stronger arguments than they had done nine years earlier, for the Standing Joint Committee agreed to both applications.

Following the amalgamation of the Maldon force with the county in 1888 the town boasted a strong police presence in the form of Inspector Halsey, Sergeant Coult and seven constables. By 1899, Inspector Halsey had been promoted and had become the Dengie divisional superintendent stationed at Latchingdon, Inspector Waterman having taken his place at Maldon. The town's police operated from their own office in the Moot Hall itself, inside which building was the centuries old courtroom and cells. The facilities there were far superior to those at Latchingdon.

While arrangements for this transfer were taking place a one-acre site in Back Lane, Southminster, was purchased for £200 and plans drawn up for a police station and courthouse. On completion these had to be forwarded to the Secretary of State, who took a full year to agree to the proposals. Work was completed by April, 1901.

Architect and builder combined to produce one of the most attractive police stations in the county. The tall, angular buildings such as those at Thorpe-le-Soken and Halstead gave way to a broader, more solid-looking structure built entirely of deep red brick outlined in grey stone. Its four cells typified the advances made both in design and comfort. Compared with the tiny, claustrophobic cells of the mid-Victorian stations, Southminster's cells are large and airy. The unfortunate prisoners

The new headquarters at Springfield, designed by Mr George Clare to replace the original headquarters, which became known as Old Court.

no longer sat in total darkness but were afforded light from outside the cell by way of an ingenious but very simple device. Beside each cell door there is a small aperture some ten inches square with thick unbreakable glass on the inside and a hinged trapdoor on the outside. Set inside this square window is a gas-jet. As darkness set in the officer on duty would walk along the corridor, light the gas and then close the hatch, directing the light through the glass and into the cell.

During the first year of its existence Southminster police station was manned only by a sergeant and one constable. By 1902 the divisional commander,

Southminster police station, built in 1901, to which the headquarters of the Dengie Division were transferred a year after its completion.

Superintendent Noah Gibbons, had moved his headquarters from Latchingdon and taken up residence at the new police station.

Not all Essex policemen were so well provided for as those in the Dengie Division, however. During 1901 the Standing Joint Committee expressed its concern over the amount of rent being charged to police officers living in private accommodation, for the force had far outgrown the facilities provided in the first stationhouses, where by the turn of the century only single men and recruits were living. The bulk of the force was living in private lodgings, for which they received a rent allowance based on their rank and the district in which they resided.

Following a number of applications for an increase in this rent allowance the Justices asked the Chief Constable to submit a return of the number of houses privately rented and the cost of such. The subsequent return makes interesting reading:-

Houses rented to the County:-	255
Total weekly rent for all these:-	£55.9s.6d
Proportion paid by the officer:-	£37.1s.8½d
Proportion paid by the County:-	£18.7s.9½d
Average rent per house:-	4s.4d per week
Officer's proportion:-	2s.11d per week
County's proportion:-	1s.5d per week

After sixteen years without a review, new pay scales were introduced on 1st April, 1901, and the division of superintendents into classes was abolished.

Inspectors and sergeants had been similarly dealt with in 1884. The new rates were as follows:-

Superintendents	Old Scale	New Scale
2nd class on appointment	120	On appointment 135
After five years	135	Five years 150
After ten years	150	Ten years 175
1st class on appt.	150	Fifteen years 200
After five years	175	
After ten years	200	
Inspectors		
On appointment	95	On appointment 100
After five years	102	two years 105
After ten years	110	four years 110
		six years 115
Sergeants		
On appointment	29s.2d	On appointment 30s.4d
After two years	30s.4d	two years 31s.6d
After five years	31s.6d	five years 32s.8d
After eight years	32s.8d	eight years 33s.10d
Constables		
On appointment	22s.2d	On appointment 22s.2d
2nd Class	23s.4d	2nd Class 23s.11d
1st Class	24s.6d	1st Class 25s.8d
After two years	25s.8d	two years 26s.10d
After five years	26s.10d	five years 28s.
After eight years	28s.	eight years 29s.2d

A brief mention in the records in November, 1902, to the effect that the county was preparing to purchase the Town Hall at Billericay "which incorporates the Courtroom, Cells and Police Station" serves to cast our minds back sixty years to March, 1841, when Billericay became the first town in the county to provide accommodation for the new police force.

In 1841 a Mr Curtis of Market House leased part of his premises at a rent of £8 a year for use as a stationhouse and lock-up. Market House and the Town Hall were one and the same, the building being designated a Town Hall in 1862 when a group of local businessmen formed themselves into a Town Hall Company and bought the premises, promptly raising the police rent to £20 a year. Built originally in 1830 at a cost of £800, the building was intended for use as committee rooms and for hire to other bodies for public functions.

Market House, or Town Hall, originally intended for use only until such time as a proper police station could be built, became as temporary as post-war prefabs for in 1903 the County Justices learned that the building was being put up for sale by auction and was expected to fetch something like £1,000. Without a moment's delay the Clerk of the Peace was instructed to negotiate the purchase of the building for not more than £950. That he succeeded for just £935 deserved congratulation.

In July, 1904, a builder from Southend was awarded a contract worth £1,311 to refurbish the police station, cells and Magistrates' Court. Inspector George Thomson and Sergeant Michael Keaven must have wondered just how "temporary" this building had become. In the event, its occupancy by the police far out-lived them both, for it was not until 1939 that the present police station and court was built at the far end of Billericay High Street and the old Town Hall turned over to Civil Defence and local government offices.

The Town Hall or Market House at Billericay which served as a "temporary" police station from 1841 to 1939.

CHAPTER TEN

Did he fall or was he...?

PC BARHAM stood at his conference point on the Ardleigh Road near Dedham rubbing his hands and stamping his feet against the bitter cold of that January evening in 1894. He had been there since 6.15 and was expecting to be met by his sergeant, John Harvey, at 6.30. If there was no sign of him by 6.45 then he could get on his way and finish his patrol. He shivered again and looked about him.

The spot at which he was standing afforded a good view towards Dedham on his right and Ardleigh to his left. Opposite stood the *Live and Let Live* beerhouse and to the right of that a pair of semi-detached labourer's cottages. Next to the cottages stood the old weather-boarded cottage of Henry Buss, the local shoemaker.

Hearing the sound of footsteps, the constable turned and saw the object of his uncomfortable wait approaching from the direction of Langham. It was exactly 6.30, Sergeant Harvey was right on time. The two men stood together for a few minutes engaged in desultory conversation before crossing the road to the beckoning warmth of the *Live and Let Live*, where they found that Tom White, the landlord, had already set down two tankards of ale. It was a curious thing, mused the constable, that whoever had devised the list of conference points had ensured that most of them were outside, or very close to, public houses! Half an hour later, and warmed through again, the sergeant and constable bade goodnight to Mr White and made their way out into the darkness. They walked around for a short while before, at 7.30, going their separate ways, Pc Barham to walk the one-and-a-half miles back to Dedham and the sergeant an equal distance to Ardleigh, where he had arranged to meet Pc Page at the *Crown* public house at 9.45.

At nine o'clock the following morning Henry Buss let himself out of the back door of his cottage and walked the few yards along the path to the well which stood in the corner of his garden. He had never given much thought to covering it over, either with the traditional roof or even boarding, for the best drinking water was always to be had at the spring just down the road; everyone in the hamlet of Lamb Corner used it.

Looking about him, Buss saw that there had been a fairly heavy fall of snow overnight and only his fresh footprints disturbed its smooth perfection. Leaning over the edge of the well, he lowered his bucket the ten or twelve feet to the water. Suddenly he froze, for there floating on the surface was a policeman's helmet! He instinctively glanced around the garden, but all was quiet and undisturbed. He looked down again, the helmet was clearly visible—so too was a pair of feet! As the realisation dawned on him that he had a body down his well, and almost certainly a policeman's body at that, he turned and ran the twenty or thirty yards to the *Live and Let Live* where he blurted out his story to Tom White.

The landlord's first question was, quite naturally, "Is it Pc Barham's body?" Buss confessed that he had no idea, for all he could see were the soles of a pair of boots. White then told him that Sergeant Harvey had been in the village the previous night and they had better be sure whom they were dealing with. It was agreed that White should go to Ardleigh while Buss went to Dedham, for the body had to be that of one of those officers. It was Tom White who was to discover its identity when a distraught Mrs Harvey told him that she had not seen her husband since the previous afternoon.

Pc Barham, brought hurriedly to the scene by Buss, was joined by White. A length of cord was brought from the cottage, a noose slipped around the feet and the body of Sergeant Harvey hauled to the surface. The constable immediately noticed a contusion and swelling around the sergeant's left eye and two small cuts near his nose. Apart from that there appeared to be no obvious injury. Pc Barham was sharp enough to check the sergeant's waistcoat pocket and found that his watch had stopped at 8.21.

Without delay Superintendent Ackers at Colchester was notified by telegraph from the Post Office at Dedham, and he in turn notified the Chief Constable. Captain Showers placed Ackers in charge of the investigation and summoned the Police Surgeon, a Mr Maille.

The circumstances as they became known were certainly bizarre enough to warrant Ackers' full investigation into the possibility of murder, for apart from the extraordinary manner in which the sergeant had met his death, there remained the mystery of what he had been doing in that back garden in the first place. The superintendent was to discover that Buss was distantly related to the dead man, having married Mrs Harvey's cousin.

The inquest was held at the *Live and Let Live* on the morning of the following Monday, 8th January. The Coroner, Mr Harrison, told the jury that they were to consider three possibilities, foul play, suicide or accident, and if they were not satisfied that the evidence indicated any of these then they must return an open verdict.

The jury was to learn that Sergeant Harvey was thirty-six years old, married, with three young children aged five years, four years and eighteen months. His wife was again heavily pregnant. He had previously served in the West Riding of Yorkshire Constabulary before transferring to Essex in 1885. He was posted to Ardleigh on 6th January, 1886, and promoted sergeant on 1st October, 1891. The unfortunate officer had therefore met his death exactly eight years to the day since arriving at Ardleigh.

Superintendent Ackers, who gave evidence of identification, Mrs Harvey being in no fit state to do so, was asked whether he knew of any other reason for Harvey's visit to Dedham, apart from the routine matter of visiting his constable. At this Ackers appeared reluctant to reply. "There was a matter that required the serious attention of the police in this neighbourhood. If you press me I will state it, but in the interests of Justice it would possibly be best not to," he said. "You may state it," said the Coroner.

Ackers replied, "Sheep have been stolen in the neighbourhood, and in consequence close attention was being paid by my special direction." The foreman of the jury cut in, "Nobody has considered that he came into contact with sheep stealers," to which the superintendent replied, "There is no suspicion of that kind."

He did not elaborate on this confident reply, neither was he questioned further about it, so we are left wondering why he thought Harvey's death was unconnected with sheep-stealing.

Henry Buss said that he had been at home all night and had heard no sound, neither was there any sign of disturbance in his garden. The Coroner asked him, "When you discovered the body why did you not pull it out instead of wasting time going to Dedham? The man could still have been alive." Buss replied rather tartly that no body with two inches of snow on the soles of its upturned feet could possibly have been alive. Mr Harrison took the point.

The witness was then asked by a member of the jury, "Was Sergeant Harvey in the habit of going to your premises?" Buss replied, "Only to the window to ask how I

Superintendent H. G. Ackers, who investigated the mysterious death of Sergeant Harvey in 1894.

was getting on." The same juror then asked, "Would he go that way (through the garden) to get to your window?" The witness replied that he would not. Sensibly pursuing the subject, the questioner asked, "Did he know the well was there?" Buss confessed that he did not know whether Harvey was aware of the existence or location of the well. Perhaps the juror wondered about the family relationship between the witness and the deceased but decided not to press the matter.

The surgeon was then called and described his examination of the body. The Coroner asked, "How might those injuries have been caused?", to which Maille replied, "With a blunt instrument or by falling against the side of the well." The cause of death, in his opinion, was drowning. The Coroner then asked, "And what is your opinion as to the way he fell?" Maille replied, "I think the man must have been stunned before going into the water." At this, the jury foreman asked the obvious

A well similar to that in which Sergeant Harvey died.

question, "Is the doctor satisfied that he was not killed before he went into the well?" The surgeon gave this some thought before replying, "I should say he died from drowning. I did not detect any fracture whatsoever but only a post-mortem could determine that—and it is an easy thing to fall down that well."

The Coroner described the whole affair as extraordinary, and the jury declared themselves totally baffled. They returned an open verdict.

The funeral of Sergeant Harvey took place the following Wednesday, the coffin being borne by six of his colleagues. The Chief Constable recommended to the Standing Joint Committee that Harvey had met his death while in the execution of his duty and his widow and children were entitled to full benefits. The committee agreed and granted Mrs Harvey a pension of £15 a year, plus £2.10s. for each of the three children.

What stands out so strikingly in the evidence given to that inquest is the absence of a post-mortem. It was only the surgeon's opinion that the deceased drowned, it was only his opinion that no further injuries existed and he stated quite clearly that only a post-mortem could throw further light on these facts. So why was a post-mortem not held? Simply because there was nothing in law which said there had to be. Forensic medicine has come to the fore only since the turn of this century, and although at the time of Harvey's death autopsies were not uncommon they were neither mandatory nor conclusive.

Whichever way we turn we are still left with the one question of what Sergeant Harvey was doing in the pitch darkness of that back garden. Had he seen or heard something suspicious and gone to investigate? If so, would he not have called out to Buss to assist him, for the shoemaker was sitting only a matter of yards away in his living room.

The inhabitants of Lamb Corner entertained no such thoughts. They were convinced that Harvey's death was no accident, and for an explanation there was no need to look further than the lush green meadows thereabouts. It was plain, simple sheep-stealing.

Buss, a local man, probably knew a lot more of what was going on than the Ardleigh-based Harvey and was, the villagers thought, passing on what he heard to his relative the sergeant. The thieves got to hear about this and lay in wait for Harvey on his next visit to the cottage (his calling at the *Live and Let Live* would have confirmed the possibility of more information changing hands). A stunning blow to the side of the head and a swift bundling down the well would ensure that any knowledge he possessed, or was about to obtain, could be of no further use.

Did a fit and healthy police officer really trip and fall headlong down the well without a sound? Or did the villagers thereabouts know a lot more than was ever brought out at the inquest? Whatever the truth of the matter, there is little possibility of it coming to light now.

Sergeant Harvey and Pc Barham carried out their patrols on foot, but since the 1880's the bicycle had been growing in popularity both as a form of social recreation and as a cheap and efficient means of delivering light goods.

Inevitably the question arose of allowing constables to use pedal cycles on large rural beats. Captain Showers was, of course, aware of the advantages. Greater distances could be covered, remote areas could be visited more frequently and the time spent in responding to urgent calls could be reduced from a thirty-minute walk to a quick cycle ride. On the other hand he was equally concerned with the need for the Constabulary to retain its contact with the public.

In February, 1900, he achieved something of a compromise by declaring that only under exceptional circumstances would constables be permitted to use pedal cycles on duty. Those officers whose beats were remote from telegraph offices (in those days practically every beat in the county boasted a Post and Telegraph Office) might use cycles, and other officers might use them when required to travel outside their own areas to perform duty or when the duty was of an urgent nature and the journey long.

The rural beats continued to be patrolled on foot until the early 1930's when tradition finally gave way to expediency. Within a few years all rural officers patrolled on bicycles, which they were still required to purchase privately, and for which an allowance was granted. Naturally these men bought the cheapest cycle they could find, for new models were expensive and the allowance none too generous. This resulted in a motley collection of machines in various sizes and designs. By the early 1960's the allowance had been withdrawn and every rural officer was supplied with a standard black Raleigh Roadster.

The cycle finally gave way to the lightweight motor-cycle and then the Panda car so evident on our roads today. Many policemen, and certainly most of the general public, mourn the gradual passing of that quiet, casual but efficient means of transport.

Pc Arthur Oliver, left, and a colleague at a conference point near Ridgewell at the turn of the century. The unmade road surface is doubtless responsible for the clay adhering to the boots of both men and to the tyres of the cycle. Note the leather gaiters worn by the constable with the cycle.

CHAPTER ELEVEN

The Moat Farm Murder

THERE WAS always speculation as to how their paths crossed, the retired professional soldier, convicted forger and philanderer and the Victorian gentle-woman of independent means.

Samuel Herbert Dougall was born at Bow in 1846 and enlisted with the Royal Engineers two months before his twentieth birthday. Rising to the rank of Quartermaster Sergeant, he served for twenty-one years before retiring on a pension of 2s.9d a day. He was married twice during his army career and met his third wife, Sarah White, while working in Dublin. They were married on 7th August, 1892. In 1895, he was convicted at the Old Bailey of forging a cheque which he had previously stolen and sentenced to twelve months hard labour. While at Pentonville Prison he tried to hang himself, was declared insane and transferred for the remainder of his sentence to Cane Hill Hospital, Surrey.

It was soon after his discharge from Cane Hill that he met Miss Camille Cecille Holland, who was then fifty-three and enjoying a comfortable £6,000 legacy plus stocks and shares inherited from her late aunt. Living together as man and wife, the couple moved to rented rooms at Brighton and within a short time were negotiating the purchase of Coldhams Farm, near Clavering in north-west Essex. From Brighton Dougall and Miss Holland travelled to Saffron Walden, where they rented rooms at 4 Market Row while arrangements were made for moving into the farm. To all who knew them they appeared to be an ordinary, comfortably situated and devoted couple.

They moved into their new property, which Dougall had renamed Moat Farm, on 27th April, 1899, and a local girl called Florence Havies joined the household as a domestic servant. Within twenty-four hours she was complaining to Miss Holland of Dougall's amorous advances. Three days later, apparently quite undeterred by her previous reaction, Dougall tried to get into the girl's bedroom and her screams brought the mistress of the house running to her aid. Despite his insistence that it was all a misunderstanding, young Florrie spent that and the following two nights in Miss Holland's room.

At 6.30p.m. on 19th May, 1899, little more than three weeks after their arrival at Moat Farm, Dougall and Miss Holland drove off in the trap, calling out to Florence that they were going shopping and would be back soon. Two hours later Dougall returned alone, saying that his "wife" had decided to go on to London by train. The following morning the girl arose to find Dougall already downstairs saying that he had received a letter from Miss Holland stating that she was on holiday. Finding herself alone in the house with Dougall, Florence was prudent enough to ensure that her mother came and collected her.

Dougall lost no time in plundering Miss Holland's bank account, forging not only her cheques but also letters. One of them, addressed to the National Provincial Bank, Piccadilly, and signed "Camille C. Holland," explained that her signature might vary slightly due to a sprained hand. By similar means Dougall managed also to transfer the ownership of Moat Farm to himself, and once this was successfully accomplished he set about further improvements to the property, one of them being the filling in of a drainage ditch which ran across the farmyard.

By 1902, with a succession of local girls having come and gone, some of them leaving pregnant, the local folk had begun to wonder what had happened to "Mrs Dougall." Soon after her disappearance Dougall had summoned the real Mrs

Left: Miss Camille Holland

Opposite: Dougall is escorted from Audley End railway station on his way to Saffron Walden for questioning about the murder of Miss Holland.
Essex Police Museum

Dougall, Sarah White, to stay with him (posing as his daughter to allay any suspicion) but she had left soon afterwards. By the end of that year gossip had grown to such a degree that it was being openly bandied about that Camille Holland had never left the farm in the first place. This reached the ear of the local constable, Pc James Drew, who reported the facts to his superintendent. He in turn informed the Chief Constable.

On 28th February, 1903, Detective Inspector Marden from Romford arrived at Clavering to conduct local inquiries, and as a result of his report Captain Showers instructed Superintendent Pryke (the same officer who, as an inspector, had assisted in the investigation of the Sergeant Eves murder) to interview Dougall. He visited the farmhouse on 4th March and was told of "Mrs Dougall's" visit to London. By that time the Metropolitan Police were investigating the cheques purporting to have been signed by Camille Holland. One of them, dated 28th August, 1902, was shown to her nephew, Ernest Holland, who declared it to be a forgery.

On 18th March Dougall walked into the Bank of England and attempted to change fourteen £10 notes which he had withdrawn from the Birkbeck Bank. The clerk realised that some of the serial numbers corresponded with those recently circulated as "stopped" and invited Dougall to wait in the secretary's office. There he was asked to endorse the notes, which he did in the name of "Sydney Domville, Upper Terrace, Bournemouth." The Bank's detective was called and informed Dougall that the money had been obtained by means of forgery and that he would be arrested and conveyed to the City of London Police headquarters at Old Jewry.

During the short walk to the police headquarters Dougall made a despairing dash for freedom, sprinting down Old Jewry towards Cheapside, hotly pursued by

Detective Inspector Cox and Pc Padgham. His liberty was to be short-lived, for he turned into Fredericks Place, only to discover that it was a cul-de-sac. From Old Jewry he was taken to Cloak Lane police station and there charged with forgery. The Essex Police asked that he be transferred to Saffron Walden for questioning. The following morning Dougall was returned to Essex and lodged at Saffron Walden police station.

A search was made of the farmhouse, where it was found that most of Miss Holland's possessions still remained. The outbuildings and other parts of the farm were searched but to no avail. The moat around the house was drained and the mud carefully examined, but still no sign of her could be found. Digging then commenced, for Captain Showers was positive that somewhere on this remote farm lay the remains of Miss Holland. After five weeks of intensive but fruitless effort a farm labourer named Henry Pilgrim was traced to his new employment at Anstey in Hertfordshire. Returning to Moat Farm, he pointed out the exact line of where the main drainage ditch had once run—the same ditch which Dougall had ordered to be filled in soon after his arrival.

The police diggers got to work again, this time up to their knees in excrement, filth and slime. On Monday, 27th April, a constable discovered a piece of rag and shortly afterwards a lady's boot, inside which could be clearly seen the bones of a foot. Renewed efforts brought to light a female body, almost completely decomposed, but later identified by its clothing as that of Miss Camille Holland. She had been buried four feet down inside a hollow which had been dug in the side of the ditch and covered over with brambles.

Two days later, during a post-mortem, Doctors Pepper and Sprague discovered a bullet hole behind the right ear and subsequently declared that death had been due to a gunshot wound to the head. Dougall was charged with wilful murder.

On Monday, 22nd June, 1903, he stood before Mr Justice Wright at the Essex Summer Assize in Chelmsford and pleaded not guilty. Mr Gill, KC, leading for the Crown, outlined the prosecution's case that the accused had killed Miss Holland to gain control of her considerable assets including Moat Farm itself. Mr Elliott, representing Dougall, claimed that decomposition had been so advanced as to make

Left: The four members of the Essex Police who carried out the digging operations at Moat Farm. Detective-sergeant Scott, who found the body of Miss Holland, is seated on the left.

Opposite: The trap belonging to Dougall in which the murder is believed to have been committed.

Essex Police Museum

positive identification impossible, and that his client stood to gain nothing from her death.

The following afternoon the jury returned a verdict of guilty. The Judge, donning the traditional black cap, solemnly intoned the death sentence and Dougall was led silently away.

At that point Captain Showers, who had personally supervised the entire murder investigation, stepped forward and asked permission to address the Judge. This being granted, he read out the names of all the officers who had spent so much time tracking down the accused and those who had suffered the acute discomfort of five weeks digging, stating that it was his desire that each should receive the Judge's commendation. To this most unusual request Mr Justice Wright politely informed the Chief Constable that he would ensure their actions were brought to the notice of the appropriate authorities.

On the morning of 14th July, 1903, Dougall, pinioned and masked, stood on the trapdoor in the execution shed of Chelmsford Prison. Suddenly the Chaplain, the Rev. J. Blakemore, spoke out. "Are you guilty or not guilty?" Receiving no reply he repeated the question. "Guilty sir," replied Dougall, and was immediately plunged to his doom.

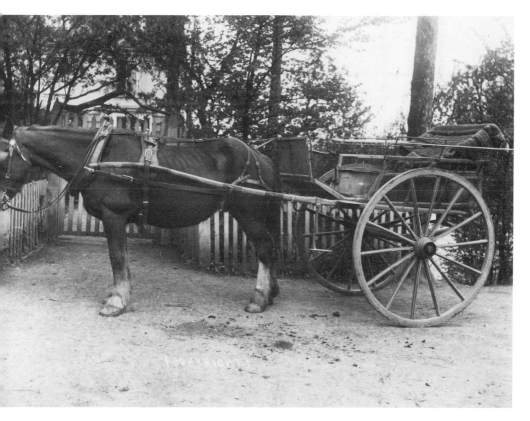

CHAPTER TWELVE

Edwardian Times

A S THE new century dawned, heralding the birth of the Edwardian era, the authorities were becoming increasingly aware of a quite different breed of constable from those of even twenty or thirty years before. The stolid "physical" policeman, so long the favourite of Victorian cartoonists, had given way to an intelligent and energetic young man eager to prove himself in a service which enjoyed the respect of the vast majority of the general public.

Although discipline and obedience still ruled both his working and private life, the Edwardian policeman was standing back and taking stock of what was happening around him. He began to wonder why his predecessors had for so long endured basic injustices, why working conditions had remained unaltered since 1840. He was beginning to ask why he should face instant dismissal if he dared "combine" or form a union, and why had it taken fifty years for his pension rights to be placed on a firm footing. He wondered, too, why after more than sixty years he was not entitled to a regular day off such as everyone else seemed to enjoy without his having to apply in writing to his superintendent for permission.

When pension funds were introduced under an Act of Parliament in 1840* it was left to the local authorities to decide for themselves how best to administer the scheme. That this important Act would require further legislation to correct its deficiencies was apparent some twenty years later when the first pensions fell due. To those first constables who had put their faith in what they had always been told were cast-iron arrangements came a rude awakening when they discovered that the Justices (who still retained discretion over the amount of pension awarded) were basing their assessment on the Chief Constable's report of the man's service record and behaviour. An applicant's pension could be, and often was, reduced in proportion to the number of times he had been punished for disciplinary offences during his service.

Essex, despite its reputation for enlightened attitudes, must share responsibility for the bitterness and hostility provoked by such treatment of men who had devoted twenty-five years of their lives to the police service, suffering all the restrictions that a disciplined service imposed.

Who was to blame for this? Was it the Justices who deliberately interpreted the Act in such a manner as to ensure some saving of public funds? Was it the Chief Constable who used the threat of a reduced pension as a disciplinary stick, or was it Parliament who should have foreseen the consequences of allowing too much discretion to rest in the hands of the local authorities?

*3 & 4 Vict. c88

Certainly so far as Essex was concerned it seemed that the Chief Constable had very little say in the matter, for although the Justices generally acted on his recommendation they were by no means obliged to do so. It was the practice in Essex for the Chief Constable to submit the names of those who were eligible for pension along with a brief résumé of their police careers. The Police Committee would study each officer's "contribution" to the county and decide whether he merited the full pension. Most of them received it, but there were still some whom the Justices declared were not deserving of a full pension, and it would be reduced accordingly. When this happened the facts were published in General Orders as "a warning to others."

It was later discovered that many local authorities, having acted on unsound advice or been guilty of downright mismanagement, found their pension funds insolvent. The Parliamentary supporters of the police argued that there should be a consistent national policy which would benefit all Constabulary officers and relieve them of their dependence on the vagaries of local administration.

As was to be expected, these proposals met staunch opposition. Some authorities saw in it yet another attempt to whittle away their centuries-old control over the Constabularies. Other, less well off, declared that they simply could not afford such generosity.

First introduced and defeated in 1882, the Bill went before Parliament again and again, always to founder on this one issue. Finally, fifteen years after the first recommendations were made by a House of Commons Select Committee, the Police Act 1890 became law, laying down in unequivocal terms the age limits, length of service and the varying degrees of pensions to be paid to members of the police service.

The constant refusal of the authorities to allow the police the opportunity to form a negotiating body ensured that any progress in the improvement of their working conditions was painfully slow. In the same way that a uniform system of pension rights had been secured by the efforts of influential friends both in and out of Parliament, so too were strenuous efforts made for the introduction of a regular rest day.

Much of the credit for the changes which eventually came about must go not to a serving police officer but to John Kempster, who founded and edited a periodical called *Police Review* which served both to provide policemen with useful reading and to ventilate their grievances.

In response to mounting pressure, the Government appointed a Select Committee in 1908 to inquire into the working conditions of Constabularies, more particularly the question of granting regular rest days. While no one appeared to oppose the implementation of a regular rest day, it was pointed out by many local authorities that the granting of such days off would effectively reduce the strength of the police if, for example, one seventh of their policemen were to be absent from duty each week. The only way to counteract this would be to increase each police force by one seventh, and how much was that going to cost the ratepayer?

Parliament took note of this very valid point when it passed the Police (Weekly Rest Day) Act 1910, which granted to every policeman as a right one day off in every seven. To allow the local authorities the opportunity to organise (and pay) for this considerable change, leave was granted for a maximum of four years to elapse before its final introduction. If, by July, 1914, any authority had failed to implement the Act then Parliament would compel it to do so.

Essex made full use of this facility, for the Act was not implemented until January, 1913, and then only by half, as is evidenced by the Force Order published on 21st December, 1912: "Each member of the force below the rank of

Superintendent David Scott in dress uniform with ceremonial sword. Next to the crown on his collar he wears the Merit Star. Superintendent Scott served in Essex from 1883 to 1920.

98

superintendent will be allowed one day's rest a FORTNIGHT...the rest day will be fixed by the superintendent. There is no objection to members occasionally, say once in each month, leaving the vicinity of their residences on their rest day provided that they arrange this beforehand with their superintendent."

Having waited two and a half years for the first regular rest days to be granted, the long-suffering Essex policeman found that the Act and its attendant benefits were not quite all that he had imagined. He was no doubt delighted to hear that an all-round increase in pay was being awarded from 1st January, 1912, but not quite so pleased to discover that the new pay packet was heavier by the staggering sum of seven pence a week!

In April of that same year the Chief Constable had received approval for an increase in establishment of three inspectors, ten sergeants and thirty constables to offset the deficiencies brought about by the Act. In March, 1914, only four months before the final deadline laid down by Parliament, Captain Showers reported to the Standing Joint Committee that following a conference with his divisional superintendents he proposed adopting the system introduced in Lincolnshire (which had been approved by the Secretary of State) and allocate only three rest days a month, the remaining days to be added to each officer's annual leave. Despite the previous increase in manpower he could not implement the three-day-a-month system without a further increase of thirty-eight men, four sergeants and thirty-four constables.

The Standing Joint Committee replied that he should "endeavour to carry out the requirements of the Act with as little increase as possible." In June the Chief Constable presented the revised figure of just two sergeants and eight constables. At the same time he proposed, for reasons of economy, yet another divisional reshuffle. The little Dengie Division (admittedly only twenty-one strong) was to disappear and become a sub-division supervised by an inspector under Rochford. The Dengie superintendent was to be transferred to Epping to replace the retiring Superintendent Terry. Maldon Borough was to be transferred to the Witham Division, and Dunmow and Walden Divisions were to amalgamate to form a new Walden Division.

By June, 1914, the county force comprised the following:-

	Supts	Insps	Sgts	Pcs	Total
Headquarters	1	1	1	7	10
Brentwood	1		6	29	36
Chelmsford	1	2	10	35	48
Colchester	1	2	7	40	50
Epping	1	2	5	36	44
Grays	1	1	8	38	48
Hinckford	1	2	6	33	42
Rochford	1	1	5	31	38
Romford	1		5	31	37
Thorpe	1	1	5	22	29
Walden	1	1	5	38	45
Witham	1	1	3	22	27
Total	12	14	66	362	454

The new pay scales introduced in 1912 were:

		Old £		New £
Superintendents	on appointment	135		150
	after two years	150		165
	after five years	170	after four years	180
	after seven years	185	after six years	195
	after ten years	200	after eight years	210
			after ten years	225
Inspectors	on appointment	100		110
	after two years	105		115
	after four years	110		120
	after six years	115		125
Sergeants	on appointment	1.10s.4d		1.12s.8d
	after two years	1.11s.6d		1.13s.10d
	after four years	1.12s.8d		1.15s.0d
	after six years	1.13s.10d		1.16s.2d
Constables	on appointment	1.2s.2d		1.3s.4d
	after six months	1.3s.11d	after one year	1.4s.6d
	after two years	1.5s.8d		1.6s.3d
	after four years	1.6s.10d		1.7s.5d
	after seven years	1.8s.0d	after six years	1.8s.7d
	after ten years	1.9s.2d	after eight years	1.9s.9d
			after ten years	1.10s.11d

With the change in the man on the beat went a change in the kind of accommodation needed by the force. An extensive building programme had by 1903 provided the county with twenty-one new police stations, but in Chelmsford the policeman's lot was just the same as it had been for sixty years. Soon after the opening of the headquarters at Springfield Court in 1844 the divisional headquarters had been transferred to offices in the Shire Hall, and sixty years later they were still there.

Just as Saffron Walden had owed its new police station to the intervention of the Inspector of Constabulary, so Chelmsford found itself with a new police station as a result of the Judges of Assize and Chairmen of Quarter Sessions complaining of the inadequacy and discomfort of their accommodation at the Shire Hall.

So it was that in 1903 the Shire Hall Committee decided to extend the courts by moving back the walls, which were then flush with the public galleries, erecting an extension on the New Street side of the building and increasing the number of cells. The first two parts of the project were fairly easy to accomplish, but where were the additional cells to be sited?

During the early months of the following year it was agreed to spend £1,500 on a plot of land at the corner of New Street and Waterloo Lane, just across the road

An architect's drawing of the front elevation of Chelmsford police station, showing the basement and subway to the Shire Hall, lower right.

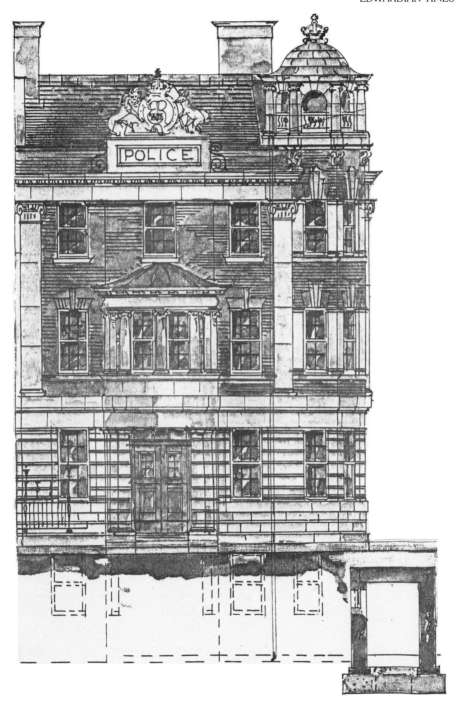

POLICE

from the Shire Hall, on which stood property owned by that old-established Chelmsford family the Gepps. On this site was to be built an underground cell-block with accommodation for twenty-two prisoners along with prison officers. A subway was to be driven underneath New Street to provide direct access to the eleven cells below the Shire Hall. This cell-block and subway would remain a part of the Shire Hall over which the police would have no jurisdiction; indeed it remains so to this day. Once that had been decided it was only a short step to the Police Committee proposing to increase still further the space in the Shire Hall by moving the police into a permanent structure of their own, and where better than on the recently acquired site in New Street?

Plans were drawn up and tenders invited for a two-phase building programme involving the Shire Hall improvements on the one hand and the police station on the other. By July, 1904, the contract had been awarded to J.S. Hammond of Romford, who quoted £5,047 for the police station and £2,950 for the Shire Hall alterations, subway and cells. The Justices insisted that the new underground passage and cells be faced with white glazed brick to match the existing cells and passages within the Shire Hall, a feature which cost an extra £360, bringing the total figure to £8,357.

The builders lost no time, and by November, 1905, the new police station, three storeys high and containing cells, offices and sleeping/living accommodation for its constables, stood ready for occupation.

There have been a number of alterations since, the most important being the subsequent purchase of Mr Gepp's offices next door to provide an extension containing a sergeant's office, typist's room, charge room and parade room. The little telephone room was demolished (the telephone being removed to the general office) to provide access to these additional offices. The police station remained operational until 1969, when a new and very much larger station was built at the far end of New Street. The old police station is presently being used by the Essex Record Office.

By 1912 it had become obvious that the old police offices in the Guildhall at Harwich were quite inadequate. As far back as the 1830's when the town maintained its own borough force the police station had comprised offices on the ground floor and two small cells at the rear. On amalgamation agreement was reached that the county Constabulary could continue using the rooms and cells for an annual rent which in 1912 stood at £75 a year.

The town had seen its population grow from 4,451 (Harwich 3,383 & Dovercourt 1,068) in 1851 to 13,528 (Harwich 7,900 & Dovercourt 5,628) in 1911. The police establishment had grown proportionately and thus exposed the limitations of the Guildhall.

In September, 1912, a site was found on the main Harwich to Dovercourt road with a frontage of 155 feet and a depth of 150 feet. While the County Architect prepared the plans for a new police station test bores at the site revealed a very unstable subsoil, and it became clear that before any building took place a reinforced concrete raft would need to be constructed.

The contract for the construction of the raft was awarded to Fawcett Construction, who had quoted £743 10s, while that for the building of the police station was granted to Edward Saunders, of Dovercourt, who had submitted the lowest tender of £7,098. By September the Police Committee were having second thoughts about the cost of this building and asked the County Architect to revise his plans. Subsequent plans revealed the main building intact, while the constables' living quarters had borne the full brunt of the cutback to the tune of £446. The concrete raft was completed in October, 1913, and the building of the main station commenced the following month. By February, 1915, all building was complete and the Harwich police moved into their first custom-built station, which remains to this day.

Rochford featured along with Harwich in being the last police station to be built before the restrictions brought about by the First World War put a stop to all building plans. Rochford's old station, built in 1846 for the use of a superintendent and two or three constables, was totally inadequate for twentieth-century needs. Its two tiny cells had long since been supplemented by those at Southend, and in addition to this the Rochford superintendent was complaining that lack of space was forcing him to hire the local Corn Exchange at four shillings a day in order that he could hold the regular pay-parades and periods of drill which were still an essential part of police discipline.

In June, 1913, a site in South Street with a frontage of 89 feet and a depth of 100 feet was purchased for £406 and plans prepared for a very impressive building containing four cells and living accommodation for four constables. As with Harwich, the committee demurred at the cost and insisted on modifications. This time the

Harwich police station, one of the two last stations built before the First World War. It was first occupied in 1915 and is still in police use.

living quarters suffered along with the cell block, both being reduced from four to three.

Of the fourteen estimates received, the lowest quoted a figure of £3,585.10s. Unable to reduce this any further, the committee awarded the contract to Myall Brothers, of Southend. Work commenced in March, 1915, and was completed in exactly one year. This very fine-looking building remains operational to the present day.

Without a doubt the gravest test of the Constabulary's ability to maintain law and order came in 1912 with the great dock strike at Tilbury. The dock industry was labour-intensive, providing regular work for thousands of dockers, lightermen and stevedores. Over the years these men had formed unions and societies, many of which later became affiliated to the National Transport Workers' Federation. As the power of the unions grew and with it a desire to see the industry "closed" to all but ticket-holders repeated approaches were made to the employers to recognise the closed shop, but this they steadfastly refused to acknowledge. Employers regarded non-union labour as a potent weapon in the event of union-inspired strike action.

Steadily the rumblings of discontent grew and the docks of London deteriorated into a state of permanent crisis. In April, 1912, came the spark which was to ignite the powder-keg. A man named Thomas, himself a member of the Foreman Lightermen's Union, had been employed since 1910 as a watchman by the Mercantile Lighterage Company. Union officials complained that as Thomas's union was not affiliated to the NTWF and he was working as a watchman he should join the ranks of the NTWF and take out a ticket. This Thomas himself refused to do on principle. The Lightermen's Union thereupon called for its members employed by Mercantile Lighterage to down tools, and without its workforce the company passed on its business to another lighterage firm, whose workers refused to handle Mercantile's work. They were promptly dismissed. The unions responded with a total stoppage throughout the Port of London, and sent out a call for support to their brethren in the provinces. Unfortunately for them the response was negligible, and what little support there was petered out within a few days, only London, Essex and Kent remaining firm in their resolve.

What of the men of Essex? Responding to the call of their unions they remained, for the first week at any rate, calm and resolved. After a fortnight, though, with only their meagre strike pay coming in and household bills beginning to mount tempers flared and ugly demonstrations took place. The sight of more and more non-union workers being brought in to man the docks served only to fan the smouldering embers into flames of violence and destruction.

The Chief Constable was quick to realise that the situation was worsening by the hour and if serious trouble broke out the Constabulary would be in no position to contain it. The total strength of the Essex Police then was just 450 officers. The only course open to Captain Showers was to put out a call for reinforcements from other forces. Hurried calls resulted in the drafting into the county of no fewer than 500 officers, not only from the immediate counties around Essex but from as far afield as Birmingham. All rest days and leave for Essex men was cancelled, 114 of them were drafted into the dock area from all parts of the county and the rest were put on instant standby.

Above: The original police station at Rochford, built in 1846 in North Street and now serving as the town's Post Office.

Below: The imposing facade of the Rochford police station built in 1915–16 in South Street.

By the middle of June sporadic outbreaks of violence were becoming more frequent, the increasing anger and resentment of the strikers being directed not only against the 13,000 "blackleg" workers brought in daily to work the docks but against the police, who in their efforts to protect those workers found themselves caught in the middle of two warring factions.

On Sunday, 9th June, strikers at Purfleet held up a train carrying "blackleg" labour to the docks and a number of those workers were attacked. As policemen continued to be injured, so the number of arrests continued to rise. The magistrates dealt severely with offenders and sentences of between fourteen days and three months were imposed. On 21st June, nine such offenders who had been sentenced to imprisonment were being conveyed to Grays railway station under a foot and mounted police escort when the prisoners and police found their way barred by a hostile crowd of between 2,000 and 3,000 sympathisers. Despite appeals for them to disperse the mob remained, a solid wall of defiance vastly outnumbering the police and bringing the town centre to a standstill. Finally, a strong contingent of Birmingham Police was ordered to clear a path through the crowd, which they did with drawn truncheons. Numerous injuries were inflicted on both sides.

By early July the situation had deteriorated still further, with mobs roaming the streets, smashing windows and causing widespread damage. As the strikers became more and more desperate clashes became more frequent and trains carrying "blackleg" workers were waylaid and bombarded with missiles. One group of strikers tore down the fence at Grays railway station intent on stopping one of those trains, ejecting the driver and fireman, and then sending it off to destruction along with its complement of "blackleg" passengers.

Faced with an almost total breakdown of law and order, the Lord Lieutenant, Chief Constable and local magistrates gathered in Grays for the reading of the Riot Act, the last step before armed intervention, and three hundred men of the Dublin Fusiliers, each armed with a rifle and ammunition, were drafted in from their barracks at Gravesend. With the police now substantially reinforced with an equipped military presence the strikers wavered and then gave in. After ten weeks of anger, frustration and poverty, with union strike pay down to just two or three shillings a week for each man to feed his family, the NWTF called off the strike and ordered a resumption of work.

If the cost to the strikers had been shattering, the cost to the county had been catastrophic. Trade in the area had been brought to a standstill, smaller businesses which had relied on the huge population of dock-workers for their survival had been crippled, widespread damage to property had occurred and the general prosperity of south-west Essex had been dealt such a blow that it was to take years to recover.

By September, 1912, the county's finance office had prepared a list of accounts and expenses incurred during the period of the strike showing a total expenditure, up to then, of £8,658.12s 3d. The bill for the hire of the Birmingham Police totalled £2,619, with another £1,540 for the fifty officers from Kent and lesser sums for the other forces involved, which included Colchester Borough. Representations were made that month to the Chancellor of the Exchequer urging that as the strike had not arisen from any local trouble but was rather a national issue this very considerable expense should be met either in part or whole from central Government funds. It took the Chancellor's office three months to reply that Lloyd George himself had considered the matter but felt that "local authorities should pay all the expenses incurred in keeping law and order in their districts and any departure from this rule would be unjustified."

Despite this setback, the Standing Joint Committee for the Police had no intention of letting finance interfere with the gratitude they felt for a county force which had laboured unceasingly throughout the ten-week strike in its efforts to prevent a total breakdown of public order. Many of its members were injured, all of them were physically exhausted. "We are of the opinion," said the committee, "that great credit is due to the Chief Constable and the officers and men under him who were engaged in the districts affected by the strike for the efficient and tactful manner in which they performed very onerous and exacting duties." Awards were made as follows:-

Chief Constable	£50	
Supt Laver (Grays)	£25	(and recommended for
Supt Hastings (HQ)	£10	the King's Police Medal)
Insp Fulcher	£10	

All ranks who were engaged in these duties for four weeks or more were awarded six days' extra pay, those who were engaged for less than four weeks being awarded three days' extra pay.

The years 1910-1914 witnessed many upheavals within the county police, not least of them being the formation of a new borough force at Southend. This involved not only a reversal of the trend set by the boroughs of Harwich, Saffron Walden and Maldon but also an interesting battle of wits between the borough Corporation and the County Standing Joint Committee.

To examine these developments we must go back to 1892 when Southend, with a population then of 13,000, was granted the status of a borough under the terms of the Local Government Act 1888. Within five years Southchurch had joined and swelled the figure to 23,000 and by 1913, with the incorporation of Thorpe Bay, Westcliff, Leigh and Prittlewell, the population had leapt to 82,000. With a population well in excess of the required minimum of 50,000, Southend applied for full county borough status, which was granted with effect from 1st April, 1914.

What was to become of the county police who still patrolled the streets of the borough? By December, 1911, Captain Showers had recognised the unique situation of the town when he placed before the Standing Joint Committee a recommendation that Southend, then still a part of Rochford Police Division, should become a division in its own right with its own headquarters in Alexandra Street. His report showed that Rochford Division comprised a total of twenty-eight parishes containing a population of 93,844 and a police strength of ninety officers. The Chief Constable pointed out that twenty-six officers were stationed in rural areas while no fewer than sixty-four were required for Southend. This imbalance could be rectified by creating a separate division of Southend and supplementing the depleted Rochford Division by an amalgamation with the Dengie Division. The Standing Joint

Committee approved this step and Superintendent Jones was moved in to become Southend's first divisional commander.

This decision rather upset the Corporation, who complained that it was arbitrary. Surely, they said, common courtesy dictated that the Standing Joint Committee should have consulted them before approving a move which so affected

Southend on a rainy day at the turn of the century, when it was still part of the Rochford Division.

the borough? In this protest lay the core of a civic pride which would lead eventually to the formation of a new borough force within the county.

It was inevitable that the subject of a borough force should be raised at Southend Council meetings. Those who favoured the idea argued that the force would be controlled by and accountable to the Watch Committee instead of the County Standing Joint Committee. It was further observed that the borough, already subscribing £102 a year towards the maintenance of each of its constables, could with prudent management reduce that figure to just £75 and thereby enable the establishment to be increased to about a hundred officers without incurring additional expenditure. There were, however, many objectors to this proposal who preferred to leave the already well-established county police and its administration undisturbed.

In February, 1913, the county entered into negotiations with the Southend Watch Committee as to the best method of policing the borough. It must have been as patently obvious to the Watch Committee as it was to the Standing Joint Committee that discussions could not include any decision which would deprive the Chief Constable of his constitutional control over his force and at the same time Southend saw no reason why it should not be permitted to exercise at least some such control. A rather farcical situation developed; who would be the first to formulate a set of proposals which would satisfy the other side, yet give nothing away?

The S.J.C. had already made it plain to the borough that it would be desirable in the interests of both parties that the unity of the county police should be preserved, even though this would prove to be of no financial benefit to the county. On 30th June, 1913, the county again approached the borough asking if it was still their wish that the county continued policing the borough? If so, would they care to make some definite proposals on the matter?

Seven weeks were to elapse before the reply was forthcoming. The Corporation, they said, had no intention of making any proposals. If the county wished to continue policing an area which was shortly to become a county borough it was up to them to suggest how they were going about it, and to put these suggestions to the Corporation for their approval. The S.J.C. replied on 3rd September that they had no proposals to make; the town was a perfectly legal division of the county police and if the Corporation wanted it otherwise it was up to them to forward the necessary proposals.

This rather ridiculous situation continued until September, when the Corporation wrote to say that the county doubtless realised that time was pressing and if it still wanted to police the borough then it should say so. The county was given fourteen days in which to reply. If the Corporation thought this would force the county into making hasty decisions and rash concessions they were mistaken, for exactly fourteen days later the S.J.C. replied to the effect that they were in possession of a copy of an agreement between another county force and a borough which had been in operation for some years and appeared to be working well. The only snag was that the county failed to enlighten the borough as to what that agreement contained.

Clearly losing patience, Southend Corporation replied that if that was the best the county could do there was no point in continuing the discussions and steps would be taken as soon as possible to establish a borough force. Would the Standing Joint Committee kindly forward particulars of the service, age and records of all the county policemen serving within the borough boundary who wished to transfer to the new force.

With neither side having yet shown its hand, the S.J.C. realised it was in a difficult position. Was Southend really considering breaking away and taking with it more than sixty fully trained and experienced county officers, or was the Corporation bluffing? A week later the S.J.C. came up with a set of proposals aimed at retaining county control over the police while granting the borough the right to consultation.

Southend Corporation found the county's proposals totally unacceptable, and within a week came up with modified proposals of its own, several of which the county rejected out of hand as they tended to divest the Chief Constable of control of his force.

With neither side willing to budge on the major points Alderman Francis urged Southend Corporation to take urgent steps to raise a borough force. It was thereupon resolved to advertise the post of Chief Constable at a salary of £400 a year rising annually by £25 (Captain Showers' salary at this time was £500 plus £200 allowances). It was also agreed that the pay and allowances for the new borough police should be the same as those in the county, but it turned out they were considerably more than were enjoyed by the county, which probably explains why so many applied to join the new force.

Mr H.M Kerslake, Chief Constable and Chief of the Fire Brigade of Dewsbury, Yorkshire, was chosen to become first Chief Constable of Southend Borough Police with effect from 1st April, 1914.

		Southend Pay Scales compared with County Constabulary	
		Southend	Essex
Inspectors	on appointment	44s.	42s.3d
	after two years	46s.	43s.9d
	after four years	48s.	45s.3d
	after six years	50s.	46s.9d
Sergeants	on appointment	35s.	32s.8d
	after two years	36s.	33s.10d
	after four years	38s.	35s.
	after six years	40s.	36s.2d
Constables	on appointment	26s.	23s.4d
	after one year	27s.	24s.6d
	after two years	28s.	26s.3d
	after four years	29s.	27s.5d
	after six years	30s.	28s.7d
	after seven years	31s.	—
	after nine years	32s.	after eight years 29s.9d
	after ten years	33s.	30s.10d
	after twelve years	34s.	—

Borough constables would also be granted their full entitlement of a weekly rest day, whereas the county officers were permitted only one rest day a fortnight. The rank of Chief Inspector was added in January, 1914, Inspector Ellis from Essex being appointed to that rank. A total of three sergeants and sixty-nine constables had applied for and been accepted by the new borough force and continued wearing their county uniforms (Southend's uniform being identical) which the borough had agreed to purchase from the county at £3 each.

CHAPTER THIRTEEN

The First World War

THE YOUNG recruit surveyed himself in the mirror of the single men's dormitory at police headquarters, Springfield. His interviews and medical now behind him and his swearing-in before the Chelmsford Justices still fresh in his mind, Pc Alfred Welham checked the creases in his uniform and glanced for the last time at his gleaming boots. Satisfied with what he saw, he made his way downstairs to join the handful of newcomers awaiting the arrival of the Sergeant Instructor. It was 14th July, 1914, and the first day of their month-long basic training had begun. Six weeks later Pc Welham was dead.

Constable Percy Battle patrolled quietly along Chelmsford High Street, his eyes wandering now and again from the bustling pavements to the large white-faced clock which looked down from the Shire Hall. How many times had he looked up, just as he was doing now, to check that he had enough time to get to that conference point where the sergeant or inspector might be waiting? He smiled to himself as he remembered how, just a year ago, he had missed a similar "point" on his old beat at Brentwood. That little omission had cost him a visit to the Chief Constable and a five shilling fine! Now, with three years in uniform, he looked forward to many more days such as this, for it was August, 1914, and the sun shone down over the county town. One month later he was dead.

These two men share the sad distinction of being the first Essex constables to die in the "war to end all wars". Pc Welham, a single man, was recalled to the Suffolk Regiment before he had a chance even to finish his police training and was killed on 26th August, 1914. Pc Battle, who had joined the Constabulary in January, 1911, and had married two years later, was recalled to the Grenadier Guards in August and killed on 4th September. Pc William Burnett of Wickford (Coldstream Guards) followed in October, Pc Herbert Button of Colchester (Grenadier Guards) in November, and Pc William Goodrick of St Osyth (West Kent Regiment) in December.

From a force of 450 men no fewer than 154 left for the war. Twenty-two were killed, many more wounded—two so seriously that they could only be discharged on their return.

Essex was declared a War Zone and transformed into an enormous armed camp, with troops stationed in every town and village throughout the county. The naval port of Harwich was "closed" and anybody wishing to enter the town had first to obtain a police pass. So seriously did the Government view the situation of Essex that secret plans were made for the evacuation of the entire population to Hertfordshire in the event of an invasion.

The war affected everyone, with stringent food rationing and little or no protection against spiralling prices. Worse affected than most was the policeman, for taking into account his hours of duty, greatly increased responsibilities, restrictive conditions of service and discipline, he found himself little better off than a farm labourer.

Constables on town beats found the working day divided into three shifts, early turn from 6am until 10am and 2pm until 6pm, late turn from 10am until 2pm and

The First World War policeman. Pc 407 Charles Havers during his basic training at headquarters in December, 1913, following which he was posted to Brightlingsea.

6pm until 10pm, and night turn from 10pm until 6am. Those on day shifts were not permitted to leave their stations during the four hour "off-duty" period without express permission but were expected to remain on call and were found jobs to do about the place. No provision was made for meal-breaks except for those on night duty, who were granted a thirty-minute break. On two shifts out of three, therefore, the constable effectively worked a twelve-hour day—and as though this were not enough, he was restricted still further by having to ask permission to leave the station at *any* time, regardless of whether he was on duty or not. This restriction covered his monthly rest day, too.

The detached beat constable fared a trifle better, for he could work a discretionary duty of five hours each day with a compulsory three hours' patrol at night, generally from 8pm–11pm, 9pm–12 midnight, 10pm–1am, 2am–5am and 5am–8am. He could not choose which of these to perform but was allocated a list showing what he was to do. For the remainder of his twenty-four hours he remained on call and was expected to deal with anything which came his way, regardless of whether he was on or off duty. During these set patrols the rural officer had a number of conference points to attend, as indeed did the town constable. The sergeant, inspector or superintendent would know from the list where any officer would be at a particular time and could turn up unannounced.

It was not uncommon for a crafty rural man to cycle to his point and hide his machine behind a hedge. If no one turned up to meet him, all well and good, but an equally crafty inspector or superintendent, who had undoubtedly perfected the same technique during his younger days, would often invite the constable to "hop aboard" the County cart for a lift to his next point. The crestfallen passenger, unable to refuse such an open-hearted invitation, would then be left to walk the two or three miles back to where he had left his bicycle. This particular dodge remained a favourite "cat and mouse" game for many years. In particularly bad weather the results could be most uncomfortable!

The effects of the dock strike and other upheavals had forced upon the Government the need to look again at the implications of the mutual aid scheme which existed (and still exists) between forces. Established in the middle of the previous century, it was originally intended only for use between neighbouring forces as a means of supplementing each other in times of need and was never intended to be used as a form of massive reinforcement. Local authorities were still calling upon the military for assistance despite a report made in 1908 by a Select Committee of the House of Commons (The Employment of Military in Cases of Disturbance) that deplored the use of soldiers in civil disorders and called for the Home Secretary to be granted powers to requisition up to ten per cent of any county force for use in any area threatened by riot.

It was quite obvious that the calling in of the military was an admission of failure on the part of the police. Despite the fact that many forces had depleted their own resources in their efforts to assist Essex during the dock strike of 1912, the situation had become so grave that the military had to be called upon to quell the disturbances.

It took the Home Office just three months to react to that call for armed intervention. An urgent circular, dated 15th September, 1912, was sent to all Chief Constables and read:-

> It is of great importance that there should be in every Police district a classified register of persons whose services would be available for the assistance of the Police if any serious emergency should arise. There should be:- (a) a First Police Reserve consisting of men who are accustomed to discipline and who have been trained in the Police or the Army, or otherwise specially qualified for Police work. (b) a Second Police Reserve consisting of all those willing to be sworn in as Special Constables (under the Special Constables Act 1831). Immediate steps are to be taken to build up adequate Police Reserves which will enable them to cope with future troubles without having recourse to military aid.

On the face of it this appeared to be an excellent alternative to calling in the military. Captain Showers was nevertheless dubious about the practicalities of raising and maintaining such a reserve. Having canvassed his retired police officers he found, not surprisingly, very few of them willing after thirty years service to do it again for nothing. He reported to the Standing Joint Committee that in the absence of experienced police volunteers the only alternative was to call in ex-army personnel, and he was not exactly overjoyed at that prospect. He went on to say that some counties had already proposed a substantial increase in their regular forces, which would be of greater benefit to the community. Rather than incur the cost of a reserve force which might or might not be required, and might or might not be relied upon to assist the police, he proposed that Essex increased its regular force.

The committee instructed him to apply for an increase in establishment of fifty constables to be built up slowly over the forthcoming years. So far as the Second Reserve of Special Constables was concerned, the good people of Essex could always be relied upon to rise to the occasion in the event of calamity. Somewhat surprisingly, the Home Office agreed.

Two years later, such increases as had been achieved were wiped out when so many of the county's trained and experienced policemen were recalled to the Colours. Replacements would have to be found, and found very quickly. What was to be done?

Paradoxically, the solution lay in that Home Office recommendation of 1912 which Essex had side-stepped in an effort to build up its regular force. The second option, that of a Special Constabulary, had clearly to be adopted without delay.

At a specially convened meeting of the Standing Joint Committee on 15th August, 1914, a strategy for policing the county was thrashed out and an appeal for volunteers published. Its content, serving well to illustrate what was expected of them, read as follows:-

It is desirable that during the War there should be a Volunteer Police Force to aid the County Police in the preservation of peace and good order. All those not within the limits of age prescribed by the Territorial Force who are willing to serve (without remuneration) are asked to enroll their names at the nearest Police Station with as little delay as possible. They will only be asked to serve in their own town or parish. The service will be voluntary but it will be under the control of the Home Office and its operations will be regulated by the terms of the Police Act. It will be composed of British citizens of good physique who will form themselves into groups or squads serving under a Sergeant of their own nomination who will be responsible for discipline and duty spells of the squad.

The spell of duty will be four hours a day and arrangements will be made to avoid interference as far as possible with the men's ordinary occupations. The Special Constables will be employed in the neighbourhood of their homes and will make their own arrangements for food. They will be equipped with a truncheon and will wear an armlet on the left arm.

It was resolved that there should be at all times not fewer than 500 Specials available for duty, with a reserve list to fall back on if the need arose. Each constable was issued with a striped armband (similar to those worn by the regular Metropolitan

Police) upon which was exhibited the insignia of his rank, truncheon, whistle, peaked cap and police cape. The rank insignia were as follows:-

Chief Special Constable: silver crown between two silver stars mounted on a circle of two inches diameter in blue cloth.
Special Chief Superintendent: silver crown and silver star on a two inch circle of red cloth.
Special Superintendent: silver crown on two inch circle of green cloth.
Special Sergeant: letter 'S' in brass.
Special Constable: letter 'C' in brass.

These men had to be enrolled, sworn-in, trained, drilled, supervised and administratively maintained. With the envisaged minimum of 500 men Captain Showers realised that the control of what amounted to a second full-strength Constabulary would require the full-time occupation of its commanding officer. Both he and his superintendents were already heavily engaged with the welter of wartime emergency regulations and Home Office instructions, so somebody had to be found who would be willing to devote his energies to this new force.

Such a man was Captain Matthew Ffinch, of Hoe Mill, Maldon, a retired officer of the South Staffordshire Regiment and a Justice on the Witham Bench. By September of that year the Standing Joint Committee had approved Captain Ffinch's enrolment as a Special Constable, whereupon he was immediately placed in command of the organisation, training and duties of the Special Constabulary. His first instruction to the new Constabulary covered their duties and read as follows:-

(1) Special Constables are to patrol all roads on the constable's beat and constantly inspect wires and posts, buttresses and arches, roadways of bridges and all culverts under the roads and railways. All vulnerable points liable to outrage should be guarded.
(2) Take notice of all passers-by and stop and question any who look like foreigners, and if he suspects them of being German or Austrian, to demand their permits (which he must very carefully read). All vulnerable points are to be guarded between sunset and sunrise.

Thus was the Special Constabulary of Essex brought into the twentieth century.

Captain John Unett, who succeeded Captain Showers, made it his first job when he took over in May, 1915, to obtain approval for Captain Ffinch's appointment as a full-time police superintendent for the duration of the war. This, of course, entitled Ffinch to receive the pay of a superintendent. In his memoirs Unett was to say of the Special Constabulary, "At the end of the war the (regular) force was 180 below its proper establishment, the deficiency being made up by the Special Constabulary. Until the war there were no Special Constables in Essex, but from its small beginnings in 1914 the Special Constabulary grew until, in 1918, it comprised a well-disciplined, willing and capable force of 10,000."*

Compared with the devastating blitzkrieg of the Second World War, the air-raids of the 1914-1918 war pale into insignificance. Yet it must be remembered that Britain's population had never before been subjected to air attack, and the sight of hostile aircraft over the fields of East Anglia and the sound of bombs as they detonated on our towns created an entirely new concept of war. From 1915 to 1918 German aircraft flew over Essex on no fewer than sixty-three occasions (fifty-four by

*The author has been unable to find the source for this statistic, for records of the day (1917) show 4,348 Special Constables with a further 1,357 held in reserve. Only about 500 were ever fully utilised.

night and nine by day), releasing a total of 536 bombs—many of them dropped by hand from the cockpits. Fortunately casualties were extremely light.

During the early hours of Sunday, 24th September, 1916, a squadron of Super Zeppelins, nearly 650 feet long and 78 feet in diameter, crossed the Essex coast en route again for London. One of these, the L-33, was struck by anti-aircraft fire and slowly descended over the village of Little Wigborough, near Colchester. At a height of less than 150 feet the shouts of its crew could be plainly heard as they fought desperately to keep their craft airborne. Slowly it fell beyond a distant ridge and the watchers, disappointed at being unable to follow its path, turned towards their homes. Suddenly, the entire neighbourhood was lit as if by some mighty flare. Trees and houses stood out in stark relief as the whiteness turned to brilliant red and then slowly, very slowly, died away. Commander and crew, having brought their ship to earth, had disembarked and then touched off the gas-filled cells to send their contents fire-balling into the night sky.

Satisfied that nothing was now left which could be of any use to the British, the German commander ordered his twenty-two men to empty their weapons, formed them up into ranks and marched them out on to the Colchester road. A short while later a very startled Special Constable, resplendent in peaked cap and armband, found himself confronted by this rather formidable group, the leader of which asked the way to the nearest Army post. Wondering what on earth he was expected to do, the Special Constable followed the group along the road towards Colchester.

Before long the column came upon the solitary figure of Pc 354 Charles Smith, who having heard that the airship had come down was on his way to the scene. He walked boldly up to the German commander and informed him that both he and his men were under arrest and that he, Pc Smith, intended conveying them to Colchester police station. Chatting amiably on the way, the German inquired of the constable, "Do you think the war will soon be over?" to which Smith replied, "Well, it's over for you at any rate!"

Arriving at Colchester at two o'clock in the morning, Pc Smith handed over to the duty inspector what must surely have been the strangest batch of prisoners he had ever encountered. Shortly afterwards a military escort arrived to convey the Germans to a prisoner-of-war camp. That very day Charles Smith was to learn that the Chief Constable had ordered his immediate promotion to sergeant and had awarded him the Star of Merit "for his coolness and judgment."

From that day forward this little-known constable became something of a celebrity, known to every member of the force as "Zep" Smith. Many years later another generation of policemen were reminded of his exploit when they read of his death on 24th April, 1977, just short of his 95th birthday.

The crew of another Zeppelin were not so lucky as the men of the L-33. Part of the same squadron which had crossed Essex that night, the L-32 was attacked and severely damaged by British fighters near Romford. Slowly turning for home, it began to lose height over Billericay. A mighty explosion ripped it apart and sent both airship and crew plummetting to earth. There were no survivors.

There is no doubt that the pay awarded to the new Southend Borough Police caused considerable unrest throughout the county, prompting a call for a further increase just two years after the 1912 award.

The wreckage of the Zeppelin L-33 at Little Wigborough. The arrest of her crew led to Pc Charles Smith being awarded the Star of Merit and gaining the nickname of "Zep" Smith.

The request was presented in a somewhat unusual manner in that it was made on behalf of their men by the superintendents. With no union to protect the policemen's interests and "combining" still a serious offence, it is clear that the superintendents maintained a watchful eye on things. Their letter, dated 19th June, 1914, and addressed to the Chief Constable (who if not the originator would certainly have been aware of its content long before he received it), was signed by Superintendent Raglan Somerset, the Deputy Chief Constable, and Superintendents Hastings, Lennon, Mule and Cowell. It highlighted yet again the vexed question of police pay being based entirely on local agreement. It read, "Attention is to be directed to the pay of the new Southend Borough Force which is materially higher than the county force. Further, in the Metropolitan Police the maximum pay of a constable is 1s.4d to 4s.10d per week more than the pay of an Essex sergeant. These differences must, of course, have a serious influence on the question of recruits for the force as well as creating a general feeling of dissatisfaction. Having regard to the increase in the cost of living and to the fact that the police in different parts of the country have had considerable increases in their pay.... the pay of the Essex Police should be made at least to equal that of some of their colleagues near them."

Captain Showers plainly sympathised with the application and forwarded it to the Standing Joint Committee for consideration. The pay award of 1901 which had increased the wages of a constable by roughly five per cent had been quite considerable, reflecting as it did the gradual rise in the cost of living over the previous fifteen years. The pay rise of 1912 represented only two per cent and was of little or no benefit. With a war-induced spiralling of the cost of living the Essex Police considered themselves justified in asking for their first substantial increase in thirteen years.

The application remained with the Standing Joint Committee for three months before it was approved, and another month with the Secretary of State for his endorsement. By December, 1914, rising costs had already taken their toll and another application was made for a supplementary award to take into account the damage inflicted by that six-month wait. Again the months slipped by with no word from the authorities. Prices continued to rise almost daily, swiftly engulfing the pay award of the previous year. With the working day getting longer, their duties becoming more and more demanding and their pay being overtaken by rampaging inflation, policemen throughout the county grew more and more discontented.

Evidence of this manifested itself in a letter published in March, 1915, in the *Essex Chronicle*. Signed "Boy Blue", it was undoubtedly the work of an angry and frustrated Essex officer, illustrating not just the mood prevailing at the time but the widespread reaction to a well-publicised agreement between the Home Office and a number of forces (not Essex) for the payment of a supplementary weekly award called a "War Bonus".

> It is announced that all members of the Metropolitan Police are to receive an additional 3s. per week owing to the increased cost of living and the extra work, and that all members of that force will be paid a full day's wages for every rest-day lost in consequence of the war. The Essex Police are wondering when on earth their turn will come? I, for one, am disgusted to think we have been so long without a rise in pay, and more so to think that no compensation has been given us for the annual leave we lost last year (or, to be correct, I should say our weekly rest days, as that is what our annual leave consists of at present).
>
> Last Autumn we petitioned for a rise in pay and our worthy Chief Constable placed it before the Standing Joint Committee at their meeting in December when it was put to a sub-committee to consider. There, I suppose, it still remains... We are all in the hopes that we shall be given a little more than one farthing an hour (an allusion to the 1912 pay award) when we do get it. When a man makes application to transfer to another force he is politely told that the Essex Police is not a training ground for other forces. From what I hear I can assure the authorities that if something is not very soon done for our welfare several other forces will benefit by having their trained men.

If ever a letter deserved study it was surely this, for it encompassed the feelings of every policeman. Resentment, anger, frustration and despair are all there. Its demands were not outrageous, nor its tone abusive.

A month later, on 14th April, 1915, the committee announced that it had reconsidered the pay scales in question, compared with the pay scales of various other forces and found that Essex compared favourably with those forces. They saw no reason to increase the original pay award further but had considered "as a matter of urgency, the subject of an additional grant to partially meet the cost of living caused by the war..." The report went on to recommend a grant of two shillings a week to all members of the force commencing on 1st April, 1915, and continuing for the duration of the war.

This bonus continued to be paid until the end of the war, being increased several times in ratio to the rise in the cost of living. In 1916 the status of the married man was recognised when his allowance went up to 3s. a week plus 9d a week for each child under the age of fourteen (the single man's allowance remaining at 2s.). By September, 1917, the grant rose to 7s. for the married man plus 1s.9d a week for each child, and the single man's to 5s. In October, 1918, came a reversion to the original scheme in which every officer, married or single, was paid 10s. a week while the children's allowance rose to 2s.6d a week.

In the midst of the upheavals caused by the war Essex policemen and their employers learnt that the Home Office had ordered the retirement of Captain

Superintendent Raglan Somerset, Deputy Chief Constable under Major Poyntz and Captain Showers.

Showers as Chief Constable. When in 1912 he had reached the age of sixty-five Captain Showers had been given a three-year extension, but five years was the maximum extension allowed and at any time during that period the Secretary of State could withdraw his consent.

That was precisely what had happened. The Secretary of State was in no way obliged to justify his decision, which was most likely prompted by the strategic position of Essex and the size of the force, then numbering 450 men, and protests by members of Essex County Council at the Chief Constable's enforced retirement at such a time had no effect. The Standing Joint Committee had to ask for his resignation.

119

Immediately after his resignation had been so reluctantly accepted Captain Showers applied for, and was granted, the post of Chief Constable of Colchester Borough Police (fifty-nine men), replacing for the duration of the war Colonel Hugh Charles Stockwell, who had been recalled to active service. Despite all the provisions of the law Showers held this appointment until 1919, when he finally retired at the age of seventy-two.

Just a few months after his departure from the county scene came the retirement of his deputy, Superintendent Raglan Somerset, who had moved from Nottingham in 1882 to become Deputy Chief Constable under Major Poyntz. Although still only sixty, Raglan Somerset could boast a total of thirty-seven years police service—he had been appointed a superintendent at twenty-three.

Showers, a man of charm and charisma, had more than a whiff of aristocracy about him but was yet shrewd, tough and capable, as much at home chatting to a constable on a rain-swept corner as he was sipping tea in the great drawing rooms of the day. Raglan Somerset was a quite different man, solid, loyal and dependable, remembered perhaps for his eccentricities and strange hobbies. One such was the keeping of monkeys in cages behind headquarters; many a constable recalled hearing him bellow, "Recruit! Recruit! Go down to Chelmsford and fetch me some bananas for my monkeys!"

Captain Showers handed over the reins of office as Chief Constable of Essex to Captain John Alfred Unett, who for just three years had been Chief Constable of Preston, in Lancashire. Chosen from no fewer than seventy applicants, Captain Unett was a further example of the man with a military background who chose a police career after nearly twenty years' service in the Army.

The eldest son of a retired officer of the 3rd Hussars, Unett had seen action in the Boer War with the East Yorkshire Regiment, being awarded the Distinguished Service Order for his services, and had retired in 1908 determined, as he put it, "to become a chief constable." His first step was to approach a relative by marriage who was Deputy Commissioner of the City of London Police, with the result that he was taken into the Deputy Commissioner's office for three months to learn the rudiments of police command.

His appointment in September, 1909, as Superintendent and Chief Clerk under Colonel Henry Daniell, Chief Constable of Hertfordshire, provoked a storm of protest within the Hertfordshire Constabulary. Colonel Daniell, whom Unett had met while with the City of London Police, had deliberately flown in the face of Home Office instructions which ruled that "when vacancies occur in the office of superintendent, inspector and sergeant it is desirable that encouragement should be given to meritorious men serving in subordinate stations by their promotion to the higher ranks when they are qualified."

The furore appeared to have little effect on John Unett, for he was later to say that the twelve months he spent in Hertfordshire were the happiest of his life. But when Colonel Daniell retired just a year after Unett's appointment, which carried with it the position of Deputy Chief Constable, history repeated itself. Unett found himself passed over, although Colonel Daniell had made no secret of the fact that he regarded Unett as his natural successor, and he was forced to serve under a new Chief Constable whom he rather sourly regarded as "a total stranger to the county."

Not surprisingly Captain Unett sought an appointment elsewhere, and in 1912 obtained the post of Chief Constable of Preston Borough Police. Three years later he heard his name announced as the successor to Captain Showers. He faced his most crucial test, for he was taking command of a force of some 450 men in a county which had been declared a War Zone, and greatly increased responsibilities had

Captain J. A. Unett, who became Chief Constable in 1915 at a time when Essex was facing particular wartime difficulties.

been placed on every member of the Essex force, whose strength diminished rapidly as the war progressed.

The formation of the Special Constabulary in 1914 had done something to make up for the loss of manpower. The incorporation of women into the police service was another way, but it was only very grudgingly accepted. In the case of Essex, to say that it was grudgingly accepted is to understate the truth.

Mrs Nott-Bower, sister-in-law of the City of London Police Commissioner, herself an ardent supporter of women's rights, summed up the opposition when she said, "It's a curious thing that many people seem quite amused when the necessity for appointing Women Police is first suggested to them. Apparently the chief idea conveyed to their minds is one of stalwart Amazons in blue serge hauling drunken navvies to prison! Few people realise the scandalous indecency involved by sending young officers to collect information in such cases as concealment of birth, or abortion, or cases of a similar nature that involve intimate, personal investigation."

The First World War, though, was to change many things, not least of them being the recognition of woman's worth. The war saw women flocking in their thousands to replace the menfolk in mills, factories and offices, driving vehicles of every size and description, and setting up mobile canteens and nursing stations wherever the army was gathered. Many joined the various nursing corps and suffered with the men all the deprivations of active service.

Recognising their worth, although more as social workers than as policewomen, the Metropolitan Police approached the National Union of Women Workers to ask them to organise patrols in parks, on railway stations and around the numerous army camps springing up all over London. Within months 500 volunteers were engaged, forming a nucleus from which there gradually spread a nationwide system of women patrols dealing with wayward girls, begging children and domestic situations. They

The Brightlingsea Section of the Colchester Division in 1915. Sergeant Josiah Scott is seated, with Constables Garrett, Chaplin and Havers standing behind him.

One of two policewomen serving
with the Romford Division in 1918.

had no police powers and wore no uniform save a dark costume. They displayed on their left sleeve an armlet bearing the initials N.U.W.W. and carried a type of warrant card signed by the local Chief Constable authorising them to call upon the regular police for assistance.

Before the end of the First World War the Metropolitan Police could boast its own regular women police. But what of Essex? Were they, as they had so often been in the past, right behind their Metropolitan colleagues? They certainly were not!

By February, 1918, however, Captain Unett was obliged to acknowledge that voluntary patrols in Brentwood and Romford under the leadership of Mrs Cantill and Miss Newton were proving quite effective. These ladies had been approached by the Romford Justices, alarmed at the increasing number of young girls coming into the area to hang around the army camps, and asked to organise patrols in those districts. Following their success the Chief Constable suggested the employment of six women, to be divided equally between Brentwood, Romford and Grays, for a trial period of six months. They were to be uniformed in a similar style to that of the Metropolitan Policewomen and to receive full pay. By December, 1918, Unett declared himself satisfied with their performance and granted a further six-month extension. But on 31st October, 1919, with the thanks of the county authorities ringing in their ears, those few women found themselves unemployed. It was to take twenty-five years, another world war and widespread public demand and criticism before Essex gained for itself the dubious distinction of being the last county force to allow women a permanent place within its ranks.

The return of peace might see the disbandment of the women police, but it did not see the end of all Captain Unett's problems. During the early months of 1918, he was faced with a particularly tricky problem. He had been notified that the Special

123

Constabulary, recruited only to replace those men away at war, was to be disbanded as soon as hostilities ceased. He knew that many months would elapse before the ranks of the regular Constabulary were brought back to full strength. How, during that interim period, was he going to manage without the Specials?

It was a problem he willingly shared with the Standing Joint Committee, and much midnight oil was burned while they pondered it. Finally, they resolved to fall back on what the Home Office had wanted them to do in the first place, form their own locally administered First Reserve.

Unett was well aware of his predecessor's lack of success in obtaining volunteers in 1912, but circumstances had changed drastically since then. He studied again the recommendations made in that Home Office document and discovered to his delight that the First Reserve should "consist of men who are accustomed to discipline and who have been trained in the Police or Army, or otherwise specially qualified for Police work." That was it! The Special Constabulary had been engaged in police work for the past four years, they were disciplined, trained and qualified.

Without delay he set about devising a scheme for the establishment of a Police Reserve consisting of seven inspectors, twenty-one sergeants and 252 constables, to

Men and women of the Romford Division in 1918. Without exception all the men sport moustaches.

be divided into seven companies of one inspector, three sergeants and thirty-six constables, each company to be attached to a divisional headquarters and subject to the orders of the divisional commander. A retaining fee of 10s. a man would be paid quarterly in advance and an allowance made of 8s.6d a day for inspectors, 7s. for sergeants and 6s. for constables, payable only when called out on duty. The estimated cost of such a force would be in the region of £1,000, with an annual cost thereafter of about £210. The daily cost to the county would be 12s.2d per man, but only when called out for specific duties.

Armed with these plans he approached the Special Constabulary. Yes, they said, they were interested, but not on those terms! They wanted better conditions of service, better allowances and, more than anything, greater recognition than they had received during the war. They reminded Unett of their request in 1917 for the issue of proper uniforms to replace the cap and armbands. Had he not thrown up his hands in horror and declared that the county could never bear the expense? Did he remember their request for a Special Constabulary war medal, and had not that been ignored? Did he recall the numbers of Special Constables prosecuted in the magistrates' court for disobedience of orders when they failed to turn up for night duty after a twelve-hour day in their own businesses? Yes, indeed, such prosecutions had taken place. Improve our conditions, they said, and then we will consider joining your peacetime reserve.

Somewhat chastened, Unett set about revising his plans. Many more months were to pass before agreement was reached and approval obtained from the Secretary of State, and it was 3rd September, 1919, one month after the formal disbandment of the wartime Specials, before the Essex Special Constabulary Reserve was formed.

Briefly, the conditions of service were that service would be entirely voluntary and unpaid, though out-of-pocket expenses would be paid for actual duty performed, and that members would only be called upon in times of grave emergency or on important occasions. Those who performed duty would be subject to the orders of the regular police, but it was agreed that duties would be performed only within the division to which they were attached and in those areas where they would have done duty prior to the disbandment of the wartime Special Constabulary. An important condition was that a full issue of uniform and equipment would be made to every man, and equally important was the fact that any member could terminate his agreement at any time he wished.

One item included in Unett's original plans, the 10s. retaining fee, was missing. This was rejected on the grounds that it was likely to "bind" a man and deprive him of his right to quit at any time he wished. Another benefit similarly rejected was the graded system of out-of-pocket expenses; everyone, it was decided, should be paid the same.

Finally, on 25th September, 1919, a letter was received from the Secretary of State revealing that a Special Constabulary Medal was to be awarded "as a mark of His Majesty's appreciation of the good services rendered by Special Constables during the late war..."

CHAPTER FOURTEEN

The Police Strike

THOSE POLICEMEN who remained on the beat during the First World War found themselves with nothing, apart from the rather meagre War Bonus, to protect them and their families from the wartime rise in the cost of living. By 1918 the cost of living had more than doubled, and some not merely found themselves facing poverty but were dismissed from the police service through falling into debt.

Inequality of pay and conditions between one force and another, coupled with the increasing workload due to the war, created a situation so volatile that only a small spark was needed to set it off. That spark came in August, 1918, when a member of the Metropolitan Police was dismissed for engaging in police union activities.

For some five years there had been growing a clandestine organisation calling itself first the Metropolitan Police Union and then, as its numbers grew, the National Union of Police and Prison Officers (NUPPO). The dismissed officer had hardly gathered his things together when NUPPO stepped out into the open and threw down a challenge to the Prime Minister, Lloyd George, and Home Secretary, General Smuts. Three demands were made: the immediate reinstatement of the dismissed officer, the recognition of a Police Union and a substantial increase in police pay. Unfortunately, the Metropolitan Police Commissioner, Sir Edward Henry (a retired Colonial civil servant), was not available to receive these demands, for although well aware of the rising discontent he seems to have dismissed all talk of strike action as mere sabre-rattling and taken himself off to Ireland for a holiday. It was left to his deputy to deliver the ultimatum to Downing Street and to receive Lloyd George's firm and unequivocal "No" to the demands.

By midday on Friday, 30th August, 1918, six thousand Metropolitan Policemen had failed to report for duty, and by evening the strike was total. The badly shaken Lloyd George lost no time in ordering the Army to patrol the streets and stand guard on strategic points. The Home Secretary, who also happened to be on holiday in Somerset, was recalled and Sir Edward Henry hurried back from Ireland to offer his resignation, which was accepted.

A hastily arranged meeting took place between Lloyd George and the strike leaders, despite the fact that in meeting them and discussing their grievances he was acknowledging their existence and position of control. The police leaders emerged content with the Prime Minister's assurances that the dismissed officer would be reinstated, that none would be disciplined for their involvement in the strike, and that immediate steps would be taken to grant a substantial increase in pay and recognition of their union, on condition that its implementation would be delayed until after the war.

True to his word, Lloyd George saw to it that the police officer was reinstated and that all ranks were granted an immediate pay rise of 13s. a week (bringing the constable's pay to £2.13s.), and also set up a committee under Lord Desborough to review the entire structure of police pay and conditions on a national basis.

In 1919, with the war over, talks commenced with the new Commissioner, Sir Neil Macready, on the subject of a police union. The incredulous constables heard that Lloyd George was denying having ever promised recognition! On a basis of such mistrust little further could be achieved, and in March, 1919, his patience exhausted, Macready called off negotiations and refused to entertain any further approach on the subject.

A short while later an incredible thing happened. The Government had organised a National Industrial Conference involving numerous trade unions from all over the country. NUPPO, doubtless tongue in cheek, applied for admission. An error on the part of a Ministry official resulted in permission to attend this conference being granted. The Home Secretary was furious when he got to hear of it, and declaring that it was nothing more than a clerical error reaffirmed the Government's total opposition to any form of police union.

During a mass meeting in Trafalgar Square the call went out for another strike for recognition. All were awaiting the result of a Bill then being debated in Parliament containing recommendations of the Desborough Committee. NUPPO knew full well that Desborough had already recommended substantial increases in police pay, and if this was accepted by the police membership the demand for recognition would slide into obscurity. With the Bill due to complete its passage by 1st August, on 31st July NUPPO called upon every police force in the country to strike. To their considerable embarrassment NUPPO found that of the 60,000 who could have responded, only 2,364 actually supported the call, and more than 1,100 of these were in London. The provinces had totally rejected the call and remained at work. The sacrifice of those 2,364 men was total, for all were dismissed and none of them reinstated. The Government, still determined to deny the police any form of affiliated trade union, seized upon the Desborough recommendations for a watered-down version of the same thing, a Police Federation.

The authorities in Essex had been fully aware of the pressures building up in the Metropolis. In an effort to combat the feelings of helplessness and despair shared by all ranks Captain Unett set up what he called a Representative Council (later renamed the Representative Committee) in August, 1918. Three superintendents and four inspectors were elected to sit on this committee, along with one sergeant and two constables from each division in the force, all of them freely elected by their colleagues. They met at headquarters under the chairmanship of the Chief Constable and were permitted to air their views and grievances without fear of reprisal and to discuss without deference to rank any matter which materially affected the welfare of the Constabulary members. Thus a full year before Desborough was to publish its findings Essex was operating a democratic system of representation. The committee died a natural death, however, when the Police Federation was formed. By 1919, when the call went out for strike action, the Essex Constabulary, confident that a substantial pay rise was in the offing and engaged already in setting up its own locally-based negotiating machinery, turned away from the suicidal path of the militants.

Not every Essex policeman had been appeased by these developments and some still voiced support for strike action. To those was directed a Force Order, dated 30th May, 1919, incorporating a Home Office letter spelling out the Government's total opposition to a TUC-style union and assuring every Chief Constable full Government support if he were forced to dismiss any of his members for participating in or encouraging others in any form of strike activity. Captain Unett declared that any Essex officer who failed to report for duty in support of this action would be instantly dismissed and forfeit all service counting towards his pension. However, he "confidently expected that the wiser judgment of the majority will lead to no such action being necessary."

Within forty-eight hours of that instruction being read out to divisions yet another followed, unashamedly aimed at those who might still have been wavering, and reassuring those who had decided to remain at their posts. It read, "The Chief Constable desires to thank and congratulate all ranks for the manner in which they have performed their duties during the very trying past five years. All ranks have performed these duties, and many hours of additional duty, with a splendid spirit of willingness and zeal quite regardless of the number of hours duty required of them. Annual leave for all ranks will, for this year, be extended by five days."

Not a single member of the Essex Constabulary joined in strike action—nor later joined those who did strike in the dole queues.

The Desborough Report was presented in two stages, the first on 1st July, 1919, and the second on 1st January, 1920. The basic issues it recommended for implementation were as follows:-

(1) an immediate and substantial increase in pay for all ranks back-dated to 1st April, 1919, with an immediate payment of £10 to every man while the final figures for these awards were being worked out.
(2) the standardising of police pay and pensions throughout the country.
(3) the abolition of rent allowances, the total cost to be borne by the local authorities.
(4) the formation of a Police Federation to represent the service in future negotiations on pay and conditions, each force freely to elect its members on to Constables, Sergeants and Inspectors Branch Boards, and these boards to be consolidated for negotiating purposes into Joint Branch Boards.
(5) the creation by the government of a department within the Home Office with special responsibility for the conduct and welfare of the police.

The government not only accepted these recommendations but went on to assist the local authorities with a substantially increased Exchequer Grant which would cover half the total cost of the police and not, as formerly, only half of the men's pay and clothing. This one factor alone cost the government £18 million that year, against only £7 million spent on the police in 1914.

The Police Committee in Essex showed commendable zeal in implementing the report, the £10 interim payment (recoverable from central government) being made and draft pay scales in accordance with those suggested by Desborough and based on those approved for the Metropolitan Police being forwarded to the Secretary of State for confirmation. They were swiftly returned, the sergeants' and constables' scales being approved, and the senior ranks endorsed with "suggested" alternatives which increased the Chief Constable's pay and reduced that of the inspectors and superintendents.

The policeman was to benefit still further with the abolition of rent allowances, for until then each officer had been required to pay two-thirds of his rent while the county paid the other one-third. Now the county must pay the total sum. This put a few more shillings a week into the pocket of the policeman but was to cost the county an additional £3,000 a year.

Despite government assistance by way of the Exchequer Grant Essex was still liable for greatly increased expenditure. Long-term cutbacks had to be achieved, but where? There was little that could be done about pay and pensions, for these were now set on a national level, so savings had to be made on an internal basis. The Police Committee tackled it two ways.

As far back as June, 1918, the Standing Joint Committee had anticipated the problem of what they were to do when a hundred and fifty or more officers returned from the war requiring accommodation. Only a small percentage of these had been housed in single men's quarters at the various police stations, the majority having been in rented lodgings which had long been let to other occupants. Aware of its

Police houses built in 1924 at Plough Corner, Romford. The author spent some of his early years with the county force living in one of these.

Grays police station just before rebuilding in 1930.

obligation to return each of these men to the same location and station he had occupied before call-up, they embarked upon a plan for the immediate purchase (so far as finances would allow) of cottages and houses throughout the county with a view to renting them to the returning constables, little knowing that Desborough would, just a year later, abolish police rents.

By December, 1918, four cottages had been purchased in Quarry Road, Grays, at a total cost of £1,000, and in March, 1919, another four houses in Braintree were purchased for the same sum. By the end of that year three more houses at Halstead had been bought for £180 each, and negotiations were being conducted for the purchase of plots of land on which to build houses at Tilbury and Romford.

The acquisition of both houses and land heralded an entirely new concept in police accommodation, the custom-built police house. Within ten years the county owned forty-seven such houses, seventy-five more were rented and a further hundred and seventy-two represented lodging accommodation for which the police tenant received a rent allowance. This figure was to grow dramatically over the years until by the middle 1960's, when approval was given for officers to purchase their own houses, the number of police-occupied county-owned houses fell. At the present time (1985) the number of county-owned police houses stands at 488 actually occupied by policemen, with a further 150 leased to other bodies.

The other method of cutting costs involved a complete reshuffle of divisions. Thorpe and Colchester were amalgamated to form the new Clacton Division, its headquarters being transferred from Colchester to Clacton; Witham Division disappeared within the Braintree Division; Dengie Division (along with Maldon) was transferred to the Chelmsford Division, and Rochford was swallowed up by the Brentwood Division. The county was now reduced to nine divisions, namely Braintree, Brentwood, Chelmsford, Clacton, Epping, Grays, Romford, Saffron Walden and headquarters.

Following this reshuffle, Superintendent Scott with over thirty-seven years service and Superintendent Smith with nearly thirty-three years retired on pension,

130

while Superintendent Page was transferred to headquarters to become the first Assistant Chief Constable.

Pay Scales from 1st April 1919

	Old			New	Revised*
Superintendent on appt.	165			430	400
after two years	180	one year		447	415
after four years	195	two years		465	430
after six years	210	three years		482	445
after eight years	225	four years		500	460
after ten years	240				
Inspector on appt.	115			320	310
after two years	120	one year		330	320
after four years	125	two years		340	330
after six years	135	three years		350	340
		four years		360	350
Sergeant on appt.	1.13s.10d			5.0s.0d	
after two years	1.15s.0d	one year		5.2s.6d	
after four years	1.16s.2d	two years		5.5s.0d	
after six years	1.17s.4d	three years		5.7s.6d	
		four years		5.10s.0d	
		five years		5.12s.6d	
Constable on appt.	1.3s.11d			3.10s.0d	
after one year	1.5s.8d			3.12s.0d	
after two years	1.7s.5d	one year		3.14s.0d	
after four years	1.8s.7d	two years		3.16s.0d	
after six years	1.9s.9d	three years		3.18s.0d	
after eight years	1.10s.11d	four years		4.0s.0d	
after ten years	1.12s.1d	five years		4.2s.0d	
		six years		4.4s.0d	
		seven years		4.6s.0d	
		eight years		4.8s.0d	
		nine years		4.10s.0d	
		ten years		4.12s.6d	
		seventeen years		4.15s.0d	
		twenty-two years			

In January, 1920, Captain Unett's services during the Great War were finally recognised with the arrival of a letter from the Home Office telling him his name was being submitted to the King for appointment as an Officer of the Order of the British Empire (Civil Division).

To most people the award of an OBE would have been a cause for celebration. Not so John Unett! Any elation he felt when he opened the envelope was quickly dispelled when he read the letter, for he was clearly being nominated for the lesser Order of the British Empire and not Commander of the British Empire. He had already heard on the grapevine that a number of Chief Constables had been nominated for the CBE, including his own deputy, Captain Ffinch! Unett, having

*revised following Home Office objection.

commanded one of the country's largest and most important coastal constabularies during those crisis-torn years, was quite confident that nothing less than a CBE would come his way. Allowing himself only two or three days to mull the matter over, he penned a reply asking that his name be excluded from those being put forward for the OBE.

Too proud to indicate any reason for such a refusal, he was later to acknowledge that he had acted rashly, for he was to find that this refusal was to cost him dear. For the next ten years his name did not feature on any approved list. In the New Year Honours List of 1931 he found himself the recipient of the King's Police Medal.

To a bustling and rather self-important man, never forgetful of his Army rank and inordinately proud of his DSO, this official snub, as he saw it, came as a body blow, and from that moment Unett's interest in the police service ebbed away. Never an easy man to work with, he became unpredictable, irritable and aloof.

His visits to the numerous police stations throughout the county became so infrequent that many a constable was later to boast of never having clapped eyes on the man. Almost by way of reply his wife Daisy, having already earned widespread praise for her untiring work for the war effort and the needy, threw herself with renewed vigour into voluntary work.

Captain Unett continued in the post of Chief Constable in spite of such troubles until in the Spring of 1932 he suffered a recurrence of an illness for which he had undergone a serious operation nine years earlier. Despite the attention of surgeons and specialists he grew steadily worse and died on 6th December, 1932. He had seen the force through the most hectic five years of its history, the years of the First World War and the cliff-hanging days of the Police Strikes, and if he was not the most dynamic of Chief Constables it is at least fair to give him credit for that achievement. Only he and those who trod the corridors of power knew just how much he owed to the loyalty and capable management of his deputy, Superintendent Alfred J. Offord.

It fell to Superintendent Offord both to lead the force during the time Captain Unett spent on sick leave in 1932 and to help his successor to take up the reins of office.

Captain Unett's successor was Captain Francis Richard Jonathan Peel, a direct descendant of Home Secretary Sir Robert Peel who had played so important a part in the setting up of the modern police force. While still at Malvern College, Worcester, in 1915 he had volunteered for service with the Royal Field Artillery, into which he was commissioned the following year. Posted to France, he fought with great distinction and earned swift promotion, a Mention in Despatches and, in 1917, the Military Cross.

With the war over he returned immediately to his studies and secured for himself a place at Cambridge University, where he gained his BA (Honours) in just four terms. In 1920, having determined to make the police his career, he began looking around for a suitable force. He could easily have turned to his Uncle Phillip (later Sir Phillip) Lane, then Chief Constable of Lancashire, a large and prestigious force, but instead he chose a path which was to earn him the respect of all those he was later to command; he joined the Liverpool City Police as a beat constable.

No doubt had he joined the Lancashire Constabulary he would have found himself in no time at all commanding a comfortable division somewhere in that county. Instead he pounded the beat in what was probably the toughest and most dangerous port in the country, at a time when Sinn Fein activities were at their height and many policemen (including Pc Peel) patrolled their beats armed.

Within two years he had been promoted sergeant, in 1926 he became inspector and chief inspector in 1928. In 1931 he saw advertised the post of Chief Constable of

Captain Sir Jonathan Peel, the first Chief Constable of Essex to have risen through the ranks.

Bath City Police, and within months of applying for the position found himself at the age of thirty-three the country's youngest Chief Constable.

Following the death of Captain Unett, Peel travelled with many other applicants to Chelmsford where, on 1st March, 1933, it was announced that he had been selected from an original total of nearly two hundred candidates to become not only the youngest-ever Chief Constable of the county but the first to have attained that position from the rank of constable.

By the end of April of that year the Acting Chief Constable, Superintendent Offord, satisfied that his new chief had settled in, retired after thirty-three years service. His successor was Superintendent John Crockford who, as an inspector, had headed the Essex team of investigators into the murder of one of the county's policemen. Peel's long and industrious career with Essex had begun.

CHAPTER FIFTEEN

The Murder of Pc Gutteridge

AT THREE o'clock in the morning of 27th September, 1927, Pc George Gutteridge walked quietly along the country road from his house in Stapleford Abbotts to Howe Green. It was a fine night, not too dark and with just enough autumnal chill in the air to warrant his wearing a cape. Across the undulating countryside he could see patches of white mist gathering in the hollows of fields and woodland. Approaching Grove House, a large residence standing in its own grounds at the top of Howe Green hill, he was met by Pc Sydney Taylor, the Lambourne End constable. The two men stood together for about twenty minutes or so talking in low tones before Pc Taylor glanced at his watch and observed that it was just turned twenty past three and he was going home to his bed. Bidding his colleague goodnight, he turned and made his way down Hook Lane towards Lambourne End. Gutteridge remained at his point for a few more minutes to complete the regulation half an hour wait before he too turned for home. It was then just 3.30am.

The constable had covered a distance of only 600 yards when he heard the sound of a car coming along the road behind him. He stopped and turned, wondering who could be out at this time of the morning. As the vehicle approached he flashed his torch and signalled it to stop. The driver had either failed to notice him or was deliberately ignoring his signal. Quickly pulling his whistle from its pocket, Gutteridge gave a loud blast and almost immediately the car stopped. He walked up to it, making a mental note as he did so that it was a Morris Cowley, index number TW 6120, and flashed his torch in at the two occupants. Asking them where they had been, he received the reply that they came from Lea Bridge in London and had been out doing some car repairs.

"Where exactly have you been?" said Gutteridge. As the driver began to stammer a reply he was interrupted by the constable, "Is this car yours?" The passenger cut in with the reply that it belonged to him. At this the officer asked, "Then what is the registration number?" Before the man could reply the driver retorted, "You'll see it on the front of the car." This unhelpful remark served only to draw from the constable the observation that he knew full well what the number was, but did he, the driver? "I can give you the number," said his companion, "it's TW 6120."

His suspicions now aroused, Pc Gutteridge put away his torch and drew from his pocket a notebook and pencil. Unseen by the officer, the driver's right hand had already slid down into the pocket of the car door, and as Gutteridge turned to make use of the car's headlights the driver's hand emerged clutching a heavy revolver. Suddenly, in quick succession, two explosions rent the night air as two .45 calibre bullets smashed into the constable's left cheek. The impact sent him reeling backwards across the road where he struck the grass verge and collapsed, rolling over on to his back.

Moments later the gunman clambered from the car and walked over to look down at his helpless victim. "What are you looking at me like that for?" he said, and bending down took careful and deliberate aim. Twice more his finger squeezed the trigger and twice more the constable's face took the full force. These were not haphazard shots, for the bullets had been directed into each of the officer's eyes. Pc Gutteridge died instantly. Hurried footsteps returned to the car, the engine roared to life and a few minutes later peace descended once more over the quiet Essex countryside.

Some minutes before six o'clock that same morning, Mr William Ward, a motor engineer with a contract to deliver mails for the Post Office, drove his car along the Stapleford Abbotts road. Rounding a bend he involuntarily swerved to the left when he saw a pair of legs protruding into the roadway. Stopping the car he walked across to the huddled form and, despite its obvious injuries, recognised Pc Gutteridge. Lifting the constable's hand he found it cold and stiff, and looking around he saw a trail of blood running across from the centre of the road to merge into the now congealed pool around the officer's head. A pencil was clutched in the right hand, a pocket-book lay nearby and the policeman's helmet lay just a few feet away. Hurrying the 250 yards to Rose Cottage, Ward awakened Mr Alfred Perritt and both men walked back to the body. There Perritt stood guard while Ward drove on to Stapleford Tawney post office and telephoned the police at Romford.

Detective Inspector John Crockford (later to become Deputy Chief Constable) attended the scene with other officers, but it was only after the body had been removed to the Royal Oak public house, Stapleford Abbotts (and then to Romford mortuary), that Detective Constable Norman found the first vital clue. He was standing looking at the pool of blood when he suddenly bent down and prised loose a spent .45 bullet embedded in the road surface. Until then this bullet had been concealed by the officer's body. Just two or three inches away lay another bullet.

The bullets were of supreme importance and were at once despatched to ballistics experts in London.

In the meantime a post-mortem examination of the body revealed some very interesting characteristics about the powder burns found around the eyes of the murdered officer. At least one of the bullets fired had certainly been propelled by a type of black powder which had not been manufactured since 1894. The rifling marks on those bullets were photographed. All the police had to do was find a man who owned a .45 revolver and ammunition of some vintage.

The first real breakthrough came at six o'clock that same evening when a Mr Albert McDougall, of Brixton, told police that at seven-thirty that morning, just four hours after the murder, he had left home to go to work when he almost bumped into a Morris Cowley car parked in the passageway beside his house. Squeezing past the car, he put his hand on the radiator and found it was still warm. When he arrived home that evening and found the car still there, he took a closer look. The front nearside mudguard, he saw, had been torn away from the running board. Making a note of the index number, TW 6120, he went out and reported the matter to a patrolling constable in Brixton Road.

Inquiries quickly established that the Morris belonged to a Doctor Lovell, of Billericay, who had reported the theft of his car the previous night. Detective Sergeant Hearn examined the vehicle and found, adhering to the front "dumb irons" (springs protruding from the front of the car) a small quantity of what appeared to be tree bark. This he carefully scraped off into an envelope. The car was then driven to Brixton police station for further examination.

Once there, an empty cartridge shell, marked RL IV, was found on the floor beneath the passenger seat and a number of spots and splashes of blood were discovered near the steering wheel. Taking a note of the mileage reading, Sergeant Hearn drove out of London to the spot where the officer's body had been found and thence via Ongar and Brentwood to Billericay. The recorded journey was 36.8 miles. Fortunately Doctor Lovell was in the habit of noting his daily mileage and from this the police were able to establish that the Morris had taken this route on the night of the murder.

During the evening of 20th January, 1928, a number of Metropolitan Police officers were keeping observation on the Globe Garage in Northcote Road, Clapham Junction. The man they were waiting for was Frederick Guy Browne, a man with numerous convictions going back to 1911. This time he was wanted for questioning concerning the theft of a Vauxhall car which had been stolen at Tooting the previous November and then sold to an unsuspecting buyer in Sheffield. Taken in part exchange for the Vauxhall was an Angus-Sanderson car.

Another man wanted for complicity in this particular theft was a William Henry Kennedy, a thirty-six-year-old army deserter with a criminal record very similar to Browne's. Kennedy was believed to work with Browne at the Globe Garage.

The patience of the officers was finally rewarded when a grey Angus-Sanderson car drove into the garage yard with Browne at the wheel. Minutes later he was under arrest. After initial questioning he was searched by Detective Inspector Barker, who found in the suspect's waistcoat pocket a pair of artery forceps , and in his hip pocket twelve .45 bullets. Shown these, Browne said, "That's done it, now you have found them it's all up with me." From his right hand jacket pocket was taken a stocking mask with holes cut out for the eyes, ears and mouth. At the same moment Detective Constable Bevis entered the workshop carrying a .45 Webley revolver in one hand and six bullets in the other. The fully loaded gun (he had ejected the bullets as a precaution) had been found in the pocket on the inside of the driver's door of the Angus-Sanderson.

Browne took one look at it and said, "Ah! you've found that, have you? I'm done for now."

The searching continued and brought to light sixteen .45 bullets wrapped up in a handkerchief and various items of medical equipment such as tweezers, bandages, lint and sticking plaster. A compartment behind the driver's seat in the Angus-Sanderson was found to contain another fully loaded .45 Webley revolver. The detectives, already aware from a tip-off that Browne might know something of the Gutteridge murder, were now amassing before his very eyes some very formidable evidence indeed.

Browne's home in Battersea was also searched. There, the officers recovered from the top of a wardrobe a .45 Smith & Wesson revolver along with two boxes of ammunition.

Browne was at that stage held in custody charged with the theft of the Vauxhall car. The hunt was now on for his friend Kennedy.

At dusk on 25th January, 1928, Detective Sergeant William Mattinson of the Liverpool City Police knocked at the door of a boarding house in Copperas Hill, Liverpool. Identifying himself to the landlord, he was allowed to enter and search a room rented only the week before by a Mr & Mrs Kennedy. There the officer found a magazine for an automatic pistol. Within a short time Mattinson had organised a team of detectives (including two officers from the Metropolitan Police) to keep the house under observation.

All evening they waited, then just before midnight Sergeant Mattinson suddenly caught sight of a familiar figure walking along the road. Followed at some distance by

Dr Lovell's Morris Cowley car, used by the murderers of Pc Gutteridge.   *Essex Police Museum*

three of his colleagues, Mattinson set off at a fast walk. Turning into St Andrew's Street, the sergeant quickly caught up with the figure who was wearing an overcoat with the collar turned up about his face and a trilby hat pulled down over his eyes. As Mattinson drew level the man's hand came up and held on to the hat brim in an attempt to hide his face, but the officer had already recognised him.

"Come on, Bill," said Mattinson. Suddenly, the man—it was Kennedy—swung round and withdrew his right hand from his overcoat pocket. The muzzle of an automatic pistol was thrust into the sergeant's ribs and a moment later a distinct click was heard. For one long, dreadful moment Mattinson stood there wondering why he had not heard the bang or felt the impact of a bullet.

Grabbing Kennedy's gun hand, the officer managed to twist his arm up into the air and then struck the gunman in the face with his right fist. Wrenching the pistol around, he managed to turn the gun on to Kennedy himself and force him struggling back up the road, yelling as he did so for assistance. Moments later his colleagues had Kennedy secured, while Mattinson sank to his knees feeling quite sick. Later at the police station he happened to walk past Kennedy, who said to him, "I'm sorry, I've no grudge against the police but you should be in heaven now . . ."

Kennedy was charged at that stage with being concerned with Browne in the theft of the Vauxhall car and taken under escort back to London. The following day he was interviewed by Chief Inspector Berrett and charged with the murder of Constable Gutteridge.

When the two men stood together in the dock at the Central Criminal Court on

Captain Unett, the Chief Constable, leads the cortege as it arrives at Warley Cemetery. Immediately behind the coffin, with their arms around each other, are Pc Gutteridge's two children, a twelve-year-old daughter and a four-year-old son, and their mother.

23rd April, 1928, applications were made both by Mr E.F. Lever, defending Browne, and Mr F. Powell, for Kennedy, for them to be tried separately. Kennedy had made a very long written statement to the police implicating Browne in the murder, but Browne's defence would be that he had never been near the scene of the murder and knew nothing of the crime, the two men's Counsel told Mr Justice Avory. On the other hand the Solicitor General, Sir Boyd Merriman, K.C., M.P., who led for the prosecution, contended that the two men had been charged as principals, the case for the Crown was that they were commonly engaged together on a joint purpose which resulted in murder, and there was no reason for them to be tried separately. The judge agreed and rejected the defence applications.

During the next five days evidence was heard from more than forty prosecution witnesses. Ballistics experts were called from Woolwich Arsenal to prove beyond doubt that the Webley revolver found in the pocket of the Angus-Sanderson car was the murder weapon, and that much of the ammunition found in Browne's possession was identical to that used in the murder. Most telling of all was the written statement made by Kennedy which described in great detail the events leading up to the murder, the stealing of the Morris Cowley, the murder itself and the drive back to London, during which they ran off the road and struck a tree.

The defence put up by each of the accused was quite different. Browne simply denied all knowledge of the murder and invited the prosecution to prove every point it made. Of Kennedy's damning statement he said, "It's a fairy tale from beginning to end, it's a concoction," and later, "it is one pack of wilful or imaginative lies, either wilfully told or misled by some kink of the brain, I should think. I cannot imagine anything outside a penny-dreadful that could have been written with so much care." The evidence given by Browne, and his cross-examination, took up practically the whole of the third day.

The following morning Mr Powell addressed the court to explain why Kennedy had decided not to go into the witness box, where he would have been subjected to cross-examination by both the prosecution and Counsel for Browne. Kennedy was convinced, said Mr Powell, that all the evidence placed before the court served only to prove his innocence, and as he had told the truth in his written statement to the police there was no need to say it all over again on oath.

"My case is that Kennedy did not know that Browne had a revolver till he heard the two shots," he said. "It follows that he could not have been a party to the shooting." Referring to Kennedy's statement that he begged Browne not to shoot a second time, he said, "Does that show the monster and callous brute? Does it not show that although he may be a burglar he is not a murderer?"

Mr Justice Avory, in his summing up, told the jury that Kennedy had already admitted his involvement but he was denying participation in the actual shooting. Could he have taken steps to prevent Browne firing those final two shots, which had undoubtedly killed the officer? Had he not, after the murder, reloaded the revolver (dropping that cartridge on the floor as he did so) and handed it back to Browne? Why had he done so if not to enable Browne to use it again if stopped by the police? Could he not have refused to hand the revolver back, or even thrown it from the car window? And what of Browne? Kennedy stated quite emphatically that Browne had fired the bullets which had killed Gutteridge. Bearing in mind that he was being charged with wilful murder, how much reliance could be placed on his statement?

The jury took only two hours and twenty minutes to return a verdict of guilty against both defendants. Browne and Kennedy were both sentenced to death.

Less than a month later the Appeal Court heard submissions by both Counsel that a miscarriage of justice had occurred when the trial judge had refused to have the defendants tried separately. It was alleged also that Mr Justice Avory had not given as full a summing up as he could have done and that he was wrong to criticise Kennedy for deciding not to give evidence on oath. After all, was that not his right? The Appeal Judges, after listening to the most protracted arguments, declared themselves satisfied "that the evidence was overwhelming and as plain as a pikestaff, and it would still have been as plain as a pikestaff if the appellants had been tried separately. There was also nothing in the Judge's criticism that was unfair." The appeals were therefore dismissed. On 31st May, 1928, Browne was hanged at Pentonville Prison and Kennedy at Wandsworth.

The grave of Pc Gutteridge in Warley Cemetery.

CHAPTER SIXTEEN

The Great Leap Forward

T HE FIRST motor car to be used for police purposes was purchased, as one might expect, for the use of the Chief Constable.

Towards the end of 1909, Captain Showers sought the permission of the Standing Joint Committee for the hire of a car on the grounds that "it would save a great waste of time in travelling by train to see my Justices at the different Benches, and to pay surprise visits to police stations and is also an absolute necessity in cases of serious crime to enable me to be on the spot to investigate with the least possible delay." The committee thought long and hard before granting permission for a trial period of six months at a cost not exceeding £50.

Needless to say, Captain Showers was quite able to justify the use of the car and continued to hire such a vehicle on a six-monthly basis for the next five years. Whether he subsequently changed to a smaller model or whether the hire charges became cheaper as the years progressed is not clear, but by 1913 the half-yearly rental had dropped by over fifty per cent to £24.10s.6d. In December, 1913, it fell to £22.8s.6d, climbing again in July, 1914, to £29.1s.9d and then to £38.14s.3d in January, 1915.

At this point, perhaps because of inflation or due to the commandeering of every motor vehicle the Army could lay its hands on, costs rose dramatically. The Chief Constable pointed out the economic wisdom of purchasing a good second-hand car for something less than £200 rather than continue paying exorbitant charges for a vehicle which never became the property of the county. The Police Committee agreed.

The first county-owned motor car was a 10/12hp Belsize saloon, delivered just in time for Captain Showers to admire it before he handed over the reins of office to Captain John Unett in May, 1915. At first a constable was employed as chauffeur but by the end of 1915 the Police Committee was persuaded to sanction the employment of a civilian chauffeur (duly kitted out in fine livery) at a wage of 30s. a week. This arrangement lasted less than a year, for it then became apparent that with Constabulary pay being outstripped by the cost of living a constable at 27s.5d a week was cheaper to employ than a civilian chauffeur!

The motor car's potential was not lost on the Chief, for by December, 1916, he was reporting to the Police Committee that as the Constabulary now maintained only eleven of its authorised seventeen horses, and considering how expensive they were becoming to feed and stable, it would be a good idea to phase them out in favour of motor cars. He suggested starting with the horses owned by the divisional superintendents, but before doing so he would pass on his Belsize car for a superintendent's use over a twelve-month period and study that officer's report as to its suitability for divisional work.

That lucky man turned out to be Superintendent Lindsay Fulcher, of Braintree, who took delivery of the Belsize in July, 1917. A year later he submitted his evaluation as a result of which the Police Committee authorised the Chief Constable to negotiate the purchase of four new Ford cars at a cost not exceeding £300 each. The county found it had plenty of time to organise the financing of these new additions, for there was a twelve-month waiting list for these particular vehicles, the Model T.

By 1920, all had been delivered and taken into service. Two more second-hand Belsize cars had been purchased for £250 each, along with two more Fords and an Overland saloon. Each of the county's ten divisional superintendents was thus fully mobile.

Determined not to be left behind in this surge of mechanisation, Sergeant Haggar of Castle Hedingham submitted a report to the Chief Constable in 1921 outlining just how large a territory he covered and how many miles he walked each day to supervise and visit the constables on their outlying detached beats. He owned a motor-cycle and would be willing to put it to police use if Captain Unett agreed. In those days even the use of a pedal cycle was frowned upon, so it must have come as a considerable surprise to everyone concerned when the Chief Constable agreed.

In September, 1921, the cheeky Haggar applied for a motor-cycle allowance—and got it! The Police Committee, who held the purse-strings, had some difficulty in

Superintendent Fulcher in the Chief Constable's Belsize car after it had been delivered to Braintree for its twelve-month divisional trial. The car was sold in 1923 for £100.

determining just what should be allowed, for no such allowance existed in the books of the day. They finally granted him the handsome sum of four shillings a week. Six months later the bold sergeant declared that this was just about enough to buy a gallon of petrol and that he was out of pocket on the deal. His allowance was raised to six shillings a week.

The 1930s witnessed a great surge in the use of modern technology. One of the most important recommendations to come out of the Desborough Report was the establishment within the Home Office of a department responsible for the co-ordination of nearly two hundred separate police forces throughout the land and the initiation of a cohesive pattern of administration.

The majority of these forces, particularly the smaller city and borough forces, were still autonomous and insular, jealous of their traditions and for the most part resentful of anything which smacked of "outside interference". Yet none could deny that the criminal was becoming increasingly mobile and was steadfastly refusing to heed the various police boundaries through which he passed.

The sum total of organised inter-force co-operation was the Metropolitan Police Criminal Records Office, which had been formed as far back as 1871 and by the thirties provided a central records and information service. The *Police Gazette* was also published daily by Scotland Yard and its details of wanted or missing persons were distributed nationwide.

In 1933, the Home Office set up a committee ostensibly to enquire into the subject of detective training (after all, a rational system of criminal investigation was as good a place to start as any, considering that every force in the land suffered from the same malady). It soon became apparent that this basically straightforward exercise was developing, by accident or design, into a thorough examination of the country's police resources, equipment and attitudes. The committee's report, published five years later and incorporating evidence gathered from as far afield as Canada and the United States, showed only too clearly how far behind other developed countries Britain had fallen, and how parochially-minded still were British attitudes. The recommendations of this committee led directly to the establishment of regional detective training centres, criminal intelligence bureaux, scientific aid laboratories, two-way radio systems, fingerprint and photographic departments, the training of police dogs and a radical shift in policy towards the employment of policewomen.

Quite obviously the cost of implementing all this was extremely high, so high indeed that many smaller forces held up their hands in horror and declared themselves unable even to consider such involvement. To this end a "Common Police Fund" was organised under which the Home Office undertook to pay part of the cost of these improvements while the force concerned paid the remainder on a sliding scale based on its size.

While all this was going on Essex was taking advantage of yet another Home Office scheme, for motor patrols. By 1930, the Home Secretary found himself coming under increasing pressure to do something about the effect of huge numbers of motor vehicles. At that time traffic on Britain's roads had risen from a mere handful of vehicles to 2.2 million in just twenty years and deaths had reached 6,500 a year (fifty years later, by 1981, proper instruction and road safety consciousness had

A nasty head-on crash at Margaretting about 1933. Looking at the tangled wreckage is the Margaretting detached officer, Pc 320 Victor Jordan. On the right an A.A. man takes notes.

caused a drop in that figure to 6,010 deaths despite an increase in vehicular traffic to 19.3 million).

The time had come, the Home Secretary decided, to inaugurate an entirely new concept in policing, the motor patrolman. By the end of that year a circular had been sent to a number of local authorities and Chief Constables in which it was made plain that the Government considered the use of motor vehicles as not simply advantageous but essential, stressing that the subject of organising motor patrols was of such urgency that the Home Office would make available substantial grants from the Road Fund Revenue and regard motor patrols "as material to the proper efficiency of the police". Most local authorities, and certainly Essex, saw in these words some indication that if they did not take immediate steps to set up these patrols they could be regarded as "inefficient" and the Exchequer Grant (paid from central funds to assist each authority with the maintenance of its police) could be in jeopardy.

Within three months Captain Unett had completed his plans for the formation of a special motor patrol group consisting of twenty men based at Headquarters under Superintendent Totterdell, who had been promoted from Detective Inspector at

144

Romford for this purpose (Totterdell, incidentally, became the county's first detective superintendent a year later).

By September, 1931, ten 549cc Triumph motor-cycles costing £45 each had been delivered, followed by three 16hp Austin cars at £310 each. A year later two 14hp Vauxhalls were added to the fleet along with a powerful "pursuit car"—a 30hp Ford V8 capable of speeds up to 80mph.

One of the first things Captain Peel did when he took office in 1933 was to review the whole question of motor-cycle patrols. He was not at all keen on this form of transport, arguing that the attention of the rider was fixed more on controlling his machine than on what was going on about him, that it was impossible for a single rider to deal with speeding motorists as the law required corroboration by a second officer, that cars were more efficient for transporting numbers of men to the scene of an emergency, and last but not least that during the previous year a hundred and three days had been lost through sickness and accidents brought about by constant exposure to bad weather—a fact that had led, he said, to a dramatic drop in the number of volunteers for this type of duty. By December, 1934, he had received authorisation to disband the motor-cycle patrols in favour of cars.

Some of the ten Triumph motor-cycles purchased in 1931 and their riders at Springfield Court.

In 1937, the Home Office introduced further measures in their fight against road deaths, taking the form of widespread publicity on road safety and the introduction of the Experimental Motor Patrol Scheme (soon to become labelled the "Courtesy Cops"). Unfortunately policemen themselves had received no more training than anyone else and were therefore somewhat ill-equipped to criticise or instruct the public in good road-sense. A group of driving enthusiasts, headed by Lord Cottenham, an ex-racing driver and acknowledged expert on the subject of "defensive driving", were contracted by the Home Office to devise a system of training for police officers. The system they taught fifty years ago is still in use today.

That year the Metropolitan Police Driving School was opened at Hendon, and in May two Essex officers, Inspector Postons and Pc Murray, joined eighteen others from various parts of the country on the first Advanced Driving Instructors' Course. After three months they returned and set about creating a team of locally-based driving instructors. Two more driving schools were then opened by the Home Office, one at Hutton, in Lancashire, near Preston and the other at Witham in Essex. Based at the old police station in Guithavon Street, the school continued to be financed from Whitehall funds until the outbreak of war.

For those Essex officers attending Witham the daily instruction took them far beyond the boundaries of their county, many round trips being of 200-300 miles and necessarily passing through other police districts.

This scheme proved so successful that the Home Office asked Essex to continue running it for a further six months beyond the allotted two years—a request readily acceded to since the Home Office was footing the bill!

Essex was slowly building up its fleet of cars, but although in daily use and proving a valuable asset they, unlike their Metropolitan counterparts, suffered from one serious defect—they had no radios. London's police, then as now wholly financed by the Home Office, had funds enough to forge ahead with new techniques

The staff of the Essex Police Traffic Department in 1938 with two Triumph Dolomites.

and by 1934 had not only perfected the mobile radio (so far as one was then possible) but had established their own Information Room at Scotland Yard.

Essex entered into negotiations with the Home Office on how the force was to be equipped and more importantly who was going to pay for it. In January, 1936, while these talks continued, four Essex constables, Pcs Leonard, Orchard, Priestley and Scott were sent on yet another three-month course, this time to the Metropolitan Police Wireless School at Hendon, where they were taught morse. By the middle of that year two 21hp Hillman Hawk cars were sent to Hendon to be fitted with radio receivers. Unfortunately, the roofs of these rather splendid cars had to be cut off and replaced by canvas hoods as the "metal box" effect caused serious problems with reception.

Thus the county took delivery of its first wireless cars crewed by trained officers, but it was still without its own transmitters. The originator of a message had to telephone Scotland Yard and ask them to transmit the call. How then, if the car had no transmitter, was the receipt of that message acknowledged? For routine signals it was simply assumed that they had been received. The more important message incorporated the words "please acknowledge". Then, no doubt muttering under his breath, the patrol officer would have to find the nearest police station from where he could telephone the fact that he had received the call!

This Heath Robinson set-up continued to operate throughout the war, with a total of thirty-four cars comprising the Traffic Department (Headquarters 23, Brentwood 3, Laindon 3, Grays 2, Newport 1 and Romford 1). In 1946, the Home Office finally agreed that Essex should go ahead with its own transmitters and receiving stations, the masts for which were erected at Headquarters, Great Bromley, Warley and Saffron Walden. This work took another two years to complete, and ten Wolseley cars became the first Essex vehicles to be fitted with two-way radios in 1948.

A Hillman Hawk traffic car introduced in 1936. The fabric hood was fitted to improve radio reception.

CHAPTER SEVENTEEN

The Second World War and After

IF NOTHING else the First World War had served to provide the civil authorities with an almost perfect blueprint for tackling future emergencies, and when war broke out again in 1939 the lessons and techniques learned twenty years earlier had only to be adapted to meet the new situation.

South-east England again became the battlefield of the Home Front and the peaceful air of the shires reverberated to the sound of aerial dogfights, the rumble of army convoys and the noise of hastily erected camps and airfields. For the second time in living memory food was rationed along with clothing and petrol.

For the people of Essex the "phoney war" of 1939-40 came to an end on the night of 30th April, 1940, when a German minelaying aircraft crashed at Clacton after being damaged by anti-aircraft fire from a battery near Harwich. The pilot apparently tried to land on an area of open ground near Victoria Road, but the aircraft overshot and came to rest against one of the houses in Victoria Road, its cargo of mines exploding and demolishing that house and damaging scores of others. The occupants of the house died together with the German crew of four.

Two policemen died in November the same year when a stick of bombs, probably intended either for Marconi's works in New Street, Chelmsford, or the nearby Hoffman roller bearing works, straddled the police headquarters at Springfield. In spite of the fact that an air raid warning had been given Pc Alexander Scott and Pc Maurice Lee were caught just outside the Chief Constable's house as the bombs exploded, Scott being killed instantly and Lee dying shortly afterwards in hospital.

Though they were the only Essex policemen to die on duty in air raids on the county, the police found themselves greatly involved in rescue and other work during air raids on Colchester and other places. Later in the war they had to deal with incidents when V1 "Doodlebugs" on their way to London exploded short of the target. During the final year of the war no fewer than 511 flying bombs fell in Essex, as well as four hundred of the 1,115 V2 rockets fired across the North Sea at targets in Eastern Britain.

Despite all its tragedies the war still had its lighter moments, as when two Belgian pilots escaped from their country in 1941 in a biplane they had secretly made ready for a North Sea flight. As they landed they saw the word HOLLAND painted across the roof of one of a group of buildings, and it was only when they eventually met Sergeant Percy Brown of Thorpe-le-Soken, who was on his way to investigate their landing, that they learnt that the word formed part of the legend Holland Motors, of Holland-on-Sea. They had been convinced they had made a serious navigational error and had merely crossed the Belgian border into occupied Holland.

The effects of the war brought enormous pressures to bear on the police. Unexploded bombs had to be sealed off, population evacuated from certain areas, crashed aircraft guarded and their crews recovered, devastated areas searched and survivors cared for, and beaches, harbours, estuaries and possible landing sites patrolled day and night. In the light of all this the Government decreed at the outbreak of war that no constable should be called up for military service. By December, 1939, the order had been rescinded and no fewer than 101 Essex officers—nearly a quarter of the Constabulary strength—were recalled to the Colours. In 1941 a call went out for volunteers for the RAF which resulted in another seventy-three officers leaving the force, and in the following year conscription was introduced, affecting all police officers under the age of twenty-six and depleting the force by another 117 constables. In all, a total of 291 officers left the Constabulary to serve in the armed forces*, of whom twenty-four were killed in action.

To fill these enormous gaps the Special Constabulary and auxiliaries consisting of a First Reserve (retired police officers) and War Reserve (men who met the physical and educational standards of the police and who would otherwise have been called up for military service) were mobilised. They wore the full uniform of the regular police, differing only in that the peaked cap was worn instead of the helmet and the words "Special Constabulary" or "War Reserve" were displayed on the sleeve. The War Reserve constable was committed to full-time employment with the police, drew the same pay (£4.10s a week) and was subject to the same discipline, hours of duty and shift work as a regular policeman. Nearly 350 auxiliaries were employed in Essex, enabling the policing of the county to continue despite conscription and a ban on regular police recruitment.

There was no escape for the fairer sex. Many volunteered for services such as the Women's Land Army or the Women's Auxiliary Police Corps. Formed in 1941, the WAPC not only replaced men who had been recalled to the Colours but staffed the many offices and departments which had been created as a result of the emergency. They received the same pay as employees of the county council, and in order to distinguish them from other civilian workers they were issued with uniforms, a very drab and much disliked brown overall. By March, 1943, no doubt due to the protestations of these fashion-conscious ladies, the much smarter police uniform was adapted for use (bearing in mind there were no policewomen then) bearing the initials WAPC in metallic letters on the shoulders.

At first just twenty-one members were recruited and posted as clerks and telephonists at headquarters and divisional stations at Braintree, Brentwood, Chelmsford, Clacton, Epping, Grays, Romford and Saffron Walden. As civilians they performed no street patrols, but now and again they were allowed some relief from office tedium to act as escorts for female prisoners being conveyed to court or prison.

Their position remained unchanged until early 1944, when with history repeating itself in the shape of countless army camps packed with American and British servicemen prior to D-Day and the presence of no fewer than eighteen fighter and bomber stations throughout the county (compared with only six during the first war) the waywardness of teenagers caused more than a little concern. Again the cry

* Army 165 RAF 98 Navy 24 Marines 4

went up for policewomen, but the county had none. Captain Peel, despite the vigour which had earned him a CBE in the 1943 Honours List, subscribed to the views held by so many of his contemporaries that there was no permanent place for women in the police service.

Essex held out against these demands until December, 1943, when the Standing Joint Committee set up a sub-committee to study the problem. However, the entrenched views of the opposition resulted in the committee agreeing that the whole question be shelved for another two years.

As soon as the result of the vote became known the might of Whitehall was brought to bear to force another debate on the subject. On 21st April, 1944, with the diehards still insisting that any approval for such a scheme must be on the understanding that women would be "additional to the wartime establishment of the force," agreement was reached to employ women and the Chief Constable was instructed to advertise for an inspector, a sergeant and twenty-three constables. This "temporary arrangement", like many others, was to become permanent.

In July of that year there arrived on a three-month secondment a slim, quietly spoken thirty-five-year-old woman police sergeant named Dorothy Jordan, who had joined the Metropolitan Police in 1936 and had been promoted in 1942. Superintendent Day at New Street police station, Chelmsford, received her courteously but informed her that no provision had been made for her accommodation as the living quarters over the station were for male constables only; Dorothy contacted a friend in London who knew some people in Chelmsford and was able to organise a flat for her in New London Road.

Shortly afterwards two young women just demobbed from the services became her first recruits (one would have expected at least some of the WAPC members to have been the first, but in fact only one volunteered, Miss Joan Hurley, who later became a sergeant). So ingrained in them was service discipline that Miss Jordan had constantly to remind them not to march along the road with their arms swinging but to walk at a more leisurely pace, the better to observe their surroundings.

The only concession made for these women was that they were not required to work full night duties, and much of their time was spent on foot patrols about the town. For the first few weeks Sergeant Jordan accompanied her charges on patrols and routine inquiries, for being untrained they were unable even to obtain simple statements without guidance.

Attitudes which had prevented women joining the Constabulary for so long did not disappear with the arrival of the new recruits, and if the powers-that-be had decreed that the county should have its women police it could do little to prevent open disapproval being shown by the rank and file. Paradoxically, it was the very camaraderie of service life which was to bring about an improvement in the situation, for as more and more ex-servicemen joined the police they brought with them their acceptance of women in uniform, but that was to take some years.

All too quickly Miss Jordan's three-month stay in Essex came to an end and she returned to her duties in London. Essex, though, was far from finished with her, for her personality and professionalism were sorely missed and there was no suitable replacement. Captain Peel, despite his private thoughts on the subject, decided that if Essex must have its women in the ranks it might as well have the best. He again approached the Metropolitan Police Commissioner and suggested that Sergeant Jordan might be persuaded to apply for a permanent transfer to Essex, on the understanding that if she accepted her promotion to inspector would be guaranteed. For such a woman this was a tempting challenge, and after much thought she applied for the appointment, and of course got it.

In November, 1944, she stood before the Chelmsford Justices at the Shire Hall to be sworn in as the first woman police inspector of the Essex Constabulary. That

Inspector Dorothy Jordan.

done, she reported to headquarters where Captain Peel waited to welcome her. It was only then that she discovered that Essex had no woman inspector's cap in stock. Before entering the Chief's office she persuaded an inspector to lend her his cap, and bravely (or desperately) donning it, she marched into Peel's office, stood to attention and saluted. He took one look at her, leaned back in his chair and burst out laughing. "What on earth have you got on your head?" he asked.

A short while later, properly accoutred in Essex uniform (and cap), she took on the task of building up her small force of women. There was still opposition to contend with, but she could learn to live with that as she assiduously applied herself to the job in hand. Two women sergeants were selected to assist her, a Miss Danby, who had travelled all the way from the Midlands, and a Mrs Kirk, who had transferred from Colchester Borough Police.

Seven years later Miss Jordan married George Hodges, the superintendent in charge of police training, but continued with her work and achieved another "first" when she was promoted to chief inspector in 1955. Mrs Hodges retired in 1963 after twenty-six years service and lives quietly with her husband just a stone's throw from headquarters, where she still maintains ties with the women's branch—now numbering 250 officers.

One of the most bitterly opposed recommendations to come out of the Desborough Report was on the subject of amalgamations. The suggestion that forces operating within populations of 100,000 should be abolished and merged with their neighbours brought forth such opposition from the local authorities that Home Office plans for its implementation were thwarted at every turn.

The first breakthrough for the Government came in 1942 when the Home Secretary, Herbert Morrison, asked Parliament to sanction regulations made under the Emergency Powers (Defence) Act for the forcible amalgamation of certain forces if he was satisfied that it was necessary for the benefit of naval, military or air operations. The reason for this, he said, was to rationalise the policing of those areas particularly affected by the war at a time when no fewer than 183 separate forces, of which thirty-one could boast a strength of fifty men or less, still operated throughout the country. With these "emergency powers" secured he immediately set about consolidating some two dozen forces in the South and South-west of England.

In 1945 Chuter Ede, who had succeeded Morrison as Home Secretary, went still further when he introduced a Bill designed to compel reluctant local authorities to accept amalgamations "in the interests of efficiency" but at the same time agreeing that no merger should take place without a local inquiry and the sanction of Parliament. The passage of this Bill, later to become the Police Act 1946, was difficult and protracted, many opponents viewing it as nothing more than a widening of the wedge first driven in in 1942, and yet more proof of the government's intention of creating at the very least regional forces if not a national police force. The figure of 100,000 was re-introduced and the Bill became law in April, 1946. Within a year no fewer than forty-five forces had disappeared from the map of Britain.

With a population of 52,000, Colchester found itself a casualty. Colchester Borough force, the lone survivor of the four original county borough forces in Essex, had been formed in 1836 and was therefore older than the county force which was to take it over. On 1st April, 1947, the borough handed over its men, equipment and buildings to the county police, and Colonel Hugh Charles Stockwell, who had held the office of Chief Constable for an incredible span of thirty-four years, quietly retired.

At the time the Police Act 1946 was making its way through Parliament a young station inspector resumed his duties with the Metropolitan Police after war service with the Royal Navy. He was John Cyprian Nightingale, the son of a Chelsea schoolmaster, who had joined the Metropolitan Police as a twenty-one-year-old aspiring constable in 1935, reporting to Peel House for his three months basic training.

John Nightingale's career got off to a flying start when he emerged from Peel

House as top recruit. He pounded the beat in north London for eighteen months before being selected for a course at Hendon Police College, the police equivalent of Sandhurst, at the end of which he passed out as a junior station inspector.

In 1950 he was appointed Commandant of the Police Training Centre at Ryton-on-Dunsmore, near Coventry, and three years later he moved to No 5 Police District Training Centre at Eynsham in Oxfordshire. He was well established on the

Sir John Nightingale, Chief Constable from 1962 to 1978.

promotion ladder by the time he returned to his old force in 1956, but his days with the Metropolitan Police were numbered.

At the beginning of 1958 he bade farewell to the force he had served for twenty-three years to take up duties as Assistant Chief Constable (Operations) under Sir Jonathan Peel in Essex. The two men were certainly no strangers to one another, for they had met on many occasions when the Essex Chief Constable visited Eynsham for the passing-out parades of Essex constables. Within a short time of his arrival in Essex John Nightingale was appointed Deputy Chief Constable, and when Sir Jonathan retired in 1962 he became the first Chief Constable of Essex to be appointed from within the force.

Two years after John Nightingale took over as Chief Constable another Police Act reinforced the 1946 Act by allowing the Secretary of State compulsorily to amalgamate forces "in the interests of efficiency." Under this Act the local authorities would first be invited to combine their forces voluntarily, and if this failed or one of the authorities refused on grounds unacceptable to the Home Secretary he could order the amalgamation .

It was under this Act that the Home Office in May, 1966, laid plans before Parliament for the amalgamations of a number of police forces, including Southend and Essex. It was hoped, said the Home Secretary, that the two authorities could agree to a voluntary scheme; Southend could rest assured that the decision to require the amalgamation in no way reflected on the efficiency of its police force. This news came as a shock to the borough, at that very moment preparing to select a new Chief Constable.

The county raised no objections to the proposal so long as suitable agreement could be reached with Southend, but the Southend Watch Committee expressed complete bewilderment as to why, if their force was efficient, it should be necessary to combine with the county and asked for an early meeting with the Home Office to express their views.

On 23rd November a deputation headed by Mr Norman Clarke, chairman of the Southend Watch Committee, met the Under Secretary of State, Mr Dick Taverne, at the Home Office. They strove to convince Mr Taverne that the borough had special problems and should be allowed to remain independent. If all else failed, they proposed that the town should at least become a "district" within the county force, with its own Assistant Chief Constable stationed in and responsible for the borough. The man they had in mind for this was Chief Superintendent H.J. Devlin, who had become Acting Chief Constable in January, 1965.

All this was to no avail. The Home Secretary, his opinion reinforced by the recommendations of John McKay, the Inspector of Constabularies within whose area Essex fell, whose report had come out strongly in favour of amalgamating the two forces, declared that there were insufficient grounds to justify his changing his mind. Further exchanges took place in an effort to arrange a personal meeting with the Home Secretary, but none bore fruit.

The borough advised the Home Office on 3rd February, 1967, that it was unable to agree terms with the county and that, in their view, such a merger would give the county authorities a complete monopoly of administrative services which could only result in a reduction of standards in Southend, a loss of service to the public and expensive inefficiency. Since they were still bitterly opposed to amalgamation no useful purpose could be served by continuing the negotiations.

Clearly the Home Secretary would soon exercise his statutory powers and order a compulsory amalgamation. On 6th March, 1967, notice was given that the two forces would combine "not earlier than 1st April, 1968, and not later than 1st April, 1969." On 22nd March Southend responded by objecting "in fundamental principle to the entirety of the proposed scheme on the grounds that it is wholly misconceived and that it is not expedient in the interests of efficiency." The county borough went on to say that in the event of a forcible merger they would be asking for the setting up of an ad-hoc corporate body to administer the police, with one-third of the police authority composed of borough representatives, and for the appointment of an Assistant Chief

Constable for the administration of the borough. The Home Secretary replied that the points made did not constitute specific objections but rather an objection to the entire scheme, which he was not prepared to entertain at that stage.

This play on words served only to aggravate the county borough and the resulting correspondence grew even more curt, the Watch Committee advising the Home Office that it wished to avail itself of the right to put its case before a public inquiry into the matter. This took place under the chairmanship of Mr Edgar Fay, QC, on 26th September, 1967, and lasted four days. The borough reaffirmed its total opposition to the scheme, saying it wished only to retain its existing police force. Essex, having expressed no opposition in the first place, and only now and again having put forward such suggestions as it thought useful, remained neutral.

Evidence was heard from a number of witnesses, including the HMI, Mr McKay, and the ensuing arguments were both long and technical. One issue raised was the Secretary of State's refusal to give a detailed reason for his decision to amalgamate the forces, this refusal being described by one witness (Mr E.C. Durham, representing Eastwood Ward Residents Association) as "very high-handed." At the end of the day the chairman came down firmly on the side of the government, declaring "that there is nothing in Southend's objections which ought to prevent the making of the amalgamation scheme by the Secretary of State." On 8th November, 1968, the formal Order was made to take effect from 1st April, 1969.

Southend had come a very long way in less than a hundred years. Once such an insignificant corner of Essex as to warrant the attentions of only one sergeant and two or three constables, it had grown to be a division in its own right and then a borough force which, by 1967, totalled 393 men (just five short of its authorised establishment). Its size was such that when it passed to the county the town became not one but two divisions, Southend Eastern incorporating the eastern half of the borough and the urban district of Rochford, and Southend Western incorporating the western half along with what had hitherto been the county areas of Canvey Island, Benfleet, Rayleigh and Hullbridge.

The movement of these areas into Southend caused considerable problems elsewhere and led to a realignment of divisional boundaries far to the west of Southend. With only Clacton and Grays divisions remaining unscathed, Harlow division was enlarged to encompass Saffron Walden and Braintree division was divided into two, Braintree and Halstead sub-divisions being taken over by Colchester and the Witham sub-division by Chelmsford. Brentwood too was relegated to sub-divisional status under Basildon.

Were the fears of Southend's Watch Committee justified? Although the strength of the new divisions subsequently rose to some 430 men, they incorporated a much larger area than the borough force had covered. The argument still put forward by Southend is that in real terms the town suffered a decrease in police manpower.

Certainly, there was considerable resentment among the rank and file of borough policemen at what they saw as an unnecessary and ruthless axing of an efficient and much-respected force. It was only to be expected that some years would elapse before the older borough men came to terms with their new status, but as one ex-borough officer said, "We are all policemen, aren't we, wherever we serve."

CHAPTER EIGHTEEN

The Marine Section

FROM TIME to time over the years the subject of policing the Thames and its estuary was raised, discussed and shelved. The Metropolitan Police, descendants of those cutlass-wielding employees of the Port of London Authority and East India Company who had guarded the nation's wealth in the ships and warehouses of London's dockland, were being quietly left to get on with it.

In 1914, an anxious Port of London Authority wrote to Essex County Council pointing out that the lower reaches of the Thames from Dagenham to the sea "were totally unsupervised," and that as they (the PLA) were bound under the Thames Conservancy Act to provide protection on the river, was it not time that Essex took similar steps to protect its own waterfront?

Essex resolved that in the absence of statutory persuasion the matter should be allowed to rest. And there it rested for forty-five years.

The Second World War came and went, leaving in its wake only slight signs of improvement in the austere conditions which gripped the nation. Food was still rationed, raw materials were in desperately short supply and factories and mines worked flat out to repair the ravages of the war years. Inevitably the black market continued to flourish and so did crime. Thefts from docks, warehouses and ships were such that the Metropolitan Police could be forgiven for casting yet another accusing eye at Essex, implying as it did so that if the county could not be relied on to look after its own interests the Metropolitan Police would be forced to patrol the entire river, regardless of boundaries.

The end of 1948 saw a decision made to introduce a "presence" on the Thames by way of a sergeant and four constables stationed at Tilbury. Having no wish to squander its money, the county turned its eyes to the Isle of Wight where an ex-RAF seaplane tender was up for sale. In March, 1949, three Essex officers who had volunteered for the new Marine Section accompanied two civilian engineers to Ryde to bring back the county's first patrol boat. Sergeant Cranfield (ex-Merchant Navy and Colchester Borough River Section), Pc Howard (ex-Royal Navy telegraphist) and Pc Ward (holder of a Coastal Master's Certificate) arrived at the mooring to find a decidedly run-down and seedy looking boat still clad in its wartime coat of dove grey. After a voyage that was delayed by bad weather the boat arrived at Wapping on the Thames, where Metropolitan Police marine engineers were waiting to start work on her.

The *Vigilant*, as she was later named, was a hard-chine (flat-bottomed) craft, with a length of forty feet, a beam of nine feet and drawing only two and a half feet. Powered by twin 100hp Perkins diesel engines, the boat was capable of a top speed of 20 knots. During the three months it took to strip and renovate her (including the fitting of the newly acquired RT radio) the volunteer officers spent their time with the Metropolitan Police Thames Division studying maritime law, local tides and currents, and general patrol routine.

By the time they were ready to commence duty Kent had acquired its own boat, and from the outset close liaison was maintained with that county in respect of patrols and shift duties, one side working a week of early turns (6am-2pm) while the other side worked late turn (2pm-10pm). Whichever craft was on patrol, its crew kept a weather eye open on the other's shoreline and responded to all calls from both sides of the estuary. Night duty was not normally performed, although there was always a crew on standby for such. This very sensible arrangement with Kent continued for a number of years.

In 1959 the *Vigilant* was replaced by a modern custom-built craft. Built at Shoreham-by-Sea, it was brought overland to Essex and commissioned the following month by Lady Peel, wife of the Chief Constable. *Vigilant II*, as she was named, had a length of forty-two feet, a beam of eleven feet and a draft of three feet six inches. Originally powered by twin Perkins 100hp engines, subsequently replaced by Ford Turbos, the new vessel had a top speed of seventeen knots. The new boat was a

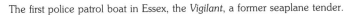

The first police patrol boat in Essex, the *Vigilant*, a former seaplane tender.

displacement craft, whereas the first *Vigilant* had been designed to plane on top of the water at speed; although slower than her predecessor she was a far superior boat to *Vigilant* and more seaworthy.

Since then, both craft and manpower have increased, *Vigilant II* being joined in 1967 by the *Alert* which covered Bradwell, Mersea, Brightlingsea and the Blackwater estuary. In 1970 came the *Watchful*, based at Burnham-on-Crouch and covering the Crouch peninsula. In 1972 the *Alert* was replaced by *Alert II* and ten years later came the *Alert III*. In 1977 came *Vigilant III*. From the original volunteer crew of four there has now grown a Marine Section composed of an inspector, two sergeants and sixteen constables based at Southend, Bradwell and Burnham.

The police launch *Vigilant II* on patrol near Canvey Island.

CHAPTER NINETEEN

Into the Computer Age

FROM ITS earliest days the structure of police divisions remained unaltered. The busiest centre of activity was naturally chosen as the divisional headquarters and there the superintendent concentrated the bulk of his constables. He was assisted by an inspector and perhaps two or three sergeants who were responsible for the day-to-day supervision of the men. Further afield the rural area was administered by a second inspector who had charge of one or two section sergeants and a number of detached beats.

Altogether a simple and effective chain of command for a simple and uncomplicated way of life. Times changed all that, though, for the massive growth in population and subsequent rise in the number of police has resulted in such a proliferation of senior ranks that there are now divisions in which a chief superintendent is assisted by two superintendents (one each for urban and rural), chief inspectors in charge of sub-divisions, inspectors in charge of each town shift (about a dozen constables) and one or more inspectors subordinate to the rural chief inspectors. Only the role of sergeants remains relatively unchanged.

The recruit, on completing his three months training at police college (for Essex men this was at Eynsham Hall in Oxfordshire), was invariably posted to a divisional station where he would receive close supervision and be placed, whenever possible, under the wing of an experienced constable. As time went by and his knowledge and abilities increased he would move outwards to the sub-divisions where he encountered a marked slackening in the degree of supervision. From there he could join a section or be selected for detached beat work, at which stage of course he was expected to be capable of working efficiently with the minimum of guidance.

While his town-based colleagues continued round-the-clock policing, the detached beat officer was left very much to his own devices during the day but expected to perform a mandatory patrol at night on a set system of "points". The extent of this patrol varied over the years from five or six hours at night down to one or two, but by the 1960's he was working a five-hour discretionary day duty followed by a set three-hour patrol during the evening or night. Eventually, most rural officers were relieved of the necessity of cycling around deserted country lanes in the early morning by being allowed to perform the duty as observer in the divisional area car. The drawback, in terms of hard policing, was that he was then liable to be sent anywhere in the sub-division either in response to calls or to supervise vulnerable areas, and his own beat was thereby neglected.

This situation was not lost on Mr John Nightingale, who appreciated that while most rural beats "died" after midnight the travelling criminal did not cease his activities, and there was far less possibility of his being caught at three in the morning than at midnight. He therefore introduced a scheme to provide cover during those hours by the use of vehicles (mostly mini-vans) manned by section or sub-divisional constables to patrol those unsupervised beats, thereby supplementing the centrally based area car. In addition lightweight motor-cycles were purchased to provide greater cover and swifter response to calls for assistance. The mechanisation of the detached beat officer had thus begun, pre-empting by two or three years the famous Home Office scheme designed to provide increased cover to unprotected areas.

Unit Beat Policing, as it became known, was a brave and very expensive attempt to extend police cover by way of re-arrangement rather than by increasing the existing manpower. It was rightly argued that most towns had grown dramatically as more and more housing estates catered for the growth and shift in population, and as most were situated in peripheral areas few, if any, had the satisfaction of seeing a regular foot patrol. It was proposed that these areas be divided into beats to create in effect urban detachments with a constable actually living within the community and, like his country colleague, being left to decide for himself how best to administer it. Unlike his rural counterpart, though, he was not required to perform mandatory night patrols. Thus, it was hoped, the inhabitants would come to identify with their own "Bobby" who in turn would develop a keener awareness and knowledge of those living around him. In addition to the Residential Beat Officers (as they were called), further cover would be provided by mobile patrols, each driver being responsible for two of these beats. All beat personnel were issued with pocket radios tuned in to their divisional stations.

From the outset there were many critics of the scheme and the question on everyone's mind was not so much "how many men will it save" but "how are we to find the men to implement it?" Divisional superintendents themselves were by no means unanimous in their support, for they knew full well that no two divisions were alike; each operated in direct relation to the needs of that particular area.

For example, Clacton and Southend demanded the maximum concentration in their town centres and seafront areas, particularly during the hectic summer season. Both towns were served by the railway which brought in visitors by the tens of thousands. At any time of the day or night disturbances could break out among trippers the worse for drink and immediate reinforcements would be required. Where were these reinforcements coming from? Why, the very men who had been moved out to police the quiet residential areas.

Other divisions, such as those incorporating Saffron Walden, Ongar and Braintree, were almost entirely rural in character, with much smaller concentrations of population and dozens of quiet, law-abiding villages around. The more the scheme was studied the more it became obvious that only certain divisions would benefit. Harlow and Basildon appeared appropriate, for both were new towns with well-planned centres and clearly defined suburbs. Even so, the superintendent of one of these felt moved to declare that his area was populated by rehoused Londoners who had failed so far to develop any community spirit and had shown a marked lack of enthusiasm for the police. The other divisional commander acknowledged himself totally "sold" on the idea.

However well-intentioned and theoretically workable it might have appeared at the outset, its practical application was often less than rewarding. The intention that

Panda cars should represent nothing more than an aid to foot constables was doomed from the start, and superintendents who had imposed a limit of thirty miles a shift (that done, the constable was then expected to get out and walk) were being forced to concede that it was impractical as the role of the Panda changed from "beat" vehicle to "swift response" unit. Calls which had previously gone out to area cars were being routed instead to the Pandas, for the simple reason that the area car was often miles away while the latter was known to be in the immediate vicinity.

Another by-product of the thirty-mile limit was that no constable, however dedicated, would willingly walk around a deserted housing estate in driving rain or bitter cold while his warm, comfortable car stood at the kerbside. With his daily quota used, he was more inclined to sit and watch the world go by. So why was his supervising officer not detecting this and pushing him on? He would certainly have done so under orthodox policing, for then the constable was required to make a "point" once in every hour regardless of weather; and not only were these points designed to ensure that he covered his beat but the officer faced disciplinary proceedings if he missed one. Now that the pocket radio had rendered him instantly available the points system was abolished.

Manpower shortages had also created a situation in which the newly-arrived recruit would find most of the experienced constables hived off to residential beats or engaged on important station duties. Consequently, town centres were being patrolled by comparatively inexperienced officers who were not only themselves suffering from lack of tuition but were expected to impart to the newcomer what little worldly wisdom they had acquired. It was therefore not uncommon to see a constable of only a few months service taking out a recruit to show him the ropes he had barely mastered himself.

Neither was great provision made for such "invisible" factors as court appearances, court duties, prison escort, sickness, annual leave and courses, to say nothing of sudden emergencies requiring additional manpower.

Gradually the situation worsened until the day arrived when recruits from the police training centre were being sent direct to headquarters for a driving test (or indeed a driving course), for the whole concept of policing had changed. At the point where these constables stepped into the nearest Panda car with only the barest beat tuition the die was cast, for these men were being thrust into situations armed only with theoretical knowledge and their wits or common sense to see them through.

Inevitably the public began to wonder what had happened to the familiar "Bobby" on the beat, the reassuring sight of a uniformed figure at the street corner, the man who knew every shopkeeper, troublesome youngster or local villain. Eventually, it needed only one bold Chief Constable to say, "Enough is enough. I am putting my men back where they belong, on the streets," for others to follow suit. More and more policemen are to be seen walking their beats and re-establishing that lifeline of communication so vital in a society which prides itself on being "policed by consent."

The Unit Beat system is not dead; indeed, its concepts are laudable and many lessons have been learned on both sides. Perhaps the biggest mistake made was in believing that it would save manpower, whereas hard reality proved the opposite.

Hot on the heels of Unit Beat Policing, and particularly one of its more successful features, the collator, who was responsible for establishing and maintaining criminal records and intelligence at a divisional level, came the Police National Computer. More than any other single factor, this technological marvel has transformed the daily life of Britain's police to such an extent that they are left wondering how on earth they managed to get by for so long without it!

Mr Robert Bunyard, who became Chief Constable in 1978.

Formed in 1970 as a result of a joint project between the Home Office and the Metropolitan Police, it was designed to give up-to-date information about crime and criminals to every officer down to beat level. Hitherto, this information had been catalogued and stored in thousands of files at Scotland Yard, but however sophisticated the indexing its sheer physical volume inevitably brought about delays.

In terms of space saving, manpower and accuracy the benefits of computerisation were enormous. So successful was it that by the end of 1974 the Metropolitan Police had suggested to the Home Office the benefits of extending the system nationwide. By that time information on stolen/suspect vehicles and their owners was already available at the touch of a button, and by 1975 fingerprint records were added. Between 1977-79 came criminal names, wanted and missing persons and disqualified drivers. In practical terms it meant that vehicles stolen hundreds of miles away could be recovered within hours, and more effective observation maintained on vehicles suspected of involvement in crime. Arrests, too, were often made in circumstances which would not previously have been possible.

Another facet of this extraordinary facility was the Broadcast System whereby a force could relay urgent messages to other forces, for example along a motorway, alerting them to the approach of a suspect vehicle or wanted person and thereby reducing to a minimum the time spent in telephoning each force individually.

Now acknowledged to be one of the most advanced and sophisticated computer-controlled systems in the world, the National Police Computer functions through a network of channels to five hundred terminals installed in police stations all over the country, and links between London and those outlying forces are such that not only can those forces extract instant information but can in return provide a reciprocal service in the form of local information.

Thus a constable on the beat in Maldon or Saffron Walden can now obtain information about a suspect or his vehicle without the suspect knowing he is interested. A far cry indeed from the day when a telephone had to be found and time-wasting delays were accepted as normal.

Modern technology has led to dramatic changes in the type of recruit being attracted into the service. Gone are the days when the basic requirements were the ability to read and write, do simple arithmetic, exercise sound common-sense (intelligence was a bonus) and impose one's will by sheer physical presence. Over the last twenty-five years standards have risen so much that it is not uncommon for university or college graduates to attend for interview clutching degrees, diplomas and sheaves of A- and O-levels.

Despite these advances, or perhaps because of them, there are still many who fear the coming of a national police force and condemn (as did the miners during the 1984-1985 dispute in the coalfields) mutual aid between forces. Far better, they feel, to be arrested by one of their own "Bobbies" than by an "outsider". Yet the question of a national force has its roots as far back as the birth of our constabularies. Many influential nineteenth-century politicians advocated such a policy, and not least among its local supporters was John McHardy himself, who deemed it to be "the greatest blessing that could be conferred upon the country".

Mutual aid has always been with us, and law-abiding folk everywhere have been more than grateful for the agreements reached, voluntarily at first during the early days, and later reinforced by various Acts of Parliament. Where would we be without such agreements? Can we really contemplate a situation where a neighbouring county, beset by strife and public disorder, cries out for support which it knows will never come? To some the assistance which each force is prepared to lend its neighbour smacks of "national policing"; to the majority it is simply common-sense.

While Chief Constables remain answerable to their local authorities, supported but not controlled by a democratically elected government, there can be no police state. The very basis of British policing remains embodied in the opening words of this book—a policeman is a citizen and a citizen a policeman.

Yet with all that has changed, the basic role of the Essex policeman has not altered. The principles on which Captain McHardy founded the force more than 140 years ago are still those on which the modern "Bobby" models himself, and though he may sit at a computer keyboard or at the wheel of a car, today's Essex policeman still remembers that first Chief Constable's advice that "the more respectful and civil the Constabulary are, the more they will be supported and respected by the public."

Harwich Borough Police

THE MAYOR and Aldermen of the Borough of Harwich exercised their ancient rights by maintaining control over the parish constables and street watchmen from the Guildhall, a fine red-brick building dating from 1601 and rebuilt in 1767. At the rear are two offices which were once the cells used to accommodate prisoners awaiting trial in the courtroom on the first floor. The building backs on to the large Bridewell which housed the long-term prisoners of earlier days.

In January, 1836, William Burton became the first Chief Constable of the borough. Often referred to as "Mr Superintendent" (a title more in keeping with his responsibilities, since he at no stage controlled more than eight or nine men), he received a regular salary of £20 a year payable in quarterly instalments of £5. Along with Mr Burton there were appointed twelve police constables, of which Harwich itself kept nine, three being sent to Dovercourt.

These constables were only part-timers, operating on a fee basis, evidenced by the following terms of reference:- "(1) A Constable in each Parish do attend at the several places of worship within his particular Parish on every Sunday during the hours of Divine Worship, such Constable to be named by the Mayor of the Borough, for which service the Treasurer is authorised to pay to such Constable the sum of two shillings for every Sunday he shall be on duty. (2) Constables shall attend every Saturday night the public houses in each Parish to prevent any disorders and to see that the Order from the Justices for closing the same is attended. For this duty the Constable shall be paid 1/6d for every such duty. (3) The Treasurer shall pay to such Constable for any loss of time in the execution of their office as the Mayor shall direct, not exceeding the sum of three shillings and sixpence for every time they shall be called out as Constables." The Chief Constable himself was "required to be on duty during the day to preserve the peace and prevent the frequent interruptions and stoppages occasioned by persons standing at corners of the streets and lanes of the Town." Quite obviously the "Chief Constable" was expected to do the bulk of the work.

Every effort was made by the borough to care for its constables and to recompense them for any injury or loss of wages incurred while on duty. In August, 1837, one of the borough constables, Thomas Wilding, was injured while arresting a naval deserter from H.M.S. *Fairy*. His injuries were such as to require the attention of a surgeon, who sent the Corporation a bill for £4.9s.6d. Not only was this paid but Wilding himself received £1 a week during the time he was off work and was given a reward of £1 for his devotion to duty.

At the end of 1838 there came a major shake-up within the borough's police force resulting in the dismissal of Mr Superintendent Burton and no fewer than eight of his twelve constables. One of those four remaining constables was none other than our friend Thomas Wilding, now recovered from his injuries. He was offered the post of Chief Constable and ordered to rebuild the shattered remains of the force. Incredibly, history was to repeat itself, for in 1842 Wilding received his marching orders, along with nine of his constables! Again we are left wondering why.

The next man to take over the reins of office was James Pain, who was sworn in with seven new constables—no fewer than four of which were men who had been dismissed in 1838.

Throughout the 1830's and 1840's the constables remained as part-time officers, supplemented by street watchmen who were employed to patrol the streets in return for 13s. a quarter.

By January, 1846, the people of Harwich were becoming somewhat disillusioned with their little force, for they could see growing around them the ranks of full-time, regular officers of the county Constabulary. Petitions were organised complaining of "the want of efficiency" shown by the Harwich constables. Bowing to these pressures but at the same time somewhat fearful of the cost, the Mayor wrote to Captain McHardy for advice on how the borough could be properly policed and particularly how much it would cost to maintain regular constables. McHardy replied that the cost worked out at £56 a year per constable, but he was unable to advise on the number of men required as he did not know the town. He went on to remind the Mayor of his powers to abolish the parochial system altogether in favour of a regular force. The following month the Corporation resolved to implement that advice.

Again they wrote to McHardy, explaining the layout of the town and its requirements and asking once again his advice on the number of constables he would employ if he were in charge. He replied that a superintendent would be required at 25s. a week, along with three constables (First, Second and Third Class) earning 21s., 19s. and 17s. a week respectively. After discussing these figures the Corporation resolved to appoint a superintendent at 25s. a week (less £8 a year for rent and coals) and four constables all earning 18s. a week. That decision having been made, notices of dismissal went out to James Pain and his constables. Mr. Hart, the Guildhall gaoler, was also dismissed as it was felt that his job could easily be taken over by the new superintendent.

By December, 1847, the committee had interviewed and appointed a George Coleman as the first regular Chief Constable. The style of uniforms, pay, allowances, duties and equipment were all modelled on those of the county and Coleman was given the use of the two cells in the Guildhall, which were converted into police offices. Two new cells were then built in the yard at the rear.

In August, 1849, an incident took place which indicates that perhaps all was not well between Coleman and his Watch Committee. He complained that one of his constables, Pc Slater, having asked for leave of absence and it being granted, had had the effrontery to use that period in order to get married without first seeking the committee's approval! It took the members only a few minutes of discussion to determine that Constable Slater had not contravened any borough regulations, the committee declaring to the startled Coleman that they were of the opinion that he needed a rest, and whether he liked it or not, he himself was being granted ten days leave of absence!

In January, 1850, Coleman was again summoned before the committee to explain why he had personally conveyed a prisoner to Chelmsford Gaol instead of allocating the task to the arresting officer. Since a mileage allowance was paid to constables for escorting prisoners we can only assume that Coleman felt he needed a day away from his duties and also the allowance that went with it. He was told that it had been resolved there and then that the arresting officer "should have the privilege of conveying his prisoner to gaol."

In 1855, the borough followed the county Constabulary by introducing the new style of uniform, for their constables had until then been wearing the top-hat and tail coat.

An interesting event took place the following year which prompted the Watch Committee to take another exasperated look at their Chief Constable. The Town Clerk had received a letter, dated 26th June, 1856, from a gentleman called George Josselyn, who resided in Ipswich, complaining of an outrageous exhibition he had witnessed on 17th June at Bentley in Essex. A public prize fight had taken place between two bare-knuckle fighters from London, who had been accompanied by an enormous crowd which had travelled by special train from the Metropolis. Both onlookers and combatants had been dispersed by a strong force of the county police and escorted back to Bentley railway station. Who should be seen among them but Chief Constable Coleman himself—in full uniform. And as if that were not bad enough, he was then seen to board the train along with the fans!

Mr Josselyn complained bitterly of the bad example shown by the borough's chief of police and went on to declare that he "and other influential gentlemen intended to proceed against all those persons implicated—and especially against those whose duty it was to discourage and prevent breaches of the peace."

Coleman was once more summoned before the committee and invited to explain. He replied quite simply that he had received information that a prize-fight (then illegal) was due to take place somewhere in the Bentley area and had "decided to set off in pursuit." On arrival he found the fight in progress and remained only to render assistance to the county officers. At the railway station he, being anxious to return to his duties, begged leave of the guard to travel with him in the brake van as far as Manningtree in order to catch the connection back to Harwich. There was little the committee could do but accept his explanation, albeit with tongue-in-cheek, for under the Parliamentary Act a borough officer had jurisdiction in the county (a privilege not extended in reverse to county officers).

By 1856 the Mayor and Corporation were becoming rather disillusioned with their tiny force, and Coleman was ordered to "draw attention to your men as to the obedience of orders of the Watch Committee, especially as to the talking and walking with people whilst on duty, and to going into public houses and drinking therein during the time they were on duty." There was open talk now between various members of the Watch Committee that it was high time they considered amalgamating their force with that of the county. Eventually the Town Clerk was instructed to write to McHardy asking under what terms he would agree to such a merger. McHardy, no doubt hiding his delight, replied that he would attend in person the next meeting of the Committee, and there be happy to answer all questions put to him.

True to his word, McHardy travelled to Harwich and offered a great deal of advice (and encouragement) on the proposed change, informing those members that although he knew little of the town he was sure that two sergeants and four constables would be sufficient for their needs. The cost to the borough would be 23s. a week for the sergeants and 17s., 19s. and 21s. respectively for the constables, depending on their grades.

At their next meeting on 25th August the Mayor and Corporation resolved to amalgamate their police with the county Constabulary, the Town Clerk being given wide powers to negotiate the terms with the County Justices. Coleman and his constables were dismissed with effect from 1st February, 1857, the county police moved in and installed Inspector Robert Banks, along with two first class and two second class constables.

It was not very long, however, before members of the Corporation began to realise that the amalgamation was turning out in some respects to be not all they had expected. As far back as could be remembered the Mayor, Committee and Justices had looked upon their constables as something akin to personal property, and had grown accustomed to their every whim being catered for without question. It was becoming increasingly obvious that the allegiance of these new county men, and particularly of Inspector Banks, was more than a little suspect. They were showing no signs of becoming dutiful servants of the borough authorities, and worse were actually referring their difficulties to the Chief Constable in Chelmsford for guidance and instruction.

Matters came to a head in October, 1858, when a Harwich Justice named Vaux complained to the Mayor that Inspector Banks had refused to lock up a boy when ordered to do so by a magistrate (himself). The inspector was ordered to appear before the Watch Committee—a totally irregular summons, for the committee had no jurisdiction on the subject of discipline and therefore no power to order the inspector to appear before them. Nevertheless Banks appeared to put his side of the argument, and did so in such unequivocable terms that the committee felt obliged to write to the Chief Constable for clarification on the subject of "Police constables' powers and duties."

On receiving this McHardy informed the Mayor that he would travel to Harwich and make himself available to the committee.

Accordingly, on 15th November, 1858, McHardy attended the Watch Committee meeting at the Guildhall and listened with growing impatience to a list of complaints set out before him. It was quite obvious that certain members of the committee felt that the arrival of the county Constabulary had deprived them of much of their authority in the borough and that the constables working therein should be made more accountable to the local authorities than to their masters in Chelmsford (precisely the argument put forward by Southend over fifty

Harwich Guildhall, from which the Corporation maintained control over parish constables and street watchmen and their successors.

years later). McHardy took pains to explain the reasons for the various actions taken by his officers but felt nevertheless that the issues raised were too far-reaching to be resolved locally. He informed the members that he would ask for one of H.M. Inspectors of Constabulary to inquire into the matter of jurisdiction and would himself submit his own report to the county authorities.

The inquiry confirmed McHardy's undisputed right to administer his force without reference to any other authority than the County Justices (except as a matter of courtesy). McHardy's report, dated 4th January, 1859, was extremely lengthy and commenced, "All the facts I shall here adduce prove, in my opinion, the unquestionable benefit arising from the amalgamation, and justify the suspicion that the *real* cause of dissatisfaction is the discreet exercise of the powers voluntarily transferred by the authorities to the Chief Constable." He went on to outline the first complaint which concerned a young boy who had been convicted by the local magistrates of stealing a kite. He was sentenced to be taken to the police station and there whipped (not an uncommon form of punishment then). Inspector Banks, somewhat taken aback, delayed the execution of this sentence while he telegraphed his divisional superintendent for advice. The superintendent in turn telegraphed McHardy who replied that the lawful sentence of the court must be carried out. The core of the complaint was that Inspector Banks, in delaying the sentence and referring it to his superiors, had shown disrespect to the Justice who had ordered the whipping. McHardy had already explained, during his visit to Harwich, that Inspector Banks had meant no disrespect but had taken that action solely because "he was wanting in the knowledge of his duties."

Another complaint concerned the boy whom the constable had been ordered by Mr Vaux to lock up. The facts, as they turned out, were that this particular constable had come across this young lad playing marbles in the street. What passed between them is not known but whatever it was led to the constable clipping the boy's ear. The cheeky chap then picked up a stone and was threatening to throw it at the officer when Mr Vaux happened to pass by. He immediately ordered the constable to take the boy into custody and lock him up. On arrival at the police station the constable related the facts to the inspector, who promptly ordered the boy's release, at the same time telling the constable that if he had not clipped his ear in the first place the incident would never have arisen.

When Mr Vaux got to hear about this he at once complained to the Mayor that his authority had been undermined by Inspector Banks. McHardy commented in his report, "The Inspector refused to confine the boy, judging that the constable had committed the assault and not the boy, and that the offence, if any, arose out of an illegal act on the part of the constable—which I have no doubt is the opinion of the (Harwich) authorities as no proceedings have been taken against the boy, although I invited the authorities to do so to show the merits of the case. I explained that unless a magistrate by *virtue of his office* remanded a party, the inspector is justified in arming himself with good reasons before confining any party. It appeared, in this case, that the inspector felt he had no power to confine the boy."

The third complaint involved the issue of the book of instructions entitled "Rules and Regulations for the Government of the Essex Constabulary", which every constable was required to possess and upon which he relied for guidance. The borough committee complained that adherence to the regulations laid out in that book "appeared to cramp the actions of the men, especially in the suppression of offences in the streets and thoroughfares, and in the inns, public houses and beershops." McHardy countered this by quoting instances where brawls had taken place which had immediately broken up on the approach of the police, the participants scattering in all directions. In all his nineteen years experience, he said, those instructions had been found to work well and were a valuable aid to constables in the execution of their duties.

The Harwich authorities also alleged that the Constabulary was slack in bringing offenders before the courts. To this McHardy retorted, "Now, what is the fact? Out of the sixteen petty larcenies during the last year, twelve have been detected, and the only one not convicted arose when the complainant declined to prosecute. The total value of the property stolen amounted to the insignificant sum of £8, £6 of which was recovered! As further proof of the protection of property since the two years of amalgamation, not one case has occurred of sufficient importance for commitment to the Assizes or Quarter Sessions." The Chief Constable ended his report thus, "After this, I held a conference with the borough authorities with a view to ascertaining, if possible, what they really had to complain of and what they wished remedied. First, a strong feeling of disaffection that the constables were prevented from carrying canes and correcting boys at pleasure, as practiced previously to the amalgamation. This, I explained, was illegal and could not be permitted. The second was that the police did not lock up a man who was drunk and fighting. This case occurred at the last Municipal Elections when the police separated the parties and discreetly left the man referred to to be taken away by his friends. In drawing up my instructions one great end I had in view was to guard against rash, arbitrary or vexatious interference with the public, most carefully impressing on each member of the force that the smallest possible amount of violence necessary for accomplishing the object is the largest amount which the law sanctions. It has been gratifying to me, and creditable to the police, inasmuch as I have never had a complaint against any man stationed in the borough of Harwich, nor a desire expressed for an interchange." At long last, the Mayor, Committee and Justices knew just where they stood.

Saffron Walden Borough Police

THE BOROUGH of Saffron Walden (once known as Chipping Walden) consisted of the town itself and the four outlying hamlets of Sewards End, Audley End, North End and Little Walden, yet the strength of the borough force never exceeded a Head Constable and two or three constables. They were controlled by the Mayor and Watch Committee from the Town Hall in the Market Place, which also incorporated in its basement the borough gaol. This gaol was necessary not only for prisoners who had been sentenced but for those awaiting their trial in the Petty Session and Borough Quarter Sessions upstairs.

On 31st October, 1849, an incident occurred which fairly shook the town. The Chief Constable, Mr William Campling, who lived in Bridge Street, had spent the evening at the *Eight Bells* public house, only forty yards from his home. As he emerged from the *Eight Bells* he met an acquaintance, Mr William Brand, a resident of North End and bailiff to Mr Martin Nockolds. The two men walked along the street in amicable conversation until they reached Campling's house. Brand bade Campling goodnight and walked on his way.

Campling was on the point of opening his front door when a shotgun blast threw him through the door. He had been shot in both legs.

Campling staggered upstairs and called upon his horrified family to "go and see where Pettit was, or where he had been." Benjamin Pettit was a local man who lived in Almshouse Lane behind the Almshouses, and was known to have borne a grudge against Campling for having, at some time in the past, been instrumental in convicting him of some offence. Campling's word was enough for Pettit to be arrested within the hour.

It became obvious within two or three days that Campling was not going to survive his injuries. The Mayor attended his bedside, in company with Pettit, and took down a deposition in the form of a dying declaration from the injured man.

Campling gave his account of what had happened and stated that the reason for immediately suspecting Pettit "was because he had threatened me at other times, the last time was when I met him in the passage down by the Abbey Lane Chapel three or four months ago. I met him on a sudden, I think his expression was in a sort of wrath: 'you old ... you, I'll do your business for you one of these times'," Pettit was alleged to have said. Campling died from his injuries a few days later.

The Watch Committee contacted Superintendent Clarke of the Essex Constabulary at Newport, just a few miles away, and requested him to investigate the murder. Poor Clarke was utterly out of his depth, having probably never investigated a murder in his life. After some days making inquiries into a murder to which, it was quickly discovered, there was not a single witness or corroborative evidence against the suspect, Clarke gave up and returned to Newport.

The committee then appealed to the Metropolitan Police and Sir Richard Mayne sent down an Inspector Lund to take over the case.

Meanwhile the Coroner's jury returned a verdict that "some person unknown, not having the fear of God before his eyes, but moved and seduced by the instigation of the Devil, with force of arms did make an assault on the said William Campling, and the said person unknown (with) a certain gun, charged and loaded with gunpowder and leaden shot, did at the legs of William Campling shoot off and gave several wounds of which he languished on, and on the ninth of November died."

Pettit was charged with the murder, remanded in custody and conveyed to Chelmsford Gaol. Unfortunately, Inspector Lund had no greater success than Clarke in building up a prosecution case. It was a peculiar aspect of this murder that not a soul in the whole of Saffron Walden town had any doubt that Pettit was guilty of the outrage, and enormous efforts were made not so much to detect the killer as to try to prove Pettit's guilt. Within a very short time however, Inspector Lund packed his bags, presented the Town Clerk with a bill for £15.12s., representing six days work, and returned to London. The Watch Committee, in desperation, ordered the Town Clerk to take over the investigation!

Pettit finally came for trial at Essex Assizes, Chelmsford, in March, 1850, and pleaded not guilty. All that could be proved against Pettit was that he had left the *Waggon & Horses* at 9.30pm and had not returned until 11.30pm. The rest of the prosecution's case was pure speculation. After the Judge's summing up the jury took only fifteen minutes to return a verdict of not guilty.

A Sergeant Benjamin Judd is shown as having been appointed Head Constable at a salary of 25s. a week in 1852, when he was granted the occupancy of "a cottage at the back of the Town Hall" which must have been Butchers Row. This type of salary was reserved for Chief Constables of boroughs, and indeed this is confirmed when one reads his entries in the *Police Journal* of 1855-1857 in which he describes himself as Chief Constable. During this period his constables were Pc Jeavons and Pc Dewberry.

The Watch Committee appears always to have had the greatest difficulty in appointing its Chief Constables, for when Judd tendered his resignation in 1856, the Mayor, Nathaniel Catling, wrote to the police authorities of the surrounding counties offering to a suitable candidate "cash salary of £65 a year, residence free, a new suit and two pairs of boots, and a new Cape and Greatcoat every two years." The replies he received were not only discouraging but downright scornful.

Sir Richard Mayne, of the Metropolitan Police, declared "that no man can be found who is willing..." The Chief Constable of Cambridge said that he would have very great pleasure in sending an officer—if only he had one whom he could recommend! The City of London replied, "It is not an easy matter to meet your requirements, a good man is worth more wages, an indifferent man is of no value." The Chief Constable of Essex wrote "that while I have no objection to any member of the Essex Constabulary leaving it who may wish to do so, I carefully avoid selecting material for any other establishment, neither do I believe a discerning man would be tempted by any apparent advantage to leave a County Constabulary for that of a Borough."

The Watch Committee received another letter from the City of London, whose Commissioner wrote "Upon enquiry I find that Samuel Heywood is a person calculated to meet your views. He is a married man with two children, and has been in the Force since February, 1849. During that time five charges have been recorded against him:- (1) robbery on his beat, (2) two irregularities, (3) gossiping on his beat, and (4) neglect of duty." Walden's Watch Committee decided they were not that desperate.

All these inquiries having drawn a blank, the Town Clerk, Mr W. B. Freeland, wrote to his friend the Town Clerk of Colchester. This evinced the following ray of hope, "We have no man in our Force fit for a 'Head', but I have seen a person today who, I think, will suit you very well, as far as I can judge, and he is strongly recommended by our Superintendent who has known him since 1848. His appearance and manner are good and he writes a fair hand. Age 36 next Nov. His name is Oliver Kirby, married, no children, has he says remarkably good health. He was originally in the Army, as a Private, became a Sergeant but for some irregularity of no very heinous nature he got degraded to the ranks again. He bought his discharge and afterwards went into business at Gravesend as a Grocer etc but did not succeed and lost £300. He subsequently became Warden on board one of the hulks at Portsmouth, where he was for four

The red-brick police station built at Saffron Walden in 1884 and still in use a century later.

years, and left for the purpose of going to Australia but his wife would not go. Afterwards he was in the Norwich Police Force for 18 months and gave up the appointment expecting to get that of Governor to the Rollesbury* Union, Norwich, but which he lost by two or three votes, and he has been out of employ since last February. I send you a copy of some of his Testimonials which I think are very good."

Delighted with their find, Walden appointed Kirby (sometimes spelt Kerby) their new Chief Constable. Alas! within a month he was sacked for drunkenness.

In October, 1856, Inspector Harvey, ex-Cambridgeshire Constabulary, was persuaded to become the new Chief Constable at a salary of 28s. a week and the usual rent-free house at the back of the Town Hall.

Discontent and despair were beginning to set in. For years the committee had been subjected to petitions and counter-petitions on the subject of amalgamation with the county. Kerby's unfortunate departure had really been the last straw.

Captain McHardy was invited to attend a meeting of the Town Council in 1857 at which it was resolved that the county be asked to take upon itself responsibility for policing the borough. The date of 1st November, 1857, was fixed for the final hand-over.

Upon the amalgamation, Superintendent John Clarke of Newport posted an inspector and four constables to take up residence in the tiny police station in the Town Hall. They were to remain there until 1884 when a new police station was built in East Street. This remains an operational police station to this day.

*Rollesby, near Great Yarmouth.

Borough of Maldon Police

TAKING ADVANTAGE of the Municipal Corporations Act 1835 the Borough of Maldon raised a force of eleven constables to take up their duties from 1st January, 1836. These were not the regular officers we know today but, as was common throughout the land, a group of citizens willing to undertake the duties on a part-time basis. These constables were given jurisdiction not only within the confines of their borough but throughout the County and Liberties of Essex. This wide area of authority led to much bitterness when the county police was formed four years later and found that it had no reciprocal powers within the borough.

The eleven constables pursued the following occupations:-

William Barnard John Bale	} Cordwainers (workers in leather)
John Beale	Workhouse Governor
Edward Warren	Porter
Thomas Keyes	Gardener
William Doubleday	Shopkeeper
Charles Handley	Meterman (measures land, etc)
Thomas Abley James Cooke	} Carpenters
Thomas Orrell Stephen Clarke	} Sergeants at Mace

The Head Constable was the cordwainer John Bale. He received £5 a year plus 2s. a week for keeping watch on the streets of the town, particularly on Saturday nights when he had to ensure the public houses closed on time. His constables received fees for whatever duties were allotted to them by the Mayor.

John Bale was dismissed from his post in 1840 for what was described as "neglect of duty," his place being taken by the Gaoler, John Raymond, who had been sworn in in 1838.

Following the establishment of a regular county force the system of policing the borough changed considerably, and a force of seven regular constables aided by twelve Special Constables was created. Following the pattern of the county force they were supplied with uniforms and paid a weekly wage ranging from 22s.6d to 25s. each—a very handsome sum indeed when one considers that the county constables' weekly wage was 17s. to 21s. The twelve Special Constables were also paid 15s.

Using this new force a system of policing the town on a regular and permanent basis was devised whereby cover was afforded for twenty out of the twenty-four hours. In August, 1853, two candidates replied to the advertisement for a Head Constable. Both were obviously considered worthy men, for one, Frederick Chilvers, was made Head Constable and the other, John Rye, became Second Officer or Deputy Head Constable. They were "employed to give their whole time and attention to the duties of Police Officers."

Friction over the borough boundaries was always a problem. Most of it originated within the borough, for the Justices were very jealous of their responsibilities. Indeed, in May, 1881, the Head Constable was censured for "employing a County Constable to assist in a search" and the Borough Police Committee resolved that "the County Police will not be called in, in future, except in a case of great necessity, and then not without an order for the purpose from one of the Magistrates."

By 1888 a new Head Constable had been appointed. He was a county policeman, Sergeant Charles Halsey, from Southminster, then part of the Dengie Division of the Essex Constabulary. His career in the Borough was short-lived, for in that same year Parliament introduced the Local Government Act which abolished small, inefficient forces and ruled that

The Moot Hall at Maldon, from which operated both the borough police and, after 1889, the first county policemen to be stationed in the town.

boroughs with populations of less than 10,000 could no longer maintain their own forces. Maldon, with a population then of only 5,381, had no choice but to comply.

The final meeting of the Police Watch Committee took place on 22nd January, 1889, and by 1st April the borough constables who had agreed to do so were transferred to the County Constabulary. The Town Clerk approached McHardy and requested that Sergeant Colt and Pc Parrott retain their borough appointments of Town Hall Keeper and Borough Clock Winder respectively. The Chief Constable agreed, with a proviso that it did not interfere with their normal police duties.

An interesting sequel to this merger involved the career of Sergeant Charles Halsey, who rejoined Essex after the amalgamation. He remained at Maldon, where he was promoted inspector. In September, 1891, he was posted to Thorpe and there promoted superintendent in February, 1893, becoming the divisional commander of the Dengie Division at Latchingdon. It was during this period at Latchingdon that one of his Sergeants, Adam John Eves, was brutally murdered at Hazeleigh, near Burnham. Halsey participated in the inquiries into this murder and supported the widow throughout her ordeal. He eventually retired on pension in September, 1901, on completion of twenty-eight years police service.

Colchester Borough Police

WHEN IT came to organising a regular Constabulary Colchester had an altogether larger and more complicated problem on its hands than did the other boroughs of Saffron Walden, Maldon and Harwich. Until 1836, no fewer than sixteen unpaid constables had operated in the town, one for each of its parishes, supplemented by night watchmen. Like their contemporaries elsewhere they continued their normal trades and businesses during the day but were expected to patrol the streets for an hour or two at night, particularly at weekends, paying special attention to the thriving alehouses.

All this changed when nineteen full-time constables were appointed under the supervision of a Head Constable to administer the law and carry out the wishes of the local magistracy. These constables were divided into two distinct bodies called the Day Police and the Night Police. The sixteen parishes were divided into three wards and allocated to three officers of the Day Police. The importance of night patrols was emphasised when the remaining sixteen constables were formed into the Night Police.

The day-duty men commenced at 5am or 6am depending on the time of year*, and continued until 8pm or 9pm. Night duty was divided into two shifts, the first commencing at 8pm or 9pm and relieved by the second shift at 1am. The second shift then worked through until relieved by the Day Police.

During the first few months the constables were supplied with only a greatcoat, staff (truncheon) and rattle. Not until later that year were uniforms purchased identical to those worn by the Metropolitan Police, namely a black top hat, dark blue tailcoat and trousers.

The Head Constable was paid the very adequate sum of 21s. a week while the constables received only 7s. (thereby putting them on a par with an illiterate farm labourer). This state of affairs lasted only a year though, for in January, 1837, the number of constables was reduced to eight but their pay more than doubled to 16s. a week. There is nothing in the records to show exactly what brought this about but there can be little doubt that finance was involved, for in common with every other local authority Colchester must have suffered considerable abuse at the cost of maintaining such a force.

By 1842 the force had grown to two Sergeants of the Watch (one each for the two night shifts) and three Sergeants at Mace (the term then used for the day constables), along with eight night constables. They all operated from what was then the Moot Hall. This building was demolished a few years later and the police station moved to offices next to the library. There they remained until 1857 while work continued on the magnificent Victorian Town Hall, in the basement of which were built police offices and cells. The borough force was to remain in this building for very nearly a hundred years before moving to the present station in Queen Street.

One of the first public relations exercises to be carried out was the printing and distribution of a thousand cards bearing the following message to the good people of Colchester, "whenever the services of a Constable may be required application should be made to any of the above or at the Police Office next to the Moot Hall." It then went on to publish the names and home addresses of every police officer in the borough.

*…"at 5am from Lady Day to Michaelmas Day (25th March to 29th September) and at 6am from Michaelmas Day to Lady Day."

The first Head Constable, often referred to as "Mr Superintendent", was a James Appleby Neville, whose period of office lasted only a year before he was replaced by a newly-promoted Watch Sergeant named Rand. The title "Head Constable" meant exactly what it implied, the position being filled by a constable who had displayed a little more intelligence than the rest or a complete outsider eager to prove his worth. He had no authority to administer discipline or even to grant a constable time off, having to refer all such matters to the Watch Committee.

The committee sat once a month to receive the Head Constable's report and to discuss any problems which had arisen during the preceding month. Not a meeting went by without at least one or two constables having to appear before its members to answer disciplinary charges brought by the sergeants or Head Constable. Far and away the most common of these involved being drunk on duty or absent from his beat.

A source of constant aggravation both to the police and the public was the presence of numerous army camps around town. Theft, robbery, drunkenness and running fights were common enough and respect for the police during those early days was almost non-existent. The constables soon learned the futility of trying to arrest a drunken soldier, knowing full well

The police station in Queen Street, Colchester, used by the borough force and taken over by the county police in 1947.

175

that others would immediately set upon him in an attempt to release his prisoner. The officer soon countered this by the simple expedient of snatching off a running soldier's hat or belt and lodging it at the police station. Eventually, the owner—or the Military Police—would arrive to claim it, thus identifying the owner, who dared not turn up on parade improperly dressed.

Matters came to a head in 1860 when a large group of soldiers went on the rampage and "committed the most violent assaults on several of the townspeople." The police went to the barracks to summon an Army patrol but were, deliberately or otherwise, kept waiting for over an hour. In the meantime the few constables left on duty in the town fought manfully against overwhelming odds. Following this, the Head Constable, Mr O. Downes, recommended to the Watch Committee that the military be persuaded to organise a permanent patrol in the town and that suitable accommodation be afforded them. Shortly afterwards such premises, comprising two rooms, were found at Green Market.

In April, 1865, a petition was presented by all the constables of the borough requesting an increase in pay. Their reasons were the ever-increasing rents being demanded in the town, accounting for a quarter of the constable's pay, the rising cost of living, that the pay of Colchester officers was lower than any other borough in the area, and that the Metropolitan Police had recently been granted a pay rise. As a result of this, they said, a Metropolitan First Class Constable received more than a Colchester Sergeant, and a Fourth Class Metropolitan Constable more than a First Class Borough Constable. By September of that year pay increases were authorised.

In February, 1867, there appeared for the first time a plain-clothes police patrol in the town. Credit for this must go to the Head Constable, Mr Downes, who had viewed with mounting concern the steady increase in robberies, burglaries and sheep-stealing in and around the borough. In an effort to counter this he instructed Sergeant Barton and Constable Wass to perform their duties out of uniform and to mix with and concentrate on the criminal elements of the town. The Watch Committee not only confirmed this departure from recognised policing but went further by approving the payment of 3s.6d a week to each officer for out-of-pocket expenses.

By December that year Downes was expressing his satisfaction with the scheme, declaring that Sergeant Barton and Pc Wass had made a number of good arrests and had broken up an active gang of corn-thieves which had been operating at the Hythe. On hearing this the committee sanctioned the continuation of the scheme and promoted Pc Wass to Sergeant, declaring him "a permanent Detective Officer", and granting him a plain clothes allowance of £9 a year.

From the earliest days the constables of the borough had been responsible for patrolling the famous oyster beds in the River Colne, but it was not until 1891 that a separate detachment was formed, based at Colne Road, Brightlingsea. Sergeant Thomas Poole (ex-Essex Constabulary) was appointed to supervise three constables, Cornelius Simmons, Charles Absalom and Edward French. Two sailing craft, the *Alert* and *Brisk*, were purchased at a total cost of £80 and taken into day and night use.

Later that year a steam launch, the *Viking,* was purchased for £429. It remained with the detachment until 1902 when it was sold at the giveaway price of £70 and replaced by another steam launch costing £1,307.

By 1914, the Colne River Police had grown to one inspector, two sergeants and nine constables, and it remained a feature of the Borough Constabulary until 1942, when the war finally brought about its disbandment.

When the Police Act 1946 forced the amalgamation of forces in towns with a population of less than 100,000 Colchester, the lone survivor of the four original borough forces in Essex, was one of the forty-five forces to disappear. On 1st April, 1947, the borough quietly handed over its men, equipment and buildings to the county police.

Essex Constabulary 1841

BRENTWOOD	Supt.	Insp.	Const.
Brentwood	1		2
Billericay			1
South Ockendon			1
Grays			2
Collier Row			1
Hornchurch			2
Romford		1	3
Orsett		1	
Total:	1	2	12

CHELMSFORD	Supt.	Insp.	Const.
Chelmsford	2	1	10
Ingatestone		1	1
West Hanningfield		1	
Danbury			1
Writtle			2
Waltham			2
Total:	2	3	16

COLCHESTER	Supt.	Insp.	Const.
Colchester	1		1
Peldon			1
Great Horkesley			2
Dedham			2
Fordham		1	1
Mount Bures			1
Brightlingsea			1
Total:	1	1	9

DENGIE	Supt.	Insp.	Const.
Latchingdon	1		1
Southminster		1	1
Purleigh			1
Tillingham			1
Burnham			1
Bradwell			1
Total:	1	1	6

DUNMOW	Supt.	Insp.	Const.
Dunmow	1	1	2
Thaxted		1	1
High Easter			2
Total:	1	2	5

EPPING	Supt.	Insp.	Const.
Epping	1		2
Harlow			2
Roydon			1
Abridge			2
Hatfield Heath		1	
Great Parndon			1
Total:	1	1	8

FRESHWELL	Supt.	Insp.	Const.
Great Bardfield	1		1
Steeple Bumpstead			1
Wethersfield			1
Total:	1		3

NORTH HINCKFORD	Supt.	Insp.	Const.
Sible Hedingham	1		2
Belchamp Walter			2
Foxearth			1
Toppesfield			1
Bulmer			1
Total:	1		7

SOUTH HINCKFORD	Supt.	Insp.	Const.
Braintree	1	1	3
Halstead		1	2
Earls Colne			2
Stisted			1
Total:	1	2	8

ONGAR	Supt.	Insp.	Const.
Ongar	1		1
Passingford Bridge			1
Matching Green			1
Willingale Doe			1
Blackmore			1
Total:	1		5

THE ESSEX POLICE

ROCHFORD	Supt.	Insp.	Const.
Rayleigh	1		1
Rochford			2
Great Wakering		1	
Southend			1
Prittlewell			1
South Benfleet			1
Total:	1	1	6

TENDRING	Supt.	Insp.	Const.
Thorpe-le-Soken	1		1
Manningtree		1	1
St Osyth		1	1
Great Oakley			1
Ardleigh			2
Elmstead			2
Total:	1	2	8

WALDEN	Supt.	Insp.	Const.
Newport	1	1	1
Ashdon		1	1
Stansted			1
Crishall			2
Great Chesterford			1
Total:	1	2	6

WITHAM	Supt.	Insp.	Const.
Witham	1		2
Coggeshall		1	1
Tolleshunt d'Arcy			1
Heybridge			1
Hatfield Peverel			1
Total:	1	1	6
Force total:	15	18	105

Essex Constabulary 1850

BRENTWOOD

	Supt.	Insp.	Const.
Brentwood	1		3
South Weald			1
Great Warley			1
Childerditch			1
Havering			1
Hornchurch			2
Romford		1	3
Collier Row			2
Billericay		1	1
Grays			1
Crays Hill			1
South Ockendon			1
Aveley			1
Herongate			1
Orsett		1	1
Rainham			1
Horndon			1
Corringham			1
West Tilbury			1
Mountnessing			1
Upminster			1
Laindon			1
Total:	1	3	28

CHELMSFORD

	Supt.	Insp.	Const.
Chelmsford	1	2	8
Ingatestone			1
Stock			1
Writtle			1
Roxwell			1
Margaretting			1
Danbury			1
Great Waltham			1
Great Baddow			1
Great Leighs			1
Boreham			1
Rettendon			1
Total:	1	2	19

COLCHESTER

	Supt.	Insp.	Const.
Colchester	1		1
Stanway		1	1
Wivenhoe			1
Great Horkesley			1
Dedham			1
Mount Bures			1
Great Tey			1
Layer Breton			1
West Bergholt			1
Peldon			1
Abberton			1
Elmstead Market			1
Total:	1	1	12

DENGIE

	Supt.	Insp.	Const.
Latchingdon	1		1
Southminster			1
Steeple			1
Purleigh			1
Woodham Walter			1
Woodham Ferrers			1
Althorne			1
Tillingham			1
Burnham			1
Burnham Oyster Co		1	2
Total:	1	1	11

DUNMOW

	Supt.	Insp.	Const.
Dunmow	1		2
Takeley			1
Hallingbury			1
Felsted			1
Stebbing			1
Leaden Roding			1
High Easter			1
Broxted			1
Total:	1		9

EPPING

	Supt.	Insp.	Const.
Epping	1		1
Theydon Garnon			1
Lambourn			1
Roydon			1
Parndon			1
Nazeing			1
North Weald Bassett			1
Harlow		1	
Sheering			1
Hatfield Broad Oak			1
Total:	1	1	9

FRESHWELL	Supt.	Insp.	Const.
Great Bardfield	1		1
Steeple Bumpstead		1	
Wethersfield			1
Finchingfield			1
Old Sampford			1
Thaxted			2
Sturmer			1
Total:	1	1	7

NORTH HINCKFORD	Supt.	Insp.	Const.
Castle Hedingham	1		2
Sible Hedingham			1
Foxearth			1
Belchamp Walter			1
Toppesfield			1
Bulmer			1
Ridgewell			1
Lamarsh			1
Total:	1		9

SOUTH HINCKFORD	Supt.	Insp.	Const.
Braintree	1	1	4
Halstead		1	3
Earls Colne			1
Colne Engaine			1
Cressing		1	
Gosfield			1
Pebmarsh			1
Stisted			1
Total:	1	3	12

ONGAR	Supt.	Insp.	Const.
Ongar	1		1
Navestock			1
Passingford Bridge			1
Blackmore			1
Toot Hill			1
Fyfield			1
Moreton			1
Total:	1		7

ROCHFORD	Supt.	Insp.	Const.
Rayleigh	1		1
Southend		1	1
Prittlewell			1
Leigh			1
South Benfleet			1
Wickford			1
Canewdon			1
Foulness			1
Hadleigh			1
North Benfleet			1

	Supt.	Insp.	Const.
Hockley			1
Great Wakering			1
Total:	1	1	12

TENDRING	Supt.	Insp.	Const.
Thorpe-le-Soken	1		1
Manningtree		1	
Ardleigh		1	
St Osyth			1
Great Clacton			1
Great Bentley			1
Kirby			1
Bradfield			1
Great Oakley		1	
Ramsey			1
Lawford			1
Brightlingsea			1
Great Bromley			1
Mistley			1
Total:	1	3	11

WITHAM	Supt.	Insp.	Const.
Witham	1		3
Kelvedon			1
Fairstead			1
Great Totham			1
Heybridge			1
Hatfield Peverel			1
Tolleshunt d'Arcy			1
Messing			1
Great Coggeshall		1	2
Total:	1	1	12

WALDEN	Supt.	Insp.	Const.
Newport	1		1
Clavering			1
Stansted		1	
Henham			1
Quendon			1
Great Chrishall			1
Great Chesterford		1	
Manuden			1
Radwinter			1
Debden			1
Littlebury			1
Ashdon			1
Wenden Lofts			1
Total:	1	2	11
Force total:	14	19	168

Index

Illustrations in bold type